KU-485-119

Regional Party Leadership and Policy-Making in the USSR

Joel C. Moses

The Praeger Special Studies program—utilizing the most modern and efficient book production techniques and a selective worldwide distribution network—makes available to the academic, government, and business communities significant, timely research in U.S. and international economic, social, and political development.

Regional Party Leadership and Policy-Making in the USSR

PRAEGER SPECIAL STUDIES IN INTERNATIONAL POLITICS AND GOVERNMENT

Praeger Publishers   New York   Washington   London

Library of Congress Cataloging in Publication Data

Moses, Joel C
    Regional party leadership and policy-making in
the USSR.

    (Praeger special studies in international politics
and government)
    Bibliography: p.
    1. Kommunisticheskaia partiia Sovetskogo Soiuza—
Party work.   2. Russia—Politics and government—
1953-   I. Title.
JN6598.K7M67   329.9'47   73-15192
ISBN 0-275-28797-1

$\cup C$

PRAEGER PUBLISHERS
111 Fourth Avenue, New York, N.Y. 10003, U.S.A.
5, Cromwell Place, London SW7 2JL, England

Published in the United States of America in 1974
by Praeger Publishers, Inc.

All rights reserved

© 1974 by Praeger Publishers, Inc.

Printed in the United States of America

I would like to acknowledge the several institutions and individuals whose support contributed immeasurably to the study. Research was conducted at the University of Wisconsin in Madison, the Library of Congress in Washington, the Lenin Library in Moscow, and the Institute for the Study of the USSR and the Radio Liberty Research Division in Munich. The librarians and staff at all these institutions were more than helpful in providing resource materials, advice, and information. The initial research in the Soviet Union, Germany, and Washington was made possible by an international travel grant and dissertation fellowship awarded by the International Studies Program and the Graduate School of the University of Wisconsin for the 1970-71 academic year. Computer analysis for Chapters 5 and 6 was funded through grants by the University of Wisconsin Computer Center in 1973 and the Iowa State University Computer Center in 1973. Professor Brian Silver of Florida State University contributed his usual insightful criticisms and suggestions at the early developmental stages of the study. A very special debt of gratitude is owed Professor John A. Armstrong, my former faculty adviser at the University of Wisconsin, who both encouraged the initial research and remained a continuing positive source of criticism throughout the evolution of the study. Finally, the study is dedicated to the memory of my father, David Moses, who died only a brief time before its completion. His own life was characterized by a commitment to personal and intellectual integrity, which I can only hope are reflected in some small measure in this book.

LIST OF TABLES AND FIGURES

ABBREVIATIONS OF SOVIET PERIODICALS AND PRIMARY SOURCES MOST FREQUENTLY CITED IN NOTES
(a detailed listing of major Soviet sources is included in the bibliography)

BP	Belgorodskaia pravda (Belgorod)
BR	Brianskii rabochii (Briansk)
Deputaty	Deputaty Verkhovnogo Soveta SSSR (Deputies of the Supreme Soviet of the USSR) (1958-1970 Volumes)
Ezhegodniki	Ezhegodniki bol'shoi Sovetskoi entsiklopedii (Yearbooks of the Great Soviet Encyclopedia) (1958-1971 Volumes)
EG	Ekonomicheskaia gazeta
G	Gudok
I	Izvestiia
IZ	Industrial'noe Zaporozh'e (Zaporozh'e)
K	Kommunist (journal)
K(S)	Kommunist (Saratov newspaper)
KaP	Kalingradskaia pravda (Kaliningrad)
Kip	Kirovskaia pravda (Kirov)
KoP	Komsomolskaia pravda
KrP	Krymskaia pravda (Crimea)
KuP	Kurskaia pravda (Kursk)
KS	Krasnyi sever (Vologda)
XIX-XXIV KPSS	XIX-XXIV s"ezdy Kommunisticheskoi Partii Sovetskogo Soiuza: stenograficheskie otchety (Stenographic reports of 19th-24th Congresses of the Communist Party of the Soviet Union)

XX-XXIV KP Ukr	Materialy-XX-XXIV s"ezdy Kommunisticheskoi Partii Ukrainy: stenograficheskie otchety (Stenographic Reports on the Materials of the 20th-24th Congresses of the Communist Party of the Ukraine).
KomZ	Komsomolskoe zania
KrZ(Kh)	Krasnoe znamia (Khar'kov)
KrZ(T)	Krasnoe znamia (Tomsk)
Kuz	Kuzbass (Kemerovo)
LP	L'vovskaia pravda (L'vov)
M	Molot (Rostov)
OP	Orlovskaia pravda (Orel)
P	Pravda
PU	Pravda Ukrainy
PZh	Partiinaia zhizn'
RP	Rabochii put'
RU	Radianskaia Ukraina
SKh	Sel'skoe khoziaistvo
SPR	Spravochnik partiinogo rabotnika (The Party worker's handbook)
SR	Severnyi rabochii (Yaroslavl')
SRos	Sovetskaia Rossiia
SZh	Sel'skaia zhizn'
T	Trud
TP	Tambovskaia pravda (Tambov)
UG	Uchitel'skaia gazeta

VN	Vechernii Novosibirsk (Rostov)
VP	Volgogradskaia pravda (Volgograd)
VR	Vechernii Rostov (Rostov)
Vedomosti RSFSR	Vedomosti Verkhovnogo Soveta RSFSR (Gazeteer of the Supreme Soviet of the Russian Republic)
Vedomosti SSSR	Vedomosti Verkhovnogo Soveta SSSR (Gazeteer of the Supreme Soviet of the USSR)
Z(K)	Znamia (Kaluga)
Z(P)	Zvezda (Perm')
ZK	Znamia kommunizma (Odessa)
ZP	Zakarpatskaia pravda (Trans-Carpathia)

Regional Party Leadership and Policy-Making in the USSR

1

REGIONAL ADAPTATION
AND POLITICAL CHANGE
IN THE CPSU

POLITICAL CHANGE

The theme of political change in the Communist Party of the Soviet Union (CPSU) has long prompted Western scholars to detailed, if at times premature, conclusions and prognostications about the Soviet system. Among other changing political dimensions, the composition of Party membership,[1] the characteristics of personnel on leading Party organs,[2] and interest group conflict[3] have forced an awareness on the part of Western scholars to the developmental phases and adaptive potential of the Soviet Communist Party. Scholars generally concede that, short of real liberalization in the political system, political change best can be identified by differences in those who participate at any historical period in policy-making. Variations in participation have often coincided with the changing power configuration and dominant political style in the Soviet Union, from the autocratic centralism of Stalin to the populist decentralism of Khrushchev to the conservative oligarchic rule of Brezhnev-Kosygin. Any real political change in the Party over the last half-century may be questionable, but important distinctions at least can be observed in the forms and quality of participation in the political system at any given time. Furthermore, given the relative stability of the Soviet dictatorship over the last half-century, even a modification in the nature of political participation assumes greater than normal significance for the overall political system.

However aware Western scholars have been of the dimensions associated with general systemic change in the Soviet Union, they have less systematically attempted to examine the related impact of that change upon lower levels of the CPSU. With few exceptions,[4] interpretations of the CPSU have tended to assume a highly integrated and controlled monolith in which political change automatically affects

3

all levels of the Party structure in the same uniform direction. As such, many studies of the Party by Western scholars have an implicit elitist bias that stresses the role of central political figures and the extensive coordination and uniformity in the Soviet political system. This is readily understandable. Information on Party personnel and operations below the central organs rarely has been available. Although Western scholars can subscribe to Union-republic newspapers and journals, for example, as basic a source of data on regional parties as the regional press has been unobtainable outside the Soviet Union. Even for Western students in the Soviet Union, gaining access to the regional newspapers is often a very frustrating and lengthy ordeal.* Since it is unlikely that archival materials such as Merle Fainsod used in his monumental study of Smolensk will ever appear again, students of regional parties must generally rely upon secondary and scattered references to regional politics in the All-Union and Union-republic press.

Even were materials available, the operational impact of "democratic centralism" and the stated intentions of Soviet authorities have always seemed to minimize either change or regional diversity in the Party structure. Indeed, a recent study of the Volgograd oblast party, while cautiously referring to the presence of interest groups in regional decision-making, also confirms at several points the circumscribed role of regional parties as "transmission belts" of central Party policy and dictate.[5] The Volgograd party in the late 1950s seems remarkably similar to the Smolensk party of the 1930s, as described by Fainsod. Because the structure of the local Party organizations has not changed since 1930 and few differences appear among regions, research on the Party would implicitly endorse the views of Soviet authorities, who laud the essential "continuity" (preemstvennost') of the Party since the 1920s.

Treating a vast bureaucratic complex like the CPSU as a whole assumes an absolutely inflexible logic and a network of totalitarian controls throughout the structure. Such conformity was most closely approximated under Stalin, when purges, indiscriminate terror, and the secret police went far to level any variations in performance,

---

*See, in particular, the comments of Philip Stewart, Political Power in the Soviet Union, p. x. The difficulties that Stewart encountered in 1962 were very similar to those I experienced at the Lenin Library in the winter of 1970. I had originally intended to study three regional newspapers over a 25-year period from 1945. Access to the regional press before 1970 was denied by librarians, who repeatedly contended that past years of the newspapers were still being bound or had been transferred to another archival reserve.

personnel, and concerns. Yet even during the Stalin era, center-local relations allowed some independence and variation to the regional party.[6] As Fainsod has shown, the leaders in Moscow were primarily concerned with political and economic performance in the Smolensk oblast. Within limits, oblast Party leaders had the discretion to achieve these results as local circumstances seemed to dictate. De-kulakization, the assignment of grain quota to rural districts, or local worker and peasant grievances were all handled by the oblast Party leadership in the manner they felt most appropriate. Central authorities set production quotas and initiated campaigns, but the local leadership defined administrative accountability and adjusted the tempo for social and political change in the region.

Other studies have also alluded to a considerable range of variation in local Party organizations. John A. Armstrong found that personnel assignments and internal processes among the Ukrainian oblast parties occurred in an oligarchic fashion, even during the height of Stalin's excessive autocratic rule.[7] In the most thoroughly researched study of local Party organs in industrial decision-making, Jerry Hough has outlined the conditions that have facilitated a limited outgrowth of automomy among oblast parties from central intervention and uniformity in the post-Stalin era. Although they carry out policy formulated at the center, regional parties for Hough are better characterized as "prefectures" in the territorial-administrative hierarchy of the Party bureaucracy.[8] At an extreme, frequent evidence of "family circles" and wide-ranging corruption in Smolensk and other areas throughout Soviet history suggest the real limits on central control and the possibilities of regional diversity. Logically, such diversity might be assumed to arise as regional Party organizations are affected by the environments in which they are situated.

However alert one should be to the potential for diversity, regional Party organizations must be observed in the context of general political trends. An awareness of such trends is essential to comprehension of behavior at the regional subsystem level. At the same time, close analysis of subsystem behavior may serve as an important test of these hypotheses on general systemic trends.

Recent studies of the present Soviet leadership have led to somewhat inconsistent conclusions on the problems of participation and adaptation in the CPSU. Zbigniew Brzezinski and others have argued that Khrushchev's fall consolidated a basic shift in the political system.[9] An old and unimaginative elite, with its narrow concerns and perspectives, has seized power, foreclosing the recognition of alternative views and demands from non-Party institutional groups and experts in the society. Abandoning the visionary goals of Communism and the new Soviet man, Party leaders have fallen back on hackneyed credos of ideological conflict and Russian nationalism to suppress opposition and to justify their policies and rule. The position of the Party, more and more anomalous, is reasserted and defended to the detriment of needed economic and social expansion. Such expansion is possible only with the open expression and admission of influence from the broader social groups and interests in the Soviet Union. Carefully contrived compromise and administrative tinkering, which fail to move essential decisions or problems off dead center, characterize the operating mentality of the restorationist elite. The leadership and society have reached an unproductive impasse with the Party's refusal to limit its prerogatives for the sake of socio-economic development. T. H. Rigby has outlined the logical corollaries to this mode of a "self-stabilizing oligarchy": No faction will dominate, and the regime is stable in the short run as long as no major shifts in personnel or policy are permitted in the Party structure.[10]

Studies from a second group of scholars would tend to qualify the generally negative contentions of bureaucratization and stalemate in the system. They can point to arenas of policy-making where a certain relaxation in recognizing and accepting alternative views and more rationally grounded information from interest groups has emerged.[11] Others too have questioned whether there really is a necessary contradiction between an ideocratic Party elite and economic-technological progress. Jeremy Azrael's historical survey of Soviet managers leads him to conclude that, as the managerial elite are locked into the political system by temperament and vested interests, the Party can call upon their expertise without any real threat to the political status quo.[12] A study of career patterns among major Soviet officials, limited as it is to the brief period from 1958 through 1962, foresees a continued trend towards greater specialization among leading Party and state personnel. Under the peculiar Soviet system of "tutelary monism," as George Fischer argues, more major political positions in the Soviet Union will be filled by those whose careers include technical training and technical occupations in the economy.[13] Even more directly, in the previously cited study of local Party organs, Jerry Hough underlines the very gradual evolution since Stalin of rational-technical capabilities at the regional level at the same time he questions the relevance of the Weberian model of a rational bureaucracy for the Soviet experience.[14] Yet, as Hough can conclude, local Party organs can respond quite well to the necessities of recruitment, political adaptation, and economic performance.

Differences between the two interpretations of the present Soviet system should not be exaggerated. Brzezinski and others concede the presence of group conflicts over policy-making and technical recruitment among major Party personnel. They differ from the second group only in the importance attributed to the group phenomenon and the long-term willingness of the elite to accommodate expertise from outside sectors. Participation after all is relative, dependent in its meaning upon the more general nature of leadership and political processes in the Soviet Union. Groups and factions were also prevalent in the Stalin era, as Stalin would play these groups and factions off against each other to minimize opposition against himself. Indeed, no one in either group of Western scholars has doubted that even now the presentation of conflicting viewpoints on policy has achieved only partial legitimacy in the system. While politically "safe" technicians and indoctrinated enterprise directors participate on industrial problems, non-Russians, jurists, liberal intellectuals, and dissident physicists have little voice on any policy. The basic questions remain as to which groups participate, in what issues, how frequently, and with what impact. Any difference between the two interpretations is minimal, if the alternatives are considered: lethargy and bureaucratic fear of innovation or a circumscribed tolerance of opposing views and a particular Soviet pattern of incremental change.

A more fundamental difference lies in the very problem of defining the Soviet political system and political change. Brzezinski and others may be quite correct in characterizing the central leadership as unresponsive and unsuited to the general needs of Soviet society. From a narrower focus, Hough and others refer to participation and recruitment only in selected policy areas or group-Party relationships. Therefore, in discussing the "evolution" or "degeneration" of the Soviet Union, it seems essential to specify the level of the political system from which conclusions and prognostications are drawn. Most sweeping generalizations on the nature of the Soviet political system err, however, by failing to allow for the possibility of divergent trends at different policy-making levels and in different policy areas. Depending on the level of analysis, the Soviet system may appear both positively and negatively responsive to demands and needs.

The rates of socioeconomic change also differ throughout the Soviet Union. Urbanization and an expanded technical work force are common features in the Soviet Union, but they have reached varying levels in different regions and, logically, should have differential impact on the political organizations in these regions. Regions are not insulated from the general political and social trends in the Soviet Union, but regional Party organizations are simultaneously influenced by social forces most active in their own immediate locales. If political adaptation and participation should be conceived as a multivariate problem, so too should the stated relationship between political and social change. By background and temperament, the present leadership at the central Party level may be acutely out of touch with general environmental changes in Soviet society. At the same time personnel elected to lower Party organs like the regional parties and the policies adopted at the regional level may be both representative of and responsive to their specific locales. Oblasts, which have undergone different rates of social change, could have different rates of personnel turnover, different career and recruitment patterns among their Party leadership, and a varied preoccupation with policies. Political adaptation in oblasts as diverse in their socioeconomic forces as Trans-Carpathia and Novosibirsk should take on very different forms and should be evaluated on very different planes. A comparison of several regional Party organizations would provide one means to evaluate not only the processes of participation and adaptation at this Party level but also the very limits of Party autonomy below the central organs.

REGIONAL PARTY ADAPTATION

The central problem posed in this study is the extent to which regional Party organizations are autonomous and should be analyzed as equivalent subunits of a bureaucracy. Autonomy does not assume the independence of regional parties from personnel supervision and ultimate accountability to the central organs in Kiev and Moscow but the possibility that subunits of a bureaucracy like the CPSU adapt to the peculiarities and demands of their environments. Considered as equivalent subunits, the manner and degree of political adaptation among several regional parties can be compared. The study will specifically focus upon 25 of the 75 administratively nonautonomous regional parties in the Russian and Ukrainian Republics over an 18-year period, 1955 through the first six months of 1973. Excluding the Regional Areas of Eastern Siberia and the Far East in the Russian Republic, the sample comprises oblasts from all 11 major historic-economic regional areas that make up the two union-republics (See Figures 1 and 2).

Regional Areas	Oblasts
1. Northwest	Vologda, Kaliningrad
2. Central	Yaroslavl', Orel, Kaluga, Briansk, Smolensk
3. Central Black Earth	Belgorod, Kursk, Tambov
4. Volga-Vyatka	Kirov
5. Volga	Saratov, Volgograd
6. North Caucasus	Rostov
7. Urals	Perm'
8. Western Siberia	Novosibirsk, Kemerovo, Tomsk
9. Southeast Ukraine	Khar'kov, Dnepropetrovsk, Zaporozh'e

Regional Areas	Oblasts
10. South Ukraine	Crimea, Odessa
11. Southwest Ukraine	L'vov, Trans-Carpathia

Political adaptation on the regional Party level will be identified on two major policy dimensions. Issue adaptation denotes the general preoccupation with issues and problems arising from the differentiated environments of regional parties. Despite the highly articulated command structure in the Communist Party, local Party organizations may not always follow a uniform standard in defining issues and assessing the causes and solutions of problems. We would anticipate that the major Central Committee resolutions and plenums are peremptorily reenacted on the local regional level. Indeed, in his study of the Volgograd oblast, Philip Stewart found that plenary sessions and their themes closely followed corresponding Central Committee resolutions and plenums.[15] Volgograd, however, was one regional party in a particular area and in a particular time period. It would be highly significant if regional parties demonstrate some "feedback" response to regional demands and rationally allocate their attention to these demands. If regional parties respond differentially to their environments, a comparison of the 25 regions should provide evidence by differences in the kinds of issues raised and in the manner of resolving them. Plenary sessions of the oblast committees should be convened at different times, the themes of plenary sessions should be concerned with different problems, and the intermittent oblast-wide conferences and specialized sessions that serve as an intermediary link in the regional policy-making process should be convened on different issues or bring together representatives of different occupational sectors.

In order to test these propositions, plenums and conferences of the 25 regions over a simultaneous nine and a half month period of 1970 were accumulated from their descriptions in the regional press. In Chapter 2-4, the plenums and conferences will be separately analyzed and their themes compared as indicators of issue adaptation among the 25 regional parties. Variance in issue adaptation will be explained by the two dominant features in the regional environment: the levels and rates of social mobilization among the regions, and the mediating influence of the obkom first secretaries, who served in the regions during 1970.

The second dimension by which regional parties will be compared is political participation. The very concept of political adaptation implies an organization's ability to recruit into its hierarchy individuals who, by background, outlook, and qualifications, harmonize and integrate the organization with social forces in its environment. If organizations are to retain a dynamic stability, the organization must be open to participation from groups and strata on a level

FIGURE 1

Map of Regions in the Russian and Ukrainian Republics

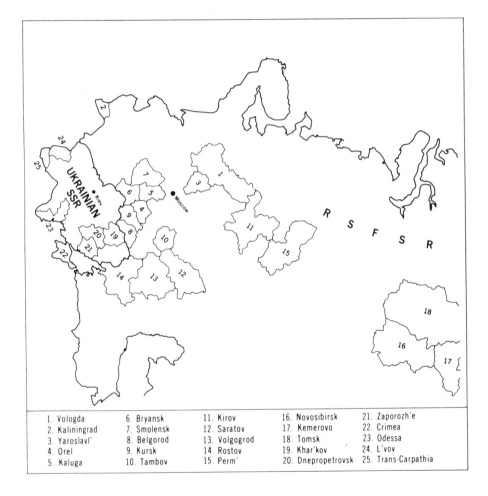

1. Vologda	6. Bryansk	11. Kirov	16. Novosibirsk	21. Zaporozh'e
2. Kaliningrad	7. Smolensk	12. Saratov	17. Kemerovo	22. Crimea
3. Yaroslavl'	8. Belgorod	13. Volgogrod	18. Tomsk	23. Odessa
4. Orel	9. Kursk	14. Rostov	19. Khar'kov	24. L'vov
5. Kaluga	10. Tambov	15. Perm'	20. Dnepropetrovsk	25. Trans-Carpathia

FIGURE 2

Chart of Russian and Ukrainian Regional Parties
in the Territorial-Administrative Hierarchy
of the CPSU
(with key Russian terms)

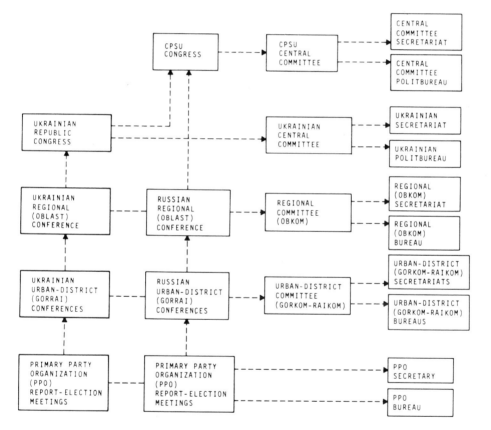

commensurate to their size and importance in the environment. As we have emphasized, Western scholars have criticized the present Soviet leadership for their very lack of "organizational adaptibility" to Soviet society. They are characterized as an aging and unimaginative elite, whose experiences and attitudes were shaped in the Stalin era; they are unwilling to promote young, technically competent specialists into responsible positions and yet are incapable by themselves of acting upon pressing socioeconomic problems.

In our analysis, participation in regional policy-making is hypothesized to have a very direct bearing upon morale among lower-level cadres and officials in the regional Party-state apparatuses. As in any bureaucracy, motivation and ambition for lower cadres and officials are logically keyed to perceived opportunities for career advancement into leadership positions at higher levels of the regions. For state or Party administrative-technical personnel, in lieu of direct recruitment into leadership positions, there must be at least some form of "virtual representation" and symbolic deference to their occupational opinions by the present oblast leadership. Participation by occupational sector representatives in plenums or other conferences that determine regional policy, for example, would be a primary means to reinforce the sense of occupational self-esteem for others in the same occupational reference group as those who participate in the plenums or conferences. Turnover rates in higher occupational levels and into the major policy-making positions such as the obkom bureau must at the same time be rapid enough to inspire the ambitions of lower cadres and officials in their present positions.

When the avenues both of self-gratification and of anticipated role fulfillment are thwarted, lower cadres and officials will be frustrated in perceived opportunities for advancement or feel that the Party leadership is unresponsive even to a formal expression of their opinions on a policy. Frustration may lead to dismay and bitterness towards the leadership or to the general system that ignores their ambitions and views. Such an absence of motivation at the lower regional levels may lead cadres and officials to adopt a minimal work strategy of doing only enough to protect themselves against criticism and demotion, but with little incentive that greater efforts or ambitions will be recognized or rewarded. Thus, to the extent that regional Party organizations do provide flexible and regularized channels of advancement and openly demonstrate a concern with the opinions of occupational sectors, the regional political subsystem adapts to policy initiatives from its own Party-state apparatchiki and to the greater social system from which these same apparatchiki have been recruited.

The importance of participation for morale and system renewal has not gone unnoticed by central Soviet authorities. Historically, purges have unleashed pent-up desires for recognition among lower cadres and rapidly promoted a new leadership stratum more deeply committed to the regime.[16] The most recent example was Khrushchev's attempted rejuvenation of the local Party organs in 1958-64. Motivated in part by his attempt to oust the opposition in the Praesidium and the Central Committee, Khrushchev's reforms began to promote younger, more technically proficient cadres into leadership positions at a stage in their careers much earlier than could have been expected within the informal structure of career opportunities. If they had survived his own fall, Khrushchev's reforms would have resulted in a significant replacement of directing personnel at the regional Party level. With expanded plenary sessions opened on a routine basis to nonregular groups and outside expertise, the plenums could have been transformed into effective forums for the dissemination of information and a limited brokerage of group opinions on policies. For the short duration of the reforms, younger cadres in all administrative and directing capacities must have been buoyed by the prospect that success indices in the factory or farm and objective personal qualifications could now lead to rapid advancement in their occupational sector—even, with the creation of a second obkom and bureau in 1963-64, into the coveted positions on the obkom bureau. With their advice solicited at expanded plenary sessions, the lower cadres and officials, who could not hope to advance as high as the regional policy elite, still had a regular channel for representatives of their reference groups and a symbolic channel to reaffirm their own self-esteem. Brezhnev and Kosygin may thus have inherited after 1964 a local Party corps that has come to expect the continuation of rapid turnover and promotion. Non-elites, who had been allowed a limited forum for their policy initiatives in expanded plenary sessions, may be less willing to submerge their opinions under Party "guidance."

In order to assess regional variations, we will compare the 25 regions in this study on two levels of political participation: (1) direct participation—the contributions of occupational sectors in the oblast work force primarily at obkom plenums; (2) indirect participation—recruitment into the regional policy-making elites (the obkom bureaus) of these 25 regions over a simultaneous 18-year period.

Direct participation encompasses all plenary sessions reported in the 25 regional newspapers over the same nine and a half month period of 1970 from which we will derive indicators of issue adaptation. Participation quotients by issue-areas and by occupational sectors have been devised from the number of times individuals in each defined occupational sector contribute to plenums during this period. We do not assume that participation rates of occupational sectors reflect their actual influence on an issue. As policy is determined in the obkom bureau, the plenary sessions, diverse specialized conferences, and meetings of the Party aktiv have a marginal impact upon decisions. As we have emphasized, however, these sessions and conferences at a minimum affect the motivation and morale of lower cadres and officials in a region. By the very act of participation in a plenum, whether to be criticized for short-comings or to be praised for positive achievements, participants and their occupational reference groups in the region are symbolically rewarded as to the key administrative role that they are perceived to perform in the policy area by the regional policy elite. As will be evident from examining the plenums and conferences during 1970, participation can signify more at times by channeling specialized initiatives to a policy of primary concern to the regional policy elite.

By indirect participation, we will examine the career-biographic characteristics of 1,108 known regional policy-makers who have served either in the obkom bureaus or other major Party-state positions of these same 25 regions from 1955 through the first six months of 1973. Of these individuals, 763 have at some time during these 18 years attained formal positions that confer candidate or full membership on the regional obkom bureaus. The remaining 345 are members of the oblast committee and potential future bureau members whose backgrounds will provide a basis from which to judge the representative capacity of the regional policy elite in the obkom bureaus to a succeeding elite at the next lower level of the regional political hierarchy.

EXPLANATORY HYPOTHESES

Consequently, if there are differences in Party adaptation and participation among the 25 regions, how could we account for this variation? Three alternative explanations will be examined in this study.

In developing a first explanation, we will attempt to assess the actual dependence of oblast Party organizations upon significant political trends at the center. The overthrow of Khrushchev in 1964 should have consistently affected turnover rates and recruitment patterns among all regional parties. Brzezinski and others contend that the Communist Party has become increasingly rigid and bureau-cratized under the Brezhnev-Kosygin regime. From 1965, the collective leadership has been committed to Khrushchev's prior adminis-tration only to the extent that institutional terror and wholesale purges are no longer legitimate means of keeping cadres in line. With the relaxation of terror, the heightened aspirations produced by the Party reforms, and the continued growth of group identity,[17] the leadership

faced a mounting morale problem among lower cadres, but without
the options of suppression or timid cooptation. The morale problem
was further exacerbated by the coup. The overthrow of Khrushchev
was a protective consolidation against the threat he posed to officials
whose careers were primarily spent under Stalin. Distrustful of
their younger subordinates, whose careers and testings postdate 1952,
and anxious to preserve the low-profile collective rule, the elite would
be reluctant to disturb the status quo with significant personnel changes
in Party-state bureaucracies. Any such changes, multiplied in the
locales, could bring to authoritative posts cadres with dubious loyalties
and commitments to the Brezhnev-Kosygin regime. The delicacy of
collective compromise at the center also argued for a freezing of
major personnel shifts. Turnover, understood in the Soviet political
context of patrons and clients, would signal a departure from collectivism to an attempt at one-man rule.[18] If the need for participation
and personnel change were greater, and alternative means to solve
the morale problem in the Party were more limited, the willingness
and ability of the collective elite to respond were less.

According to this interpretation, therefore, turnover and recruitment in the bureaus of the 25 regions should have noticeably declined
after 1964. The background, tenure, and qualifications of assigned
personnel should have changed little from those in the bureaus between
1955 and 1964. Consequently, we hypothesize that political adaptation
(by elite recruitment into obkom bureaus) declined in relation to the
central political change of Khrushchev's ouster in 1964.

An alternative (null) hypothesis might, with equal a priori logic,
state that the post-Khrushchev regime should not have affected local
Party organizations at all. With the disavowal of terror and purges,
bureaucratic indecision and compromise at the center allowed, other
things being equal, a more fluid and adaptable response at lower levels
of the political system. The collective leadership, desirous of resolving pressing issues, found it politically expedient to devolve greater
responsibility on subunits and expected them to fashion solutions
within local contingencies and personnel. For a collective leadership,
dependent for its survival on the efficacy of its decisions, political
stability and administrative efficiency both would warrant local
adaptation. Local Party organizations are situated close to daily
implementation of policies and can better weigh the practical impact
of central decisions against achieved results. Personnel in local
Party organizations also serve as convenient scapegoats for ill-
conceived decisions or inaction at the center.

The fundamental integration of the system was not threatened,
so long as the control mechanisms and personnel selection in the
local parties ultimately remained in the center. The leadership had
already indicated its willingness to decentralize by adopting a limited

version of the Liberman economic reforms in 1965. Leaders too could argue that integration has never required rote homogeneity in the Soviet system, nor has any absence of complete uniformity ever implied a weakening of central decision-making powers. Many of the oblast first secretaries in the Russian and Ukrainian Republics are, after all, members of the Central Committee. As they share in the responsibilities and prerogatives of leadership through the Committee, the first secretaries are also bound to the success or failure of the oligarchical arrangement. Trusted by the central leadership, these first secretaries had supported the overthrow of Khrushchev in 1964. Many of them had been retained in their positions since that time.

The null hypothesis thus states that political adaptation (by elite recruitment into obkom bureaus) did not change after Khrushchev's ouster in 1964, and may even have increased. Turnover rates and recruitment patterns for obkom bureau members in 1955-64 are similar to those elected after 1964. Personnel in all bureaus continue to be younger, more educated and technically qualified, and more tied by background and origins to the regions in which they were selected. Khrushchev's policy to rejuvenate the Party structure has in fact been continued under the collective leadership. At the regional Party level, the period 1965-73 can be typified as "Khrushchevism without Khrushchev."

Development of a second explanation starts with the proposition that socioeconomic differences among regions should result in varying political responses among regional parties. Whatever the general political trend, regional parties should actually vary greatly among themselves in the kinds of issues raised, in the turnover rates of bureau members, and in the background and origins of personnel. The environments in which regional parties are located influence the adaptive response of the parties. Absolute and relative rates of socioeconomic change on an aggregate level should correspond to differences in regional Party adaptation.

As previously argued, Western scholars have often overlooked the possibility of differences both in Soviet society and the Soviet political system. Contentions on the transformation or degeneration of the Soviet system may be generally valid, while inaccurate in particular situations. To avoid premature or erroneous conclusions, the level of analysis for both the environment and the political unit should be as logically and empirically congruent as possible. It makes little sense to evaluate the supposed adaptiveness of the Communist Party if we fail to distinguish the agriculturally backward from the industrially advanced areas of the country. Regional parties are directly influenced by the distribution of economic and social components in the region.

The theory of social mobilization suggests one means to assess the comparative relationship of political adaptation and social change among regional parties.[19] According to the theory, groups and strata in the society are psychologically and socially uprooted by modernization, and statistically occurring levels of modernization can be expected to result in heightened demands upon political systems. With the decline of an unskilled agricultural work force and the growth of educational levels and specialized work forces, political leaders are confronted with different problems and stresses, both in terms of the issues they are compelled to resolve and the increasing demands for political participation by newly emerging groups in the society. Housing, communal services, and crime may be common problems in all societies, but societies undergoing more rapid rates of urbanization may be suddenly overwhelmed with congested urban settings and the social displacement brought on by massive migration from the countryside to the city.[20] Ethnic, class, and professional identities may coalesce in mobilized societies. As greater numbers of minorities crowd into cities, a common language and race reinforce self-conscious attitudes among these ethnic groups; their common expectations and insecurity may spur increasing resentment against the political and cultural dominance of the majority ethnic group in the society. More students graduate from higher educational institutions. As they enter the work forces, cleavages harden in occupational sectors and bureaucracies between the older elites and these younger, more highly educated line and staff personnel. The corps of specialized cadres and technicians rapidly expands in industrializing societies. With the growth of professionalism, demands increase from this specialized stratum to participate directly in political decisions. As economic and social problems become more complex, political elites may turn more frequently to the specialists for advice or incorporate a greater percentage of them into the political leadership itslef.

Regional parties may experience these effects of social mobilization very directly. To accommodate the mobilized strata and to retain its legitimacy, the Party will expand its rate of Party recruitment to absorb these new groups. More Party members would come from non-Russian ethnic groups or professional elites. As larger numbers of students graduate from the universities and enter the regional work force, the average educational level of Party members will increase. Yet, as the composition of the regional Party changes, many of the newly mobilized groups will eventually occupy lower positions in the Party-state bureaucracies. The perennial conflict between lower-level cadres and the regional leadership is extended along the same ethnic, class, and professional cleavages in the society. Russians with comparatively little education and technical training will be directing non-Russian subordinates who graduated from higher

17

educational institutions with professional backgrounds. As the regional party becomes a microcosm of the societal divisions, commitment and performance at lower levels of the bureaucracy will dramatically decline. To remedy this situation, the Party leadership must be willing to recruit sizable enough percentages of these new cadres into higher positions. If the Party leadership adapts in this way to the latent demands of its constituency, turnover in the limited positions of the obkom bureau will increase. The background and origins of bureau officials may soon reflect the changing mix of social groups and strata. Where once bureau members were Party generalists and typically recruited from outside a region, they now are drawn from among professional-technical cadres who have spent all their careers in the same region.

Communal services, housing, cadre morale, and antisocial behavior should occupy increasing attention at obkom plenary sessions and conferences, as these problems assume more troublesome dimensions in rapidly mobilized societies. Specialists will be called upon to advise on relevant issues. All this, of course, assumes that regional parties do make some attempt to adapt. The problem may not be as simple for the leadership in Moscow, cognizant of the pressures upon regional leaders but also wary of "localism," "family circles," corruption, and withdrawal from All-Union responsibilities. Directing cadres in the region may by bureaucratic routine continue to be shifted between regions and bureaucratic sectors, in order to prevent too close an identification with local problems and political cohorts. An increase of internal recruitment from within the regional party among other factors would therefore signal a growing awareness of the morale problem by central authorities. Yet inability or unwillingness to respond on the part of regional leaders will isolate the Party even more from society at its very grass-roots level.

The second hypothesis of this study, then, states that political adaptation among the regional parties has varied directly with the levels of social mobilization in the regions. We expect to find that regions that have undergone more rapid or fundamental environmental change have higher turnover rates in obkom bureaus and different kinds of personnel assigned to the bureaus. Regions with different levels of social mobilization should also vary in the themes of plenums and specialized conferences and in the relative participation rates of occupational sectors. Social mobilization in the study will be operationalized by four regional indices of modernization: urbanization, students in higher educational institutions, technical specialists with completed higher education active in the work force, and total population with completed higher education. The indices will measure both the absolute levels of social mobilization and the rates of change over time. The null hypothesis assumes no relationship will be found between the two policy dimensions and regional social mobilization. If such a null relationship is verified by the data analysis and if political participation has actually declined since 1964 (hypothesis one), confirmation of these two hypotheses would support the thesis that the CPSU is an ideocratic and degenerating Party structure.

A third explanation assumes that the potential for adaptation in any regional party should be influenced most directly by the obkom first secretary in a region. The socioeconomic contingencies of the environment only establish certain parameters in which regional parties must operate. It is the obkom first secretary who ultimately interprets developments in the environment, defines the nature of issues, and reacts to the demands for participation.[21] In one sense, obkom first secretaries only mediate the environmental contingencies of a region. To the extent that the actions of obkom first secretaries are constrained by the environmental factors of the region, political adaptation should not be affected by the turnover of first secretaries in the same region.

In another sense, obkom first secretaries could independently influence the policy dimensions of a region. The origins and career backgrounds of first secretaries assigned to regions or to the same region over time may not be identical. While all first secretaries must respond to the same kinds of regional pressures, variance among regional parties at least in the short run could be related to differences in the attitudes and political styles of first secretaries. As one hypothesized example, obkom first secretaries born or educated in the same region to which they are assigned may be more sensitive to regional needs and cadre problems than outsiders designated from the center with no ties to the region. Obkom first secretaries with careers spent in different occupational contexts may project the prejudices of their own particular occupational concerns onto the regional parties and should differ in the relative emphasis and importance they ascribe to agricultural, industrial, or ideological problems in a region. Obkom first secretaries who reached maturity or began their political careers by entering the Party at a later period than other first secretaries may have a different set of policy priorities or may be less fearful of change than the older and more politically established first secretaries.

Our third hypothesis states that similar regions with different kinds of first secretaries (as to their careers, origins, ages) will have different themes emphasized in plenary sessions and different rates of occupational sector participation in plenary sessions and that these differences should bear a direct relationship to the background-career characteristics of first secretaries. Issue adaptation (plenary themes) and participation (occupational sectors) should vary in a consistent direction according to the first secretaries who served in the 25 regions of our sample during 1970.

NOTES

1. T. H. Rigby, Communist Party Membership in the USSR (Princeton, N.J.: Princeton University Press, 1970).

2. Merle Fainsod, How Russia Is Ruled (revised ed.; Cambridge: Harvard University Press, 1965), pp. 307-345; Philip Stewart, Political Power in the Soviet Union (New York: Bobbs-Merrill, 1968), pp. 134-177; Jerry Hough, The Soviet Prefects: The Local Party Organs in Industrial Decision-Making (Cambridge: Harvard University Press, 1969); Peter Frank, "The CPSU First Secretary: A Profile," British Journal of Political Science 1, 2 (April 1971): 173-190.

3. Peter Juvilier and Henry Morton, eds., Soviet Policy Making (New York: Praeger Publishers, 1967); H. Gordon Skilling and Franklyn Griffiths, Interest Groups in Soviet Politics (Princeton, N.J.: Princeton University Press, 1971).

4. Studies of Union-republic parties have been the most noteworthy exceptions. The perennial problem for the central Kremlin leadership has been to limit the outgrowth of nationalism and an identifiable national leadership within the republics. Examples of this genre in Western studies include John A. Armstrong, The Soviet Bureaucratic Elite: A Case Study of the Ukrainian Apparatus (New York: Praeger Publishers, 1959); Yaroslav Bilinski, The Second Soviet Republic: The Ukraine after World War II (New Brunswick, N.J.: Rutgers University Press, 1964), especially pp. 241-249; Michael Rywkin, Russia in Central Asia (New York: Collier Books, 1963), pp. 101-152; and Teresa Rakowska-Harmstrone, Russia and Nationalism in Central Asia: The Case of Tadzhikistan (Baltimore: Johns Hopkins Press, 1971), pp. 94-191.

5. Stewart, Political Power in the Soviet Union. See in particular Stewart's discussion of the "effective competence" of the obkom in plenary sessions, pp. 58-64.

6. Merle Fainsod, Smolensk under Soviet Rule (New York: Vintage Books, 1963), pp. 74 ff.

7. Armstrong, The Soviet Bureaucratic Elite.

8. Hough, The Soviet Prefects.

9. This interpretation of the present Soviet leadership has been culled from a number of sources: Zbigniew Brzezinski, "The Soviet Political System: Transformation or Degeneration," Problems of Communism 15, 1 (January-February 1966): 1-15 and Between Two Ages (New York: Viking Press, 1971), pp. 154-176; Michel Tatu, Power in the Kremlin: From Khrushchev to Kosygin (New York: Viking Press, 1970); Carl Linden, Khrushchev and the Soviet Leadership, 1957-1964 (Baltimore: Johns Hopkins Press, 1966); Frederick C. Barghoorn, Politics in the USSR (2d ed.; Boston: Little, Brown, 1972), pp. 219-240; and T. H. Rigby, "The Soviet Leadership: Towards

a 'Self-stabilizing Oligarchy'," Soviet Studies 22, 2 (October 1970): 167-191.

10. Rigby, "The Soviet Leadership," 190-191.

11. Juvilier and Morton, eds., Soviet Policy Making; Skilling and Griffiths, eds., Interest Groups in Soviet Politics; Michael Gehlen and Michael McBride, "The Soviet Central Committee: An Elite Analysis," American Political Science Review 62, 4 (December 1968): 1232-1241; Joel Schwartz and William Keech, "Group Influence and the Policy Process in the Soviet Union," American Political Science Review 62, 3 (September 1968): 840-851; Philip Stewart, "Soviet Interest Groups and the Policy Process: The Repeal of Production Education," World Politics 22, 3 (October 1969): 29-50.

12. Jeremy Azrael, Managerial Power and Soviet Politics (Cambridge: Harvard University Press, 1966), pp. 152-172.

13. George Fischer, The Soviet System and Modern Society (New York: Atherton Press, 1968).

14. Hough, The Soviet Prefects, especially pp. 289-318.

15. Stewart, Political Power in the Soviet Union, pp. 59-64.

16. Zbigniew Brzezinski, The Permanent Purge (Cambridge: Harvard University Press, 1956).

17. Group identities have been more sharply drawn since 1953, according to Milton Lodge, "Soviet Elite Participatory Attitudes in the Post-Stalin Period," American Political Science Review 62, 3 (September 1968): 827-839.

18. Rigby, "The Soviet Leadership," p. 179.

19. Karl W. Deutsch, "Social Mobilization and Political Development," American Political Science Review 55, 3 (September 1961): 493-514. For an attempt to relate levels of social mobilization to ethnic group composition and identification in the Soviet Union, see John A. Armstrong, "The Ethnic Scene in the Soviet Union: The View of the Dictatorship," in Erich Goldhagen, ed., Ethnic Minorities in the Soviet Union (New York: Praeger Publishers, 1968), pp. 3-49; and Brian Silver, "Social Mobilization and the Russification of Soviet Nationalities," American Political Science Review 68, 1 (March 1974): 45-66. The response of Communist states to varying levels of socioeconomic development has been examined on a quantitative basis by Dennis Pirages, "Socioeconomic Development and Political Access in the Communist Party-States," in Jan F. Triska, ed., Communist Party-States (New York: Bobbs-Merrill, 1969), pp. 249-281.

20. On the relationship between modernization, social displacement, and criminal behavior in the Soviet Union, see Walter D. Connor, Deviance in Soviet Society (New York: Columbia University Press, 1972).

21. On the major policy role of obkom first secretaries, see Stewart, Political Power in the Soviet Union, pp. 134-177.

THE PARAMETERS OF
REGIONAL POLICY-MAKING

The regional Party organizations are the most important coordinating link to the periphery in the Soviet political system. While the policies and goals are specified by the central Party and state organs, the primary responsibility for implementing and shaping policy in terms of local conditions rests with the regional parties. Unless the regional parties can flexibly adapt those decisions to local conditions, the relevance of these local organs as political subsystems is seriously undermined. Rote duplication of actions among the regions may satisfy the desire of the central authorities for discipline and political control, but it threatens the system's overall performance in industrial and agricultural production with that peculiar Soviet bureaucratic sclerosis known as shablonism. The post-1964 condemnation of rigid uniformity in policy implementation or shablonism under Khrushchev,[1] the increased policy discretion supposedly granted to enterprise directors since 1965, and repeated appeals for more local Party initiative[2] at least suggest an awareness by the central Soviet authorities of the necessity for some local initiative and policy decentralization. To paraphase General Secretary Brezhnev at the 24th Party Congress in 1971, the Party must avoid the equally dangerous consequences of an "anarchic lack of discipline" and a "bureaucratic centralization," which constrains initiative and activeness.[3]

EXTENT OF REGIONAL DIVERSITY

Two of the most important indications of regional Party diversity would be variation in the time periods in which obkom plenums are convened and the same issues are discussed at obkom plenums. Table 2.1 compares the themes of all obkom plenums during 1970

TABLE 2.1

Obkom Plenary Themes by Issue Sector and Month, January–October 1970

Issue Sector	Jan.	Feb.	Mar.	Apr.	May	June	July	Aug.	Sept.	Oct.	Total	Maximum Total Same Month
Industry	2	2	2	3	3	5	1	—	—	—	18	5
Agriculture	—	—	—	1	3	5	17	3a	—	—	29	17
December Plenum	12	—	—	—	—	—	—	—	—	—	12	12
Ideology	—	—	1	1	1	1	—	—	1	1	5	1
Cadres	3	—	1	2	4b	3	—	—	1	—	14	4
Organizational	6	2	1	5	4	2	9	—	1	1	31	9
Social welfare	1	—	—	—	—	1	—	—	—	—	2	1
Other	1	—	—	1	—	—	—	—	—	—	2	1
Total	24	4	5	13	14	17	27	3	3	2	113	50 (44%)
Maximum total same sector in one month	12	2	2	5	4	5	17	3	1	1	52 (46%)	—
Total obkom, plenums	13	3	3	8	9	10	17	3	1	1	68	
Of total, only organizational question discussed	1	1	—	2	—	—	—	—	—	—	4	

Note: The author left Moscow on November 5. Up to that time, only part of the October regional press had been accumulated in the stacks of the Current Periodical Room of the Lenin Library. As many regional parties were preparing for local Party conferences to elect delegates to the regional conference, the Union-republic Congress, and the All-Union Congress, it seems unlikely that additional plenums would have been convened in the intervening period. The reader should be aware, however, that the regional press was not systematically read for the month of October for all 25 regions. In later tables, September and October will be treated as one time period.

aThe three plenums held in August, like the 17 in July, discussed the July Agricultural Plenum report delivered by General Secretary Brezhnev at the Central Committee Plenum on July 2.

bThere were actually three regions that discussed cadre problems. Rostov held a plenum at which two separate cadre reports were considered.

Sources: Regional newspapers of the 25 regions, January–October 1970.

by issue sector and month. The classification of obkom plenums by issue sectors was determined by the nominal definition of the plenum themes in the agenda reports published in the 25 regional newspapers.* At first glance at Table 2.1, there would appear to be a wide distribution in the timing and discussion of topics among the regional parties. Of all plenum themes, less than 45 percent were concentrated in the same one-month period for all 25 regions. Only five regions, as an example, held industrial plenums during June, while the remaining industrial plenums are well scattered throughout the seven-month period between January and July. There is also no one period in which cadre or organizational questions dominate obkom plenums. Only 29 percent of the plenums at which these questions were raised occurred in the same month. The only themes that appear to occur other than randomly are agriculture and the December Plenum report. The 17 obkom plenum reports on agriculture during July were directly linked to the agricultural plenum convened by the Central Committee in early July. The December Plenum theme was a direct reaction to Brezhnev's report at the Central Committee plenum on cadres and economic performance in December of 1969. Indeed, by subtracting the themes of agriculture and the December Plenum from all plenum themes, only 21 of the remaining 72 themes were discussed in a simultaneous one-month period.

The same relative distribution of themes by month is shown in the column breakdown. Only 52 of the plenum themes were simultaneously considered in the same one-month periods by the regions. Again, Central Committee plenums appear to limit the overall independence of regional parties. Of the 24 plenum themes in January, 12 concerned the preceding December report, and, more significantly, 20 of the 21 substantive themes (excluding "organizational" changes) considered by the regions during July and August centered on the

---

*As it will be carefully emphasized later in this chapter, the nominal definitions of issues can be frequently misleading as to the actual nature of the policy discussed. Even if one were to accept the nominal definitions as valid descriptions, regions with an obkom plenum on the December Plenum report of General Secretary Brezhnev had to be classified into a separate issue sector labeled "December Plenum." The regions that convened plenums on this report equally stressed agricultural, industrial, cadre, antisocial behavior, and social welfare problems in their discussion and could not, even on the nominal level, be placed in one of the conventional thematic categories. As the dominant theme of the December Plenum concerned the economy, the sector will be merged with the "industrial" sector in subsequent tables, although the real distinction in emphasis between the sectors should be remembered.

TABLE 2.2

Obkom Conferences by Issue Sector and Month, January-October 1970

Issue Sector	Jan.	Feb.	Mar.	Apr.	May	June	July	Aug.	Sept.	Oct.	Total	Maximum Total Same Month
Industry	1	10	2	3	1	3	4	4	4	—	32	10
Agriculture	8	5	15a	3	7	8	2	5	7b	—	60	15
Ideology	26c	10	15	6	5	7	6	12d	7	2	96	26
Cadres	2	5	5e	3	1	5	3	3	5	3	35	5
Socialist legality	1	1	1	1	5	1	3	2	—	—	15	5
Social welfare	2	4	2	—	—	1	3	—	—	—	12	4
Total	40	35	40	16	19	25	21	26	23	5	250	65 (22%)
Maximum total same sector in one month	26	10	15	6	7	8	6	12	7	3	100 (40%)	—

Notes: "Conferences" are defined to include all oblast Party aktivs, oblast Party-economic aktivs, and oblast specialized conferences, seminars, and slety. Excluded from our definition are all regularly accuring oblast seminars, such as retraining seminars for officials in the political education network in August, and highly special oblast conferences related to nonregional events, such as the special sessions of the oblast Lenin Centenary Commissions during January and February. "Ideological" conferences include all conferences and meetings of ideological, educational, and cultural officials.

aIncludes five agricultural conferences in Kaluga oblast.
bIncludes three agricultural conferences in Kaluga oblast.
cIncludes two ideological conferences in Perm', Vologda, Smolensk, and Saratov oblasts.
dIncludes three ideological conferences in Yaroslavl' oblast.
eIncludes two cadre conferences in Rostov and Zaporozh'ye oblast.

Sources: Regional newspapers of 25 regions, January-October 1970.

July Plenum report. With these two exceptions, however, the regional parties demonstrate fairly wide-ranging and autonomous "effective competence"[4] from central dictate in the timing and in the selection of topics for their plenums.

The impression of subsystem autonomy is also confirmed in Table 2.1 by the varying time periods in which the 68 obkom plenums were convened. Only 42 percent of all obkom plenums were timed to coincide either with an All-Union Central Committee Plenum or a plenum of the Ukrainian Central Committee. It is true that the three plenums convened in August also discussed the July agricultural report. But even the addition of these three plenums to the 29 in January and July still leaves over 50 percent of the plenums with no direct relation to a Central Committee plenum at the All-Union or Union-republic levels. After subtracting the four obkom plenums at which the only theme was a dismissal of the first or second secretary, we find that the remaining 30 obkom plenums with substantive issues were unrelated to comparable discussions in the other regions of the sample. The evidence in Table 2.1 would not support the conclusion that officials in Moscow and Kiev rigidly standardize the timing and themes of obkom plenums.

Obkom plenums are only a limited segment of the policy-making process on the regional level. Much of the review of issues and problems also occurs on the less official level of oblast conferences, seminars, and meetings of the Party aktiv, where specifically designated groups or officials from the regional party and state apparatus participate in forums on particular topics. These conferences and assorted formal gatherings range in scope and specificity from the broadly based meetings of all Party aktiv in the regions to the narrowly defined seminars and specialized meetings for cadre officials, industrial enterprise directors, oblast judicial officials, social welfare personnel, or cultural-educational officials. These conferences are called at the initiative of the obkom or obkom bureau and typically are chaired by the secretaries or department directors of the obkom.

The importance of these conferences cannot be underestimated in a total appraisal of the daily policy operations and responses of the oblast party. While their function and impact may be less than formal obkom plenums, they serve as an important ongoing link to lower-level cadres in the Party, state, and economic sectors of the region. From descriptions in the regional press, these conferences appear to have important mobilizing and informational consequences for daily routines. At Party-economic aktiv meetings, the participants in the large assemblage, often numbering in the hundreds, are exhorted to return to their shops and farms to increase production or to achieve regional goals specified at the meetings. Attendance at other conferences is defined more narrowly in terms of those with common

26

responsibility for a particular functional area of regional policy, such as the oblast district and city Party secretaries. At such conferences a forum is provided for the exchange of information on the specified topic or, as in the case of cadre secretaries in 1970, officials receive detailed instructions on the means for implementing election campaigns at the lower level of the Party. As some students of the group process in the Soviet Union have argued, the linkage is not always downward. Procedures are sometimes modified as a result of feedback provided in these conferences. The conferences can reinforce group identities or provide a forum at which alternatives on a policy are expressed.[5]

The exact role and function of these formal gatherings are far from clear. As a particular example, meetings of the oblast Party aktiv actually appear to be quite similar to obkom plenums. Formally, the obkom and the obkom bureau are the only elected organs on the regional Party level. Elected organs alone have the right to make and enforce decisions binding on the regional Party organization. By right only the obkom plenums, the meeting of the oblast committee as a whole, can approve policy resolutions or change personnel under the nomenklatura of the regional Party. In the discussion of issues only the members of the oblast committee are supposed to participate. From the bitterness aroused by Khrushchev's use of "expanded" plenums and the participation in plenums by noncommittee personnel, it seems obvious that the right of participating in a plenum is a jealously guarded prerogative for committee members. In contrast, the oblast aktiv meetings are opened to participation by noncommittee Party members. As a result, the Party at times has gone to lengths to distinguish the secondary nature of oblast aktivs from the Party plenums:

> . . . It should go without saying that meetings of the aktiv are not guiding elected organs of the Party organization. Its participants are not elected or delegated by Communists, but are invited by the party committee (obkom) itself, depending on the nature of the question discussed. As a result, this meeting, despite all of its significance, has a consultative nature. Its decisions in relation to the bureau of the related Party committee have to bear a recommendatory nature. Whenever this decision is confirmed by the bureau of the Party committee, it then becomes obligatory for all Communists of the current Party organization.[6]

In reality, the sharp distinction between "elected" obkoms and "consultative" aktivs breaks down as practiced at the regional level. As shown in Table 2.1, twenty of the regions convened plenums during

July and August on the July agricultural report and only 12 of the 25 regions held plenums in January to discuss Brezhnev's December Plenum report. Yet, at the same time, the other five regions held meetings of their oblast aktivs in July and August on the agricultural report, and nine other regions convened aktivs during January, at which the central report was on the December plenum. At both the plenums and aktivs, the reports were typically delivered by the obkom first secretary. In most cases the proportion of officials from various occupational sectors in the obkom plenums closely paralleled the levels of participation in the corresponding Party aktivs.[7]

Speculation would lead us to believe that the only real difference between plenums and meetings of the Party aktiv on the same theme is the formal ability of plenums to act on personnel assignments. Regions with plenums in January and July in several occasions also appointed new industrial or agricultural directors for the obkom departments at the same plenum. Obkom first secretaries, reluctant to take immediate action against responsible apparatchiki, can prolong decisions on personnel by holding an aktiv rather than a plenum. Even in personnel assignments, however, obkom directors in 1970 frequently were identified in their positions long before official action was taken to approve them by the obkom plenums, so the formality of a plenum decision would not always appear to be necessary.

The distinction between participation in plenums and aktivs is further obscured by the number of "expanded" plenums convened by several of the regional parties in 1970. Of the 68 plenums in the sample, 11 were "expanded" plenums. "Expanded" plenums refer to meetings at which a large number of officials who are not elected obkom members are invited to participate. There does not appear to be any consistent pattern by region or topic that could account for a region calling an "expanded" plenum in 1970. The prominence of "expanded" plenums in 1970 might suggest either that the decision-making impact of the obkom plenum has been further downgraded or that certain regional leaders now have acknowledged the utility of opening participation on a regular basis to noncommittee officials. Or perhaps an inverted gradation of aktivs, "expanded" plenums, and plenums bears some relationship to the perceived importance of the issue discussed by the regional leadership. For the purposes of reliability, the themes and participants in both "expanded" and regular obkom plenums will be treated as one equivalent political forum distinct from Party aktivs, included with other Party conferences. As a prominent student of the Communist Party once concluded, however, any real distinction between a plenum and an aktiv is probably more of name than of substance.[8]

Whatever their specific role or importance, it is sufficient at this point to ask if the regions varied in the kinds of formal conferences and their timing. Table 2.2 includes all obkom conferences and meetings convened at the regional level and reported in the regional press during the first nine and a half months of 1970. Applying the same criteria as for plenum themes, we see that only 22 percent of the issue sectors were concentrated in simultaneous one-month periods. The greatest concentration in absolute terms is the ideological sector. In consideration of the Lenin Centenary, which was celebrated in April, one should not be surprised that 57 of the 96 ideologically related conferences occurred in the four months immediately preceding or concurrent with the April event. In January alone, 18 of the regions held special oblast ideological conferences to discuss the preparations for the Centenary. Agricultural meetings appear to be timed to coincide with the quarterly agricultural reviews on the regional level. Thus 15 of the agricultural conferences occurred in March, 8 in June, and 7 in September. With rare exceptions, the remaining issue sectors are well distributed over time among all regions. Conferences with cadre officials were as likely to be held in February as in September, social welfare issues to be the topic of conferences in February as in July. Overall, ideological and agricultural conferences account for over 60 percent (156) of all obkom conferences in 1970. Almost an equal number of conferences involved problems of social welfare and crime, a fact perhaps not inconsequential in the continuing controversy of applying "material" incentives or "moral" sanctions to spur the sluggish economy. By column months, the conferences are more selectively concentrated than they are by issue sectors. Of the conferences with identical themes, 40 percent were held within the same one-month periods.

A further problem arises in limiting the definition of "issue adaptation" only to the oblast plenums and conferences. The gorkom plenums of regional capitals,* the conferences called at the capital gorkom level, and the published sessions of the oblast and capital soviets also function as alternative policy forums for the discussion of particular issues on a regional basis.

Most of the industry in the regions is centered in the regional capitals, which contain a high proportion of the population. As a result, there appears to be something of an explicit and logical division of responsibility by issue sectors between the obkom and the capital gorkom of regions. Issues that were infrequently discussed in obkom plenums were more often brought up at the gorkom plenums of the capital. During 1970, 26 percent of all obkom plenums themes were on agricultural questions, 16 percent on industry, and only 2 per-

---

*Gorkom is the Russian acronym for gorodskoi komitet, or urban Party committee.

cent on problems of consumer goods and services (See Table 2.2).
On the other hand, of 54 reported gorkom plenum themes in regional
capitals for the same period, 23 percent of the themes concerned
industry, 10 percent social welfare problems, and only 5 percent
agriculture (mostly concerning technical "patronage" of industrial
enterprises for collective and state farms). Although obkom plenums
on the "December Plenum" report were not convened in Vologda,
Yaroslavl', Dnepropetrovsk, and Rostov, gorkom plenums of the
capitals in each of these regions were designated equivalent substitutes
at which the regional Party leaders did review the December Plenum.

A large percentage of educational and cultural institutes and
officials are also located in the capitals of many regions. Conferences
of these officials in several regions were called at the capital gorkom
rather than at the obkom level. As an example, Novosibirsk failed to
convene even one oblast-wide conference of scientists or cultural
officials during 1970, yet several such conferences of officials
employed directly in the city of Novosibirsk were held during the
same time period. One-fifth of the population in the capital of
Novosibirsk is employed in education.[9] Novosibirsk would therefore
suggest the need to consider obkom and capital gorkom conferences
as equivalent and alternative indices of issue concern on a regional
basis. A similar pattern developed in other regions with large numbers of their educational-scientific corps located in the capital.

Problems of social welfare and socialist legality were rarely
considered at the level of obkom plenums (See Table 2.1), yet both
were prominent themes at the published sessions of oblast and capital
soviets during 1970. This is not surprising. The officials of judicial
and consumer departments, as members of the oblast or capital
executive committees, are formally accountable to the oblast or
capital soviets, not to the obkom or capital gorkom. In recent years
the Supreme Soviet has also passed legislation that on its face would
upgrade the authority and budgetary control of local soviets for
consumer and judicial affairs in the regions.[10] Measures of regional
concern with consumer welfare or crime limited only to the official
obkom plenum themes would greatly understate their actual prominence
on the regional level during 1970.

If the nature of issue adaptation is not to be defined too narrowly,
the themes of capital gorkom plenums, gorkom conferences, and
sessions of the oblast and capital soviets must be considered in any
overall measure of issue concern on a regional basis. Our analysis,
therefore, will define issue adaptation as two regional subdimensions:
(1) obkom issue sectors—the themes of obkom plenums; and (2) total
regional issue sectors—the themes of obkom plenums and capital
gorkom plenums, obkom and gorkom conferences, and sessions of
the oblast and capital soviets. Obkom plenums, which have greater

comparability, will be considered independently for each table. The merging of plenums with the other oblast and capital sessions will provide a greater absolute total by which to compare variance among regions. Not to belabor the obvious, but, in collapsing plenums with the other informal conferences, we do not assume these other conferences and sessions are truly equivalent in importance to obkom plenums. In defining the nature of issue adaptation, as total a range of alternative political forums as possible must be taken into account.

Table 2.3 and 2.3A categorize the reporters and participants in obkom plenums during 1970 by elected or occupational position. In the principal reports or opening speeches at an obkom plenum, the nature of the topic is defined, the particular problems are identified, and the remedies are proposed. Identification of typical kinds of reporters with certain topics could distinguish the relative importance of the topic and the administrative officials with particular authority in that area. From his analysis of the Stalingrad obkom, Stewart concluded that "major" addresses are delivered by the obkom first secretary. More typically, issues perceived as less politically significant or pressing are delegated to secretaries and state officials who specialize in the particular issue area. Thus, the principal addresses on ideological and cadre questions are assigned to the ideology or cadres secretaries or to comparable state and mass organization officials, such as the first secretary of the oblast Komsomol.[11]

Failing to establish independent criteria for the importance of issues, Stewart's reasoning is somewhat tautological in that he is then led to identify the nature of a "major" issue with the delivery of the speech by the obkom first secretary. Nevertheless, the obvious conclusion from Stewart's tables is that, when issues have a higher than normal priority in a region, the first secretary himself will deliver the report to the plenum. From 1956 through 1958, at a time when Khrushchev was reorganizing industry on a national scale, the importance of the changes was registered by the fact that the plenum reports on industrial questions were delivered by the obkom first secretary.[12] Stewart notes that the first secretary at times delegates responsibility for less important reports to nonsecretaries, although usually to officials with ascribed positions on the obkom bureau.

In a minor way, then, Table 2.3 measures the relative priority of issues during 1970 and the designated administrative supervision of Party secretaries for particular issues. The obkom first secretary delivered 63 percent of all the plenum reports; secretaries with sepcialist responsibilities, 12 percent of all reports. If a secretary as a reporter defines the importance of the topic, issues varied in terms of their relative significance and the degree of authority exercised by lower administrative personnel. Not surprisingly, the

TABLE 2.3

Principal Reporters at Obkom Plenums

Position	Indus-try	Decem-ber Plenum	Agr.	Ideol.	Cadres	Social Wel-fare	Total
1st obkom	3	12	23	1	8	—	47
Secretary obkom	9	—	2	3	4	1	12
Chairman oblis	—	—	2	—	—	—	2
Chairman oblast trade-union	—	—	—	—	1	—	1
Director obkom dept.	—	—	—	—	—	1	1
Editor oblast newspaper	—	—	—	1	—	—	1
1st raikom	—	—	—	—	1	—	1
1st capital gorkom	1	—	—	—	—	—	1
Directors, railroads	2	(coreport)	—	—	—	—	2
Total	15	12	27	5	14	2	75

TABLE 2.3A

Principal Reporters at Capital Gorkom Plenums

Position	Ind.	Dec. Pl.	Agr.	Ideol.	Cad.	Soc. Wel.	Total
1st gorkom	4	4	1	2	5	—	16
Secretary gorkom	4	—	1	3	2	2	12
Chairman goris	1	—	—	—	—	2	3
Director gorkom dept.	1	—	—	—	—	1	2
1st raikom	1	—	—	2	—	—	3
Director oblast trust	1	—	—	—	—	—	1
Director and sec.-ind. conglomerate	2	—	—	—	—	—	2
Total	14	4	2	7	7	5	39

Sources: Regional press of the 25 regions, January-October 1970.

"major" issues in 1970 were those identified with the December Plenum report and the July agricultural report. In all 12 regions with plenum reports after Brezhnev's December speech (19 including 7 regions with Party aktivs on the December Report), the speech was delivered by the first secretary of the obkom. The 20 regions (25 if one includes Party aktivs) with obkom plenums as a direct response to the July agricultural plenum followed a similar pattern, with the report delivered in every instance by the obkom first secretary.

As Stewart found in Stalingrad, industrial questions in 1970 are usually delegated to the secretary in charge of industry or to the first secretary of the capital gorkom. This was the case in 10 of the 14 industrial plenums. Problems of ideology and cadres were similarly delegated to specialist secretaries or to regional officials with overlapping concerns in their elected positions. Still, while the number of plenums on cadres is too small to derive any meaningful trends, it may be more than a coincidence that 8 of the 14 reports in this area were personally delivered by the first secretary in a year when a Party Congress was pending and criticism from the December Plenum had been leveled against the poor performance of lower-level Party officials.

Only three of the plenum reports were delivered by officials who by position could be considered nonbureau members. In two of these plenums, the report was delivered by a local official in order to illustrate problems particular to his direct administrative unit. Thus, in Trans-Carpathia, general regional problems in cadres were exemplified in the report by the first secretary of the Velikii Bereznyi raikom on the progress his particular district had achieved in reassigning personnel.[13] In Dnepropetrovsk, the plenum report on railroad transport and shipping was delivered by the directors of local railroad sections in the region,[14] although in both Trans-Carpathia and Dnepropetrovsk the obkom first secretary was also said to have contributed a "major" speech at the end of the official report and discussions.

After the principal report is delivered, the agenda of a plenum allows for a certain number of speakers to address themselves to the general report or to dimensions of the policy area that relate to their own particular duties. Participation by individuals identified with particular occupational groups or sectors most likely at a minimum has an important symbolic impact on the morale of lower-level cadres in those same sectors. Although referring to the morale function of participation in the Stalingrad plenums, Stewart primarily stressed the "tutorial" function of participation as part of the decision-making process in the region—setting an agenda for lower officials in an issue area or channeling suggestions from these officials to the regional leadership.[15]

The participation by occupational sectors and issues for all plenums is summarized in Table 2.4. As the reporters in plenums, the absolute level of occupational sectors in plenums may reflect upon the sectors' general importance in the region or their relative administrative responsibility for particular areas. The secretaries in urban and district party organizations are the most heavily represented in all obkom plenary sessions, accounting for 37 percent of all discussants. This is not surprising. From previous studies of oblast committees, urban and district Party secretaries typically make up 35 to 40 percent of all oblast committee members.[16] Their rate of participation is consistently high for all issues discussed but varies somewhat according to the particular nature of the plenum issue under review during 1970. Thus, the proportional levels of urban-district secretaries are highest for agricultural and cadre questions, accounting for 44 and 41 percent of all discussants in both sectors. The stability of participation by urban-district secretaries can be noted in comparing their similar levels on the same issues in Stalingrad between 1954 and 1960. At that time, 38 percent of all participants on agriculture and 53 percent of all participants on cadre questions were drawn from the urban-district party secretaries.[17]

Urban and district secretaries were much more likely to participate in plenums on the December report than in normal industrial plenums (38 to 22 percent). In the December report obkom plenums, the general problem of industrial productivity at times was framed in the broader context of agriculture and cadres problems whose responsibility would fall more directly on the urban-district secretaries. Although only by a difference of 5 percent, officials of the oblast mass organizations with direct cadre responsibilities were also more represented in the December report plenums than in the typical industrial plenums. In contrast, officials from the All-Union or Union-republic level constituted almost a fourth of all participants in industrial plenums and only 3 percent of all participants in the December report plenums.

It might be expected that "expanded" plenums would dramatically affect the proportional levels of participation by opening up the discussion to noncommittee sectors underrepresented in the oblast committee itself. With a smaller number of representatives on the oblast committee, farm officials should displace the normally high ratio of urban-district secretaries in regular plenums. The figures for 1970, however, show only extremely marginal differences between regular and "expanded" agricultural plenums. In the seven "expanded" plenums, the percentage levels for local secretaries and farm officials were 42 and 22 percent, in contrast to 44 and 19 percent for all agricultural plenums. This finding reaffirms the conclusion that regular and "expanded" plenums are actually quite similar.

TABLE 2.4

Participation in Obkom Plenums by Occupational and
Issue Sectors (excluding principal reporters)
(in percentages)

Occupational Sectors	Plenum Issue Sectors						Total	
	Dec.				Soc.			
	Ind.	Pl.	Agr.	Ide.	Cad.	Wel.		
Obkom secretaries	4	—	1	4	3	—	2	(16)
Gorrai secretaries	22	38	44	36	41	67	37	(304)
Oblast officials[a]	9	14	23	4	3	22	15	(123)
Obl. mass orgs.[b]	4	10	1	11	10	—	5	(41)
All-Union or U.-Rep. officials	24	3	4	2	2	—	7	(57)
Farm officials[c]	2	9	19	13	11	—	12	(100)
Industrial officials[d]	13	11	7	2	9	—	9	(72)
Engineering-technical personnel[e]	10	2	3	27	1	11	5	(45)
Others	12	13	3	—	20	—	9	(74)
Total	100	100	100	100	100	100	100	
	(165)	(130)	(366)	(45)	(116)	(9)	(832)	

[a]Chairmen and deputy chairmen of oblast executive committees, directors of oblast departments and administrations, and oblast police-judicial officials.

[b]Officials of oblast trade-union organizations, Komsomol, and control commissions.

[c]Chairmen and secretaries of collective farms, directors and secretaries of state farms, farm mechanizers, brigade leaders.

[d]Directors and chief engineers of industrial enterprises and secretaries of the plant Party committees. Only five plant secretaries participated.

[e]Engineer-technical personnel on oblast or enterprise level. The personnel were classified according to their position (director of a research institute), their title (chief economist of the oblast), or their occupational function (doctor in a hospital, teacher, head of metallurgy research in an industrial enterprise).

Sources: Regional press of the 25 regions, January-October 1970.

Criticism of the Communist Party often centers upon the absence of technical and scientific representation in Party policy-making. In the analysis of participation, therefore, we should be particularly concerned with the proportional representation of officials from those sectors that might be termed the "scientific-technical" elite in the region. How well represented in the discussion of issues are they? This elite will be defined as those enterprise officials and engineer-technical personnel at the oblast, urban, and enterprise level who participate in plenums. Combined, these two sectors make up 14 percent of the discussants in all obkom plenums. As with the local secretaries, the participation levels of these two sectors vary according to the issue discussed. Not surprisingly, enterprise and engineer-technical personnel had their greatest representation on strictly industrial problems, accounting for 23 percent of all participants in the 14 industrial plenums. Indicative of the difference between normal industrial plenums and the December report plenums, both sectors fall off sharply for the 12 plenums in which general questions of industry were considered in the wider dimensions of Brezhnev's December report. The large percentage of scientific-technical personnel in the ideological sector is partly a result of the diffuse manner in which the category was defined to include educational and cultural officials with engineers and economists. Of primary importance in our analysis of participation, however, will be whether regions vary in the proportion of enterprise and engineer-technical personnel who participate in their plenums.

Measures of participation limited to obkom plenums misrepresent the total spectrum of participation on a regional basis. Table 2.3A shows the principal reporters at 38 capital gorkom plenums during 1970. While the sample is too small for generalization beyond the 38 plenums, there is a greater decentralization of responsibility and authority evident in capital gorkom plenums than at the obkom level. The only topic in which the report was consistently delivered by the gorkom first secretary was the December Plenum report. Given the predominance of industry in many capital gorkoms, it would be expected that the industrial report would always be delivered by the gorkom first secretary. Even here, as Table 2.3A shows, many gorkom first secretaries delegated responsibility for the industrial report to the second or industrial secretaries or, as in five gorkom plenums, to nonsecretaries. The reports on ideology or local consumer affairs were also typically allotted to gorkom secretaries, the chairmen of the city executive committees, first secretaries of borough parties in the city, or gorkom department heads.

The "scientific-technical" elite also participate at higher levels in capital gorkom plenums than in obkom plenums. In 19 capital gorkom plenums for which discussants were listed in the regional press, enterprise officials and engineer-scientific personnel constituted 34 percent of all participants and elected party officials at all levels constituted 29 percent. The corresponding percentages for all obkom plenums in 1970 are 14 and 39 percent (See Table 2.4). Even the latter percentage for Party officials actually underestimates the real total by excluding many secretaries of collective and state farms, classified in obkom plenums as "farm officials." The disparity between gorkom and obkom plenums holds even when the issue is identical at both Party levels. In eight gorkom plenums on industry, 19 percent of all participants were enterprise officials and 26 percent were engineer-technical personnel. By contrast, in the 14 industrial obkom plenums, only 13 percent of the participants were enterprise officials and 10 percent engineer-technical personnel. At an extreme, the reported plenums of one raikom* in a suburb just outside the city of Novosibirsk illustrate the changing adaptation pattern at lower levels of the regional party. Two plenums of the Soviet borough committee were reported in the local Novosibirsk press during 1970.[18] Of the 10 discussants in the two plenums, half were scientists or administrators of scientific-research institutes in the borough and included an academician, the director of the Soil and Agro-Chemistry Institute, the director of the Cytology and Genetics Institute, and two major officials of the Siberian Academy of Science.

Novosibirsk may be unique in the large absolute number of scientists employed directly within an urban area, and the Soviet raikom is located within a suburb with a significant percentage of the work force in research institutes (the "Academic City" of Novosibirsk).[19] Moreover, at least one of the five scientists and administrators who participated in the Soviet raikom plenums has a closer immediate background identification with the regional Party apparatus than with the scientific community of Novosibirsk. Prior to his election as deputy chairman of the Siberian Academy of Sciences, M. P. Chemodanov had been director of the science and educational institutions department of the Novosibirsk obkom.[20] In this sense, Chemodanov's formal title may be misleading as to his actual political control function within the Siberian Academy. Despite these qualifications and uncertainties, the example of the Soviet raikom and the higher proportion of enterprise and scientific personnel who participate in all capital gorkom plenums may illustrate two important factors in measuring regional Party adaptation as a whole. Lower levels of the party, below the obkom, are apparently given greater leeway to adjust membership in their committees in

---

*Raikom is the Russian acronym for raionnyi komitet, or the district Party committee (borough as subordinate unit in a city).

proportion to the levels of occupational personnel under their immediate territorial authority. Correlations between oblast characteristics and oblast committees may be drawn at too high a level to catch the real association between environment and the political system experienced at the lower and more compact urban and district Party organizations. Secondly, as reflected by the reporters at capital gorkom plenums, the resolution of issues below the obkom is more informal, less dominated by the intervention of Party officials, and, perhaps, more open to bargaining and the accommodation of alternative views. All the last points, of course, are mere speculation. The data at least suggest that the symbolic effect on the scientific-technical elite is greater overall at the gorkom and the raikom level than at the oblast committee level. It remains to be seen whether this intended symbolic effect on the obkom level varies according to different kinds of regions.

SUBSTANTIVE AND METHODOLOGICAL PROBLEMS

The tentative manner in which "issue adaptation" and "participation" have been defined points to a number of substantive and methodological problems inherent in a comparative analysis of policy-making among regional parties. While it could be argued that all research in political science is limited by the implicit values and the perspectives of the analyst, research on political phenomena in the Soviet Union is doubly confounded by the secretive and most often inaccessible nature of hard data on the Soviet system. Many of these problems are not particular to the regional party as a research topic or to the regional press as a secondary data source. Sensitive to the underlying meaning in formal pronouncements and reports by Soviet leaders, the student of Soviet politics is wary of accepting any statements of "facts" presented in the Soviet press and recognizes the great disparity that often distinguishes appearances and reality in the Soviet context. Eventually, all students of Soviet politics must reconcile themselves to findings based upon questionable secondary data and research designs constructed to fit the information the Soviets sources have made available. This does not negate the general validity of research on the Soviet system but only alerts us to the very obvious pitfalls in accepting Soviet secondary materials on their face. Yet Western analysts have begun to treat the themes and participants in Party plenums and conferences with greater seriousness.[21] Quantitative analysis of these plenums and their participants now is employed as a research technique. Although the comparative analysis of regional parties is unique to this study, the methodology and the framework were closely adapted from these previous studies.

At the same time, very early during his research the author became aware of irresolvable substantive and methodological issues that called into question either the utility or the validity of comparing issues and participants. Most of these cannot be corrected until the Soviet system itself fundamentally changes and becomes more open to direct research. Some other issues are inherent to the problems of verification in the social sciences. Indeed, in raising these issues at this point of our discussion, we may achieve the dubious distinction of being a methodological "purist," while negating any significance to the later quantitative analysis. Nevertheless, this brief excursus will serve two useful functions.

Western analysts who have compared issues and participants up to now have either not been explicitly honest enough with their readers or consciously aware themselves of the limitations. Recently, several studies have pointed to a growing reversal of research strategies in the Soviet field.[22] From an inconsistent phase of fact-gathering or deductive model-building, more Soviet-area scholars are redirecting their efforts to the rigorous operationalization of concepts, the accumulation of data, and the verification of explicitly stated hypotheses. This new trend is a welcome corrective to the field, which has been overburdened by extensive descriptive analysis with little methodological rigor or generalizing utility. At the same time, because the approach and techniques are new, scholars following this new trend (such as the author himself) must justify the use of these new techniques with as critical a self-awareness of their limitations as possible. Without a concern for methodology and substantive problems, quantification in the Soviet field is sterile and adds nothing to the traditional inductive approach. Recognition of inadequacies in our analysis, of course, does not exonerate the study. On a more practical level, by suggesting some of the obvious limitations in examining the 1970 regional press, we would only hope to alert others who might replicate this study for trend analysis or might apply the research design to other political levels in the Soviet Union.

Secondly, reference to these caveats might add to our general understanding of regional politics, knowledge of which is drawn solely from the reports on obkom plenums and assorted conferences. Although the author only had two months to read through the regional press in Moscow, his general impression was that local news is significantly underreported in the regional newspapers. Typically, at least half of each daily newspaper is filled with reprints of Pravda editorials and articles or communiqués from TASS. Articles on local issues or problems are the exception to the rule.[23] Indeed, most of what could be considered local news is taken up with reports and discussions of plenums and conferences, so an analysis of their content to a great extent validly reflects the universe of local politics available in the regional newspapers. Philip Stewart may be correct when he suggests that a careful and thorough analysis of the regional press could produce a detailed picture of oblast politics.[24] Even given the time and opportunity (both of which the Soviet officials are unlikely to grant in the near future), though, the value of a lengthy research effort expended on the regional press by itself is highly questionable. In lieu of other data to understand oblast politics, then, we must intuitively relate regional politics to more general events in the Soviet Union. We can only speculate on the real impact of these general events for particular regions, but an awareness of them and their probable importance at least enlarges the explanatory context in which any meaningful discussion of regional politics must be framed. If quantitative analysis must be applied in a self-critical manner, it must also allow for the realities of conflict and decision-making in the Soviet political system.

There are several substantive and methodological problems that arise in limiting our analysis primarily to plenums and conferences. First, the prominence of issues at the regional level cannot be understood independently of more general political trends in the Soviet Union. Studies on the political conflict in the Kremlin have concluded that Brezhnev has attempted over the last few years to consolidate his position against his opponents in the Politburo and Central Committee.[25] If a power struggle is closely involved in the emphasis ascribed to particular issues and proposed solutions, it would be expected that regional parties, many of whose first secretaries are members or candidate members of the Central Committee, are also affected by the political conflict at the center. Issues and problems may be discussed at various obkom plenums not so much because those issues are defined as relevant to a region by the first secretary but rather because the first secretary sides with one of the factions in the central power struggle. That issues are determined by political allegiances would not contradict the framework of subsystemic analysis but would require a more complex explanation of the subsystemic phenomenon.

A revealing example is the varying response to the December Plenum report on the state of the Soviet economy, delivered by General Secretary Brezhnev at an All-Union Central Committee Plenum in late 1969 and a principal policy theme considered by all 25 regional parties in 1970. Little is actually known of the specific contents of the report,[26] although rumors in the West suggested that it was a particularly bitter and candid admission of failures in Soviet economic production.[27] If so, the report either represented an unusual confession of self-guilt on Brezhnev's part, or it more subtly provided a sweeping indictment of incompetency by means of which he could hope to justify ousting Central Committee members and their political clients held administratively accountable for the poor performance. All regional parties in 1970 were presumably cued by the same policy report. Yet only 12 of the 25 regions followed up Brezhnev's report with an obkom plenum in January, and the regional parties consistently differed, over the succeeding nine months, concerning the policy priorities that they felt had been outlined by the report. For certain regions, the December report was interpreted to mean greater attention to labor turnover and work discipline.[28] In other regions, the labor discipline problem was more broadly conceived as Party "cadres" and derived from fundamental "shortcomings" of Party organizations and officials in the plants and construction sites.[29] For these regions, admission standards into the Party had to be raised, and much of each plenum report is taken up by a numerical review of Party membership in the region. In some regions, the economy and work discipline were not simply "cadres" problems but were directly attributed to outright "criminality," which diffusely equated larger-scale pilfering of property in the plants with deliberate criminal negligence on the part of industrial managers.[30] And, in still other regions, the harsh dimensions of the report were downplayed, and the economic difficulties were defined as involving social welfare. Increased productivity and discipline could only be expected if workers were provided with greater material incentives in the form of increased consumer facilities, services, and housing.[31]

In a more limited vein, certain regional parties singled out the oblast trade-union organizations among all regional cadres for the poor economic performance and the decline of labor discipline in the plants and factories.[32] The overidentification of the trade unions with workers was particularly alarming for many regional authorities. As the chairman of the L'vov oblast people's control commission noted, the trade-union organizations of a number of enterprises, organizations, and construction sites still "liberally" evaluated violations of socialist legality and the plundering of socialist property by workers.[33] The director of the Kirov section of the Gorkii Railroad was even more explicit in his criticism: In several occurrences, trade-union locals had "risen to the defense" of their workers who committed labor crimes and had requested the local judicial organs to place the offenders on bail.[34]

Real role conflict between management and trade-union officials does exist at the enterprise level,[35] and the conflict in certain regions may be serious enough to have forced unresolvable and long-term policy divisions even within the regional leadership itself. Thus, in L'vov, where the chairman of the control commission denounced the "liberal" support of workers by trade unions in 1970, the chairman of the oblast trade-union council in 1960 had been summarily dismissed for ignoring the "just grievances" of workers and "unprincipally" supporting the interests of management over those of the workers.[36] At the same time we cannot avoid the significance of the Russian phrase "ne sluchaino" (it is not accidental). The chairman of the All-Union Trade Unions Council is Aleksandr Shelepin, a political rival to Brezhnev on the Politburo.[37] Shelepin more than likely is the one major political leader most closely identified with trade-union assignments and with the performance of local trade-union councils. Criticism of trade-union leadership on the regional level may thus have been only a lightly veiled attempt to establish a case for Shelepin's further demotion from the chairmanship of the Trade-Unions Council. Selective criticism of trade-union activity in certain regions may have paralleled the relative ties of the regional Party leadership with Brezhnev, and not been a labor problem at all.

A second substantive problem is that the political year 1970 in the Soviet Union may have been atypical of the normal situation at the regional level. The relationship between issues and regional characteristics would hold, only if it could be assumed that no significant exogenous factors biased the timing of plenums and the weight assigned to policies in the regions. Yet 1970 was originally to be the year in which the Party convened its 24th Congress. The decision to postpone the Congress until 1971 appears to have been decided at the last moment and involved the ongoing power struggle in the Kremlin. At a July Central Committee plenum, Brezhnev delivered an extensive and well-publicized agricultural report on July 2. The report was printed on July 6, and it concluded with Brezhnev's reference to the convening of the 24th Congress in 1970.[38] Seven days later, on July 13, Pravda and the regional press reported that, at another session of the same plenum, the Central Committee had voted to delay the Party Congress until early 1971. The decision must have been made between the printing date of the agricultural report, July 6, and the announcement on July 13, and the postponement must have been contested. Otherwise, there would have been no reason to retain Brezhnev's reference to the 24th Congress in the published report on July 6, unless it were to discredit Brezhnev and demonstrate his minority position on the issue of the Congress.

The decision to delay apparently also caught some members of the Central Committee unaware. On July 11, the evening newspaper of Novosibirsk carried a report delivered by the Obkom First Secretary Fedor Goriachev at the obkom plenum, convened the afternoon of July 10. As a full member of the Central Committee, Goriachev either may have been absent during the plenary session when the Congress decision was made, had left Moscow after the agricultural reports and resolutions were considered, or had performed the Herculean feat of flying twice to Moscow from Novosibirsk in six

42

days and preparing an obkom plenary report for delivery in Novosibirsk on July 10. Furthermore, Goriachev had definitely been
present in Moscow during the first plenary session, for he was
reported to have been one of the participants who discussed Brezhnev's
agricultural report on July 3.[39] For whatever reason, according to
the Novosibirsk newspaper, Goriachev on July 10 began his report
on Brezhnev's agricultural speech with the highly inaccurate statement of fact: "The 24th Congress of the CPSU will be held this
year. . . ."[40]

Goriachev's faux pas was not repeated by any of the other first
secretaries in their July plenum reports. Few of the other oblasts
convened plenums as early in July as Novosibirsk, and, when they
did, the regional press was careful to delay publication of the obkom
reports for several issues. The sudden postponement, though, is
illustrative of how the Party Congress in general may have influenced
both the themes and timing of plenums and conferences during 1970.
It might be hypothesized that local Party organizations are more
likely to stress certain themes in a year of a Party Congress than
would otherwise be normal. Thus 40 percent of all obkom plenums
during 1970 concerned cadre-organizational problems (See Table 2.1),
and eight of the major reports on cadres at the plenums were personally delivered by the obkom first secretaries (See Table 2.3). This
high level of concern with internal Party affairs may be only normal
for regional parties; but, preparatory to any Party Congress, regional
parties should be more than typically preoccupied with assigning new
personnel and reaffirming cadre discipline. Similarly, 7 percent of
all issues raised at the regional level during 1970 were related
specifically to consumer social welfare problems. This average,
too, may be only normal for regional parties, but the traditional
symbolic gesture to consumer demands in a year when any Party
Congress is held should make us wary of generalizing from this
finding. Of course, in retrospect of Brezhnev's emphasis at the 24th
Party Congress on the exchange of Party cards and increased consumer goods, the stress on cadre-organizational and social welfare
issues at the 1970 regional level could have anticipated a real reversal
in priorities.

The expectation of a Congress in 1970 also may have affected
the timing of obkom plenums and conferences. During 1970, approximately half of all obkom plenums appear to have been convened
randomly, with no immediate relationship to corresponding All-Union
or Union-republic plenums (See Table 2.1). At the same time several
of the plenums that could be considered random between March and
June began to emphasize cadre-organizational problems. If the Party
Congress had been held in late summer, as originally expected, these
plenums for several regions may have been the last held before the

convocation of a regional Party conference to elect delegates to the Congress.

Regional parties would have been more likely to shore up internal Party affairs preparatory to the conference. Thus, the turnover on all levels of the 25 regions is shown in Table 2.5. While the turnover by month does not fit any exact pattern, the highest period of turnover occurs in March and April, the same time the obkom plenums begin to emphasize cadre-organizational problems. The peak is not reached again until September and October, when preparations for regional conferences once again have begun and the last obkom plenums before the regional conferences were convened.

The pattern in which cadre conferences were held in the Zaporozh'e region is typical of several regions and demonstrates how the expectation of the Congress skewed the timing of conferences. On June 6, anticipating the Congress in late summer or early fall, the obkom in Zaporozh'e convened a conference for directors of the Party-organizational departments in the gorkom and raikom Party organizations of the region. The conference was called in particular to instruct the directors on preparations for the then upcoming report-election meetings on the primary Party level, the first stage prior to the oblast Party conference.[41] On August 31, after the Congress had been postponed, the identical conference of directors was convened for the same expressed purpose with the same reporters delivering the identical speeches.[42]

The political year 1970 also may have been atypical because of the great stress placed on the Lenin Centenary at the regional level. That year was the 100th anniversary of Lenin's birth, and the occasion was used by the leadership to mount an extensive mobilization campaign. Twenty-four percent of all issues in the regions during 1970 centered on ideological matters. As mass mobilization campaigns are a general operating characteristic of the system, there may be less reason to doubt that 24 percent of the time on the regional levels is usually taken up with ideological issues. Nevertheless, in the absence of any comparable study of obkom plenums and conferences over time, one cannot be sure that either the substantive themes or the timing of plenums and conferences in 1970 are typical for any other nine and one-half month period. As the 25 regions themselves could not be randomly selected, we may actually have measured substantively unrepresentative plenums and conferences in a substantively atypical time period.

The personal context of issues in the Soviet system and the uniqueness of 1970 are only the more general substantive problems in measuring regional adaption. More immediate difficulties in methodology result from the questionable validity of the reporting in the regional press itself.

TABLE 2.5

Turnover in Party-State Personnel, January-October 1970
(turnover by administrative level and month)

Adm. Level	Jan.	Feb.	Mar.	Apr.	May	June	July	Aug.	Sept. Oct.	Total
Cadres-mass[a]	1	2	1	3	1	1	–	–	1	9
Gorkom-obkom[b]	8	5	–	11	4	5	10	3	7	53
Gorrai secs.[c]	3	8	11	6	7	4	5	3	19	66
Gor.-oblast apparatus[d]	3	–	11	–	–	4	3	2	12	35
Total	15	14	23	20	12	14	18	8	39	163

[a]First Secretary, Komsomol; Chairman, Trade Union Council; Chairman, Peoples' Control Commission.
[b]Secretaries and department directors in obkom and capital gorkom.
[c]Secretaries of urban and district Party organizations.
[d]Chairmen, deputy chairmen, departmental directors, and newspaper editors in capital and regional state apparatus.

Source: Regional press of the 25 regions, January-October 1970.

For one, plenums and conferences are selectively reported in the regional newspapers. From its inception under Lenin, the Soviet press has been utilized by the political leadership as a mobilizing agent of the population. The extensive emphasis given to certain themes and problems in the newspapers is not accidental but is intended to serve the particular needs and perspectives of the leadership. On the regional level, as a candidate or full member of the obkom bureau, the editor of the oblast newspaper is closely tied to the changing policy concerns of the regional leaders and can easily transmit them by the relative press coverage he assigns to themes in the newspaper. All this is obvious to anyone who has even a passing acquaintance with the Soviet press and its selective reporting of political reality. In comparing themes and conferences in that same regional press, however, we must assume that the reports of plenums and conferences accurately reflect the total universe of plenums and conferences held in the region over time.

More likely, quite the contrary is true, as it was even acknowledged at times in the regional newspapers. On April 8, a plenum of the Smolensk oblast committee convened to discuss the work of the oblast newspaper. The convening of a plenum on the regional press in 1970 was unusual in itself, and the editor of the oblast newspaper was later to be relieved of his position under mysterious circumstances. Most importantly, though, one of the major criticisms leveled against the regional newspaper was that too much space in the paper was set aside for reports on conferences and seminars.[43] In contrast, a plenum of the Tambov obkom on May 15 arrived at just the opposite evaluation on the proper role of the regional newspaper. According to the obkom first secretary, the Tambov oblast newspaper was remiss in failing to report enough Party meetings and conferences in order that others could benefit from the "positive experience."[44] In the comparison of conferences among regions, therefore, absolute differences actually may reflect only the relative editorial policies of the newspapers.

Even obkom plenums appear at times to be selectively underreported in the regional press. The Rostov evening newspaper of May 21 reported that an obkom plenum had been held that afternoon in the capital. The themes of the plenum were briefly listed, with the principal report on cadre affairs delivered personally by First Secretary Bondarenko.[45] The editor of the Rostov newspaper may have been premature in mentioning the plenum at all. For although a brief résumé would be expected to follow in future issues of the newspaper, there is absolutely no further specific reference either to the content of the plenum report or to the participants.* The omission could not have been unintended, for this "important" 10th obkom plenum, as it was described, was the theme of several later reported raikom plenums in the region.[46] Similarly, on July 9, Vechernii Rostov published the first in a series of letters from city officials on problems of industrial productivity in the city enterprises.[47] The letters were to serve as a preparatory forum to an important gorkom plenum, which the newspaper reminded its readers would be held at the end of August. While the series of letters continued through July, the gorkom plenum was never held. Or, if it was held (and, given all the prior publicity in the newspaper, this appears distinctly possible), for some reason it was never reported. The difference between a region such as Vologda, with three industrial obkom and capital gorkom plenums in 1970, and Rostov, which failed to convene even one, is probably the result of the relative press coverage in the regions, itself a reflection of internal regional politics and conflicts.†

The regional newspapers are also a particularly unreliable source from which to classify and compare the content of plenums and conferences. Regions will be compared in terms of the absolute formal emphasis they assign to industrial, agricultural, ideological, cadre-organizational, socialist legality, and social welfare issues. The classification is based upon (1) the nominal terms in which the themes of obkom and capital gorkom plenums, or sessions of the oblast-capital soviets, are described in the press or (2) the functional responsibility of the participants in conferences. The problem in accepting the newspaper's classification of themes is that often even

---

*The plenum was also reported in the transmission of Radio Rostov on May 26, 1970. According to the radio transmission, in addition to the discussion of two cadre questions, the plenum had released P. Tolstopiatenko as director of the obkom Party-Organizational department and replaced him with N. D. Belikov.

†During 1970 Rostov had one of the highest turnovers of major personnel among all 25 regions in the sample. Among the personnel replaced were the oblispolkom chairman (retired for reasons of "health"), the capital gorkom first secretary (transferred), the director of the obkom Party-Organizational department, the director of the oblast MVD (Ministry of Internal Affairs; retired on pension), the deputy chairman of the oblispolkom in charge of consumer affairs (transferred), the director of the obkom construction department (transferred), the second secretary of the Rostov gorkom in charge of consumer affairs (transferred), and the two directors of the Rostov city housing and commerce administrations (transferred).

a reading of the stenographic resume of the plenum reveals a great dissimilarity between the stated theme and the actual report. As an example, the Orel oblast held an obkom plenum on September 8 with the principal report by First Secretary Meshkov on organizational-political work for the 24th Congress. Nominally, Meshkov's report was on cadre policy. The printed report of Meshkov's speech to the plenum, however, gives the impression that the real theme of the plenum was agriculture. Over 80 percent of the printed speech was a detailed airing of economic successes and failures in the agricultural sector, while only the concluding column dealt specifically with the convening of report-election meetings at the primary Party level.[48]

Oblast conferences and seminars also vary significantly from what could nominally be considered their major purpose and membership. On July 1, a seminar of workers in medical establishments of Kursk oblast was convened. Nominally, this seminar is classified under the theme "social welfare" for our analysis. Yet the main report at the seminar was delivered by the obkom director of administrative organs, which has supervisory responsibilities over police and judicial organs. In light of the great emphasis placed on criminality in Kursk during 1970, the presence of the administrative organs director was ominous, as the medical workers were harangued to stop the pilfering of medical supplies.[49]

The classification of themes and conferences is thus consistent for all regions but quite arbitrary for a theme or conference in any one regional party. The problem is only compounded in comparing themes and conferences in several regions. Issues classified under cadre problems in Orel and social welfare in Kursk may have demonstrably different meaning than the same issues in other regions.

The manner in which issues are defined in the regional press relates to a further problem of "omitted" policy themes in 1970. The most glaring omission in the context of issues on the regional level is the total absence of any explicit reference to the "anti-Zionist" campaign mounted by the Soviet leadership during the early spring of 1970. Ever since 1967, there has been a growing and increasingly outspoken demand by many Soviet Jews to emigrate from the Soviet Union to Israel. Against the background of official anti-Semitism and the leadership paranoia in response to all irredentist movements in the Soviet Union, these demands have confronted the Soviet leadership with what could only be considered by them as a most damaging domestic and foreign policy problem. As indicated by the exceptionally high proportion of Soviet Jews with completed higher education in the 1970 Soviet census,* many Soviet Jews still occupy strategic

---

*No summary educational figures for Jews are included in the 1970 Census, but the proportion with completed higher education in

professional and technical positions, and their mass departure, particularly from the scientific community, could only aggravate an already faltering technical proficiency in the Soviet economy. For an ethnic minority ostensibly assimilated in Soviet society, the adamant assertion of identity among Jews after the six-day war also has ominous significance for the other ethnic groups in the Soviet Union, whose real loyalty and enduring ties to the system are, for the Soviet leadership, even more justifiably suspect. In the reasoning of the leadership, open compliance with Jewish demands could only legitimize ethnic dissent and encourage other minorities to similar action.

By 1970, the Jewish demands had become entangled in an embarrassing foreign policy dilemma for the Soviet leadership. Since the six-day war, the Soviet leadership has remained heavily mortgaged to the Arab cause in terms of continuing economic, military, and diplomatic support. Yet, if the Soviet leadership yielded to the demands on the part of Soviet Jews for wide-scale emigration to Israel, the Arab leaders by right might question the real commitment of the Soviet Union to the Arab cause. The Soviet leadership was not even able to resolve this problem along private diplomatic channels. In the early spring of 1970, Israeli leaders contributed to a campaign directed to win support from international public opinion for freer migration of Soviet Jews to Israel. The "problem" was further escalated as an international issue by the attacks of the Jewish Defense League on Soviet missions in Western Europe and the United States.

By March 1970, the response of the Soviet leadership was predictable. A carefully monitored countercampaign of loyal Soviet Jews was staged throughout the country, as Jewish scientific and cultural notables professed their devotion to the Soviet Union and denounced the allegations of discrimination by Israeli leaders. The height of the campaign was reached between March 13 and April 1. The All-Union newspapers Pravda and Izvestiia were deluged with letters of "outrage" to the editor and reports of mass rallies conducted by Soviet Jews in various parts of the country.[50]

If the Jewish issue was as prominent as the extensive coverage in the All-Union press would indicate, we would anticipate that the

---

the two republics with the largest Jewish population were 344/1,000 in the Russian Republic (RSFSR) and 195/1,000 in the Ukraine. See Itogi vsesoiuznoi perepisi naseleniia 1970 goda: Tom IV-Natsional' nyi sostav naseleniia SSSR (Moscow: Statistika, 1973), pp. 449 and 476. These figures contrast with 45/1,000 Russians in the RSFSR and 30/1,000 Ukrainians in the Ukraine.

issue would have had some parallel impact on the regional levels of Soviet society. At least as registered by the regional press in the 25 regions, however, the issue or the "anti-Zionist" campaign was never discussed at a plenum or even at a conference. Throughout March the regional press merely reprinted the Pravda and Izvestiia articles and pictures, with no intimation that the campaign was being reenacted or considered separately at the regional level. A number of blatantly anti-Semitic cartoons, apparently drawn by local political cartoonists, appeared in the regional newspapers of L'vov and Kaliningrad during March. Yet, except for these cartoons and a speech by a Professor Edelman on Judaism at a May atheistic conference in Trans-Carpathia,[51] no explicit reference to Jews or the campaign during the entire nine and a half months appeared in the 25 regional newspapers.

A review of all plenums and conferences during 1970 reveals one disturbing anomaly in the overall political vacuum on the Jewish question. On March 20, an obkom plenum was convened in the Odessa oblast with the principal theme a discussion of the creative unions of the region. The plenum stands out for three reasons. First, Odessa is the only region during the entire nine and a half months to convene a plenum explicitly on writers and artists of a region. No specific figures for writers and artists have ever been published by region.* On a comparative regional basis, the closest approximation is an overlapping occupational category of nontechnical specialists included in statistical handbooks for regions and union republics. The comparative figures for 1970 showed 26,400 nontechnical specialists (pedagogues, librarians, and cultural-enlightenment officials) with degrees from higher educational institutes employed in Odessa.[52] Three other regions in the sample had more nontechnical specialists with higher degrees in 1970 than Odessa, but they did not convene a gorkom or obkom plenum on the work of their creative intelligentsia. Indeed, the only specific cultural conference in these three regions was a seminar of theater representatives in Khar'kov on February 10, addressed in a perfunctory appeal to the Lenin Centenary by the obkom ideology secretary.[53] In contrast to the other 24 regions in the sample, though, Odessa has by far the largest Jewish population (117,000 according to the 1970 census). With few exceptions,[54] the Soviets have never published a regional breakdown of occupational groups by ethnic origins, but we might reasonably speculate that Jews are still very prominent among all writers, artists, and composers in the Soviet Union.[55]

---

*Although, as reported, in Odessa there are 3,000 members of the defined "creative intellgentsia" employed in the region. See reference by obkom first secretary in ZK, March 21-22, 1970.

The combination of a high Jewsih concentration with a high absolute total of nontechnical specialists with higher education in the regional work force is especially suspect if one takes into account the second factor—the very timing of the plenum. The plenum was convened on March 20, at the same time a mass "anti-Zionist" campaign was being staged throughout the Soviet Union and heralded in the All-Union press. It is true that an Odessa gorkom plenum in late January had already referred obliquely to "shortcomings" in the work of the cultural organs in an extended report on preparations for the Lenin Centenary.[56] Yet, whether intended or not, the significance in the timing of this plenum and its specific harsh attacks on cultural intelligentsia could not have been lost on the many Jewish writers, artists, and composers in Odessa.

Third, the tone of the report delivered by First Secretary Sinitsa was particularly critical and wide-ranging. In the March 20 published summary of the report, Sinitsa goes on to rail at all art forms, from the "ultra-modernism" in the operas and dances of the Odessa Opera and Ballet Theater to the surrealistic modernism in the advertising billboards produced by the commercial artists. The context of Sinitsa's remarks are framed in the typical Party lexicon: a lack of partiinost in art forms, creative unions "isolated" from the masses, a "grayness" in the artistic content. In addition, Sinitsa embellished his criticism with ambiguous references to a "nurturing soil for influences foreign to our ideology," which again must be read in terms of the timing of the report and the potential ethnic make-up of his audience.

All this, of course, is far from proving that the theme of the plenum was actually anti-Semitism or that the plenum was specifically called to intimidate Jewish intellectuals in Odessa. Ever since 1965, the Soviet intellectual community has been subject to increasing repressions and attacks from the orthodox Party leaders.[57] The questions remain why the Odessa Party organization alone of all 25 regions convened a plenum on problems in the creative intelligentsia and at this particular time?

Here, there is good reason to suspect the political motivations of Sinitsa that may have prompted both the timing and the veiled anti-Semitic tone of the report. In particular, the criticism of the Odessa intellectual community occurred at the same time that a pattern of corruption linked to A. I. Yurzhenko, the Ukrainian rector of the Odessa State University, had been uncovered by Pravda reporters and was proving increasingly difficult for Sinitsa and other regional Party officials to explain away. As a May article in Pravda later reported,[58] the Odessa University had been rent with corruption and bitter conflict ever since Yurzhenko had been elected rector in 1960 and had abused his official position to recruit personal friends from

51

L'vov to major faculty positions and assign university promotions and rewards solely on the basis of personal loyalty to himself. The establishment of a personal clientele and the pattern of corruption had been allowed to continue, as the Pravda article noted, despite the repeated complaints of concerned faculty and university Party officials and despite the personal investigations of regional Party officials sent to verify the "abnormal situation." While unstated, the implication of the Pravda article was that the pattern of corruption could not have gone unnoticed by regional officials nor without their tacit consent and "trustfulness." As such, the March plenum may well have been a desperate counterattack by Sinitsa to take advantage of the rabid political climate in the Soviet Union and to deflect criticism away from himself by identifying the local controversy over Yurzhenko with "foreign (albeit Zionist) influences" and attitudes among those educational-cultural officials who had complained of Yurzhenko and regional Party officials to the central authorities. In this light, it is interesting that in the plenary report Sinitsa contrasted the negative "ultra-modernism" in cultural forms with a more positive emphasis on Ukrainian nationalistic themes.

Whatever the motivations behind the plenum, Yurzhenko's "voluntary" departure as University rector in April was quickly followed on May 6 with the peremptory and unexplained removal of Sinitsa as first secretary (with I. K. Lutak, the second secretary of the Ukraine, observing the obkom plenum).[59] Only later is Sinitsa reassigned the lowly position as chief of the Ukrainian River Fleet Administration with corresponding demotions from the Ukrainian and All-Union Central Committees and his conspicuous absence even as a delegate at the 24th Party Congress in 1971.* Nor was Sinitsa the only one to be dismissed. In the following months, the obkom ideology secretary and the director of the obkom agitprop department, both positions directly linked to policy supervision in regional cultural-educational institutions, were summarily replaced without any explanation or known further assignment.† Subsequent to the related

---

*Although Sinitsa does attend the 24th Ukrainian Party Congress in March of 1971 as a delegate (XXIV KPUkr).

†Except for an interim in 1965-66, L. V. Gladkaia, the dismissed obkom ideology secretary, had held this position in the Odessa secretariat since her appointment to the industrial obkom secretariat in 1963 (PU, January 11, 1963, p. 1). The career of the former director of the obkom agitprop department, L. A. Anufriev, had closely paralleled that of Gladkaia's. He had been deputy director of the ideological department of the industrial obkom secretariat in 1963-64 under Gladkaia (P, January 7, 1964, p. 2) and had first been identified as

dismissal of the obkom second secretary in 1972,* V. V. Shcherbitsky, the Ukrainain first secretary, singled out the Odessa Party organization as a region in which in the recent past "collective leadership had been ignored in the selection of cadres" and a situation had been allowed to evolve in which "certain sectors were taken over by unqualified drifters and money-grubbers."[60]

The particularly ambiguous circumstances of the March plenum in Odessa and the very nature of the Odessa oblast should illustrate the great caution that must be used in assessing the meaning and purpose of any individual obkom plenum. The absence of any explicit reference to an issue does not necessarily discount its real significance. In the comparison of nominally identical themes among several regions, issues such as "ideology" in Odessa may have a totally different real context than they would have in other regions.

A simple ordinal ranking of issues and participation among regions also ignores the varying intensity level in which policy is considered and the varying intensity importance of certain participants. If issue adaptation is defined as the importance of issues on a comparative regional basis, that importance may have little relationship to the absolute total number of plenums on any one policy. An ideological plenum was also convened in the Belgorod oblast on October 16. There seems little reason to conclude that the Belgorod plenum to any extent was equivalent to the comparable March plenum in Odessa. Policies must be weighed by their relative priority to the regional leadership and in the context of regional political conflict. Moreover, when particular issue sectors are analyzed, the turnover of regional personnel closely identified with the issue sector, such as ideology in Odessa, may often appear as a more valid indicator of issue intensity than the number of times a problem is formally raised at obkom plenums.

The quantitative level of participation also assumes that the effect of groups can be evaluated on an ordinal scale. At times and for particular issues it may be more significant that certain personnel participate even infrequently. The participation in one oblast

---

obkom agitprop director in 1968 (P, May 8, 1968, p. 2). Replacing Gladkaia and Anufriev were A. P. Cherednichenko (RU, January 31, 1971) and P. Ivanov (P, May 31, 1973, p. 2).

*N. A. Neizvestnyi, released for "shortcomings," according to Odessa Radio, April 6, 1973. Neizvestnyi had been appointed second secretary only in 1970 (ZK, February 19, 1970) and previously had been capital gorkom first secretary, a position that would have linked him directly with responsibility for the Odessa University in the capital (PU, May 16, 1965 and February 16, 1966).

conference in Kemerovo illustrates the point. During 1970, several regions held oblast conferences of the criminal and judicial organs on the increasing problem of crime. As reported in the regional press, the mood conveyed and the participation in these conferences were almost uniformly the same for all regions. The stress was on punitive actions against law violators, and the makeup of the conferences was overwhelmingly dominated by officials from the oblast MVD and KGB (Commission of State Security).[61] The only minor exception, and it is striking because of that, was the August 12 conference convened in the Kemerovo oblast. Among the numerous police and Party officials present at the conference was the chairman of the oblast college of advocates.[62] With its potential symbolic import for considerations of due process, the presence of a legal adviser to the accused may have mollified the otherwise punitive and dogmatic tone of the discussions at the conference.

A truly accurate measure of participation would have to weigh the relative importance of individuals in certain positions or occupations and would presume prior knowledge of local political forces and allegiances that determine the actual role and influence of these same individuals in different regions. The only information available for most of these participants, of course, is the references to them and their formal positions in the regional press. Unfortunately, the regional press is a particularly unsuitable source from which to measure the qualitative intensity of themes or participants among several regional parties.

There are problems of measurement even on a strictly quantitative level. With the exception of Stewart's study for Stalingrad, no Western scholar has ever examined the participation rates and themes of oblast parties over a period of time. Consequently, there is no comparable research against which the significance of our findings can be judged. What could be considered a theoretically important difference among the regions in our sample on these two policy dimensions? How much of a relationship between regional characteristics and themes must be demonstrated to conclude that it validates or invalidates our explanatory hypotheses?

Correlational analysis would specify the exact relationship between the independent and dependent variables. Yet the regions in the sample were not randomly selected, so neither the plenums and participation rates nor the distribution of regional characteristics could be considered either a representative cross-section of the Soviet Union or randomly occurring variables subject to correlational analysis. Because of the substantive and methodological problems already raised, it was further felt that the use of correlational analysis would only exaggerate the quantitative precision of the findings. We intend the study more simply as an exploratory survey of relationships and trends at the regional Party level and much less as a definitive statistical test of alternative hypotheses. As a result, the associations between independent and dependent variables will be presented in the less statistically precise but more simply described form of percentage variation.

* * *

None of these problems can be easily overcome. Only a comparable study of the same regions at another time or a stratified sample of regions could hope to isolate the varied effect of central political conflict on the discussion of local issues, the extent to which plenums and conferences are inaccurately presented in the regional press, or the actual intensity level of themes and participation in particular regions. Additional information drawn from interviews from Party officials and participants in plenums would be required in order to gain a fuller understanding of the political context in which regional issues are formally considered and occupational sectors participate.

The time, expense, and effort in replication, though, are made more than normally difficult because the regional newspapers are only available in Moscow and on a limited basis. Interviews with officials and plenum participants are also productive only to the extent that these same individuals will candidly discuss their policy roles and regional problems. With rare exceptions,[63] local officials have not even granted interviews to Western scholars.

In the following two chapters, the themes and participants in plenums will be approximately correlated with varying characteristics of the regions and the obkom first secretaries. Yet the substantive and methodological problems will remain ones particular to the analysis. Perhaps the inability to resolve them at this time testifies to even more basic realities of the regional parties and the Soviet political system—realities that, as in Odessa, belie the precision and rigor of any quantitative measures.

NOTES

1. On the criticism of Khrushchev's policy and the nature of shablonism, see Michel Tatu, Power in the Kremlin: From Khrushchev to Kosygin (New York: Viking Press, 1970), pp. 370-373.
2. In particular, the resolution criticizing the practice of conducting Party meetings in the Yaroslavl' gorkom, "On the Practice of Conducting Party Meetings in the Yaroslavl' Urban Party Organization," Resolution of the Central Committee CPSU, November 3,

1969, in SPR, Vyp. 10 (1970), pp. 278-283. Among other criticisms leveled against the gorkom as a negative example for other local parties to avoid was that "at times Party committees without sufficient foundation obligate Party organizations to discuss one and the same problems, not taking into account the specific characters and conditions of each of them."

3. Leonid Brezhnev, XXIV KPSS, vol. 1, p. 120.

4. The term "effective competence" refers to those issues actually discussed at obkom plenums. The term is derived from Philip Stewart, Political Power in the Soviet Union (New York: Bobbs-Merrill, 1968), p. 64. Stewart found that plenums in Stalingrad were often determined by previous decisions of the Central Committee, although Stewart included all Central Committee resolutions and decrees in the category of decisions, not just resolutions passed subsequent to Committee plenums.

5. In H. Gordon Skilling and Franklyn Griffiths, eds., Interest Groups in Soviet Politics (Princeton, N.J.: Princeton University Press, 1971), Harrett and Frankel propose that conferences for industrial managers at the local levels serve as potential forums for interest articulation ("The Industrial Managers," p. 201). Barry and Berman contend that conferences on law enforcement at least may "manifest and contribute to a common identification among jurists" ("The Jurists," p. 314).

6. "On the Meetings of the Party Aktiv," PZh, no. 14 (July 1963), pp. 47-48.

7. Secretaries from the urban and district Party organizations and directors of the oblast mass organizations were more likely to appear at plenums than at aktivs; enterprise directors and workers, at aktivs than at plenums. The differences, though, are minor. The breakdown by occupational sectors in January plenums and aktivs on the December Plenum report is shown below:

No. Regions	Occupational Sectors (percent)							
	Gorrai Secs.	Obl. Offi- cials	Obl. Mass	Farm Offi- cials	Ent. Dirs.	Eng. Tech.	Other	Total
Aktivs (9)	31	13	3	11	16	3	23	100 (116)
Plenums (12)	38	14	10	8	11	2	17	100 (130)

8. T. H. Rigby, "The Selection of Leading Personnel in the Soviet State and Communist Party" (unpublished Ph.D. thesis, University of London, 1954), p. 260, cited in Ronald Hill, "Participation in the Central Committee Plenums in Moldavia," Soviet Studies 21, 2 (October 1969): 206. In the post-Khrushchev period, Hill found little

real difference in participation between a meeting of the Party aktiv and an "expanded" plenum of the Moldavian Central Committee. For the seven years of the Stalingrad obkom, Stewart found that noncommittee members constituted 48 percent of all participants in obkom plenary sessions. See Stewart, Political Power in the Soviet Union, p. 82.

9. The percentage of the city work force employed in education was cited during a March gorkom plenum in Novosibirsk. VN, April 1, 1970.

10. As an example, see the edict of the Supreme Soviet in 1971, "Fundamental Rights and Obligations of Urban and District Soviets of Workers Deputies in Cities," in Vedomosti-SSSR, no. 12 (March 24, 1971), pp. 134-144.

11. Stewart, Political Power in the Soviet Union, pp. 67-68.

12. Ibid., p. 46.

13. ZP, July 1, 1970.

14. DP, June 20, 1970.

15. Stewart, Political Power in the Soviet Union, p. 86.

16. Ibid., p. 46.

17. Ibid., pp. 69 and 79.

18. VN, June 30 and August 13, 1970.

19. On the preponderance of scientific research and academic personnel in the Academic City, see Henry R. Lieberman, "Soviet Is Reconciling Its Quest for Modernization with Communist Ideology," New York Times, December 14, 1973, p. 14. On the particular problems of political socialization the large academic community presents to the party, see R. T. Yanovskii, Intelligentsiia i ideologiia (The intelligentsia and ideology) (Moscow: Politizdat, 1974).

20. See citation of Chemodanov's position in oblast Komsomol conference reported in Sovetskaia Sibir' (Novosibirsk), June 16, 1967.

21. Primary examples are Stewart, Political Power in the Soviet Union and Hill, "Participation in the Central Committee Plenums in Modavia." Also see Michael Gehlen, The Communist Party of the Soviet Union: A Functional Analysis (Bloomington: Indiana University Press, 1969). According to Gehlen, two of the four functions performed by the Communist Party are "goal specification" and "recruitment," both conceptually approximate to "issue adaptation" and "participation" in this study.

22. Many of these studies and essays on methodology in the Soviet field are included in Frederick A. Fleron, ed., Communist Studies and the Social Sciences: Essays on Methodology and Empirical Theory (Chicago: Rand McNally, 1969).

23. Of the typical restraints on the format and layout of oblast newspapers, see Mark Hopkins, Mass Media in the Soviet Union (New York: Pegasus, 1970), pp. 212-223.

24. Stewart, Political Power in the Soviet Union, p. x.

25. Sidney Ploss, "The Rise of Brezhnev," Problems of Communism 19, 3 (May-June 1970): 1-14; Tatu, Power in the Kremlin, pp. 493-522; Frederick C. Barghoorn, Politics in the USSR (2d ed., Boston: Little-Brown, 1972), pp. 196-197, 235-236.

26. The only specific reference to the content of the December Plenum report was an editorial in Pravda on January 13, 1970 ("Towards New Accomplishments"). The editorial ambiguously described the report as a "frank" review of economic, Party-organizational, and foreign policy problems. The official Spravochnik Partiinogo Rabotnika (Party Handbook), Vyp. 10, published in September 1970 for 1969-70, still omits any reference to a summary report or resolutions passed subsequent to the report.

27. Bernard Gwertzman, "Brezhnev Reports Wide Economic Ills, Asks Tight Control," New York Times, January 16, 1970.

28. Z(K), January 23-24, 1970; KS, January 13-14, 1970; Kuz, June 11, 1970.

29. TP, May 16-17, 1970; DP, June 20-21, 1970; ZP, July 1, 1970; KaP, January 9 and 11, 1970.

30. SR, January 15, 1970; KrP, May 12, 1970; ZK, May 15, 1970.

31. Z(P), January 17-18, 1970; ZK, May 15, 1970; VP, June 26, 1970.

32. OP, January 15, 1970; LP, January 20, 1970; KiP, January 7, 1970; KrP, April 28, 1970; KaP, May 13, 1970.

33. LP, January 20, 1970.

34. KiP, January 7, 1970.

35. See the discussion of trade unions and their disputes over workers with local management and Party organizations in Mary McAuley, Labour Disputes in Soviet Russia, 1957-1965 (Oxford: Clarendon Press, 1969), cited in David Lane, Politics and Society in the USSR (New York: Random House, 1971), pp. 308-315.

36. G. V. Klimov was chairman of the L'vov oblast trade-union council at least from 1958 (PU, October 8, 1958) through 1960. See reference to Klimov's dismissal in T, September 15, 1960.

37. Tatu, Power in the Kremlin, pp. 503-508; Ploss, "The Rise of Brezhnev," p. 7.

38. Ocherednye zadachi partii v oblast' sel'skogo khoziaistva (Current tasks of the Party in the area of agriculture), Report to the Plenum of the Central Committee, CPSU, 2 July 1970 (Moscow: Politizdat, 1970), p. 48.

39. P, July 4, 1970.

40. VN, July 11, 1970.

41. IZ, June 7, 1970.

42. Ibid., September 1, 1970.

43. RP, April 9, 1970. The criticism was made by A. M. Pakhamov, first secretary of the Dukhovshchino raikom.

44. TP, May 16-17, 1970. The remarks of the obkom first secretary at the plenum, convened to discuss the Yaroslavl' resolution on conducting Party meetings, were in keeping with the original content of the Central Committee resolution, which concluded with an appeal to local newspapers to "publish materials about more Party meetings and better inform Party organizations about the positive experience in this regard." See "On the Practice of Conducting Party Meetings in the Yaroslavl' Urban Party Organization," p. 283.

45. VR, May 21, 1970.

46. As an example, see the discussion of the 10th obkom plenum at raikom plenums reported in VR, July 9, 1970.

47. Ibid.

48. OP, September 9-10, 1970. The printed report was five and a half columns long; specific reference to the report-election meetings made up only the last half column.

49. KuP, July 1, 1970. One of the obkom secretaries, V. Ye. Sharov, has apparent responsibility both for administrative-judicial organs and the consumer sector of the region. Sharov was the main speaker or participant at the legal conference on July 1 and the conference on consumer affairs on May 15. As suggested by the context of the July 1 medical services conference, the overlap may not be difficult for Sharov to maintain. Problems of the consumer sector were frequently attributed to illegal activities, falling under Sharov's other role as secretary for administrative-judicial organs.

50. The following are only selective examples of several articles from Pravda and Izvestiia: "Shame on Zionist Agents" (statement by Jewish citizens of Riga denouncing Golda Meir's statement on discrimination against Soviet Jews), I, March 13, 1970; "End Crimes" (Jewish workers of Kiev assemble), I, March 14, 1970; "Angry Protest of Millions—Rebuff to Zionist Provocateurs" (press conference to Latvian Jews in Riga), P, March 15, 1970; "Deserved Rebuff to Zionists" (Georgian Jews), I, March 18, 1970; "You Try in Vain" (letter condemns Golda Meir's statements on discrimination against Soviet Jewry), I, March 28, 1970. For an insider's perspective on the March "anti-Zionist" campaign and its impact on one Jewish scientist, see Observer, Message from Moscow (New York: Vintage Books, 1971), pp. 291ff.

51. ZP, May 24, 1970. The title of Professor Edelman's speech to the conference was "Ideology of Contemporary Judaism."

52. Narodne gospodarstvo Ukrains'koi RSR (National economy of the Ukrainian Soviet Socialist Republic) (Kiev: Gosstatizdat Ukr RSR, 1970), p. 387.

53. KrZ(Kh), February 10, 1970.

54. The ethnic composition of specialists in the regional economy is cited in the 1967 Narodnoe khoziastvo Vologodskoi oblasti za gody Sovetskoi vlasti (The national economy of the Vologda Oblast under the years of the Soviet regime) (Vologda: Gosstatizdat, 1967), p. 119.

55. As late as 1956 Soviet Jews constituted one-tenth of the writers at the 2d All-Union Writers Congress. See John A. Armstrong, "The Ethnic Scene in the Soviet Union," in Erich Goldhagen, ed., Ethnic Minorities in the Soviet Union (New York: Praeger Publishers, 1968), p. 11. A Jewish film writer and director who emigrated to Israel has estimated that 50 percent of the top Soviet film people are still Jews. See Sol Stern, "The Russian Jews Wonder Whether Israel Is Really Ready for Them," New York Times Magazine, April 16, 1972, p. 94.

56. ZK, January 30, 1970.

57. Observer, Message from Moscow.

58. "Izderzhki doverchivosti" (The costs of trustfulness), P, May 17, 1970.

59. ZK, May 8, 1970.

60. V. V. Shcherbitskii, "On the tasks of the Republic's Party organizations in the further improvement of work with cadres in the light of the decisions of the 24th CPSU Congress," PU, April 20, 1973, translated in Current Digest of the Soviet Press 25, 16 (May 16, 1973): 4 and 12.

61. The conferences were frequently a response to how the problems of falling labor productivity and labor discipline, outlined in the December Plenum report, were particularly defined in certain regional parties (supra, n. 28). Although the conferences on law and order were dominated by police officials, the most severe criticisms at the conferences were often leveled against the MVD. As an example, see conference in KiP, January 7, 1970. Other regions with related conferences between January and October include Kursk (July 1), Orel (June 27), Novosibirsk (July 15), Tomsk (July 14), Kaliningrad (April 3), Zaporozh'e (May 30), Odessa (June 15), Crimea (May 12), and Trans-Carpathia (May 26).

62. Kuz, August 13, 1970. This is the only conference or plenum at any level or in any oblast during 1970 where a jurist-advocate was reported to have participated by the 25 regional newspapers.

63. To date, three researchers have drawn extensively upon interviews with local Party or state officials for their studies: Jerry Hough, The Soviet Prefects: The Local Party Organs in Industrial Decision-Making (Cambridge: Harvard University Press, 1969); Robert Osborn, Soviet Social Policies (Homewood, Ill.: Dorsey Press, 1970); B. M. Frolic, "Decision-Making in Soviet Cities," American Political Science Review 66, 1 (March 1972): 38-52.

3

THE INFLUENCE
OF ENVIRONMENTAL FACTORS
UPON POLICY

ISSUE ADAPTATION

We could conclude from the previous chapter that the capacity of all regional parties to define and respond to local problems was not rigidly established by central authorities. All plenary themes and conferences during 1970 were shown to vary by time and issue sector among the 25 regions. The second explanatory hypothesis in Chapter 1, however, proposed a direct linkage between issue adaptation and the levels of social mobilization among regions. It is not enough to show that all regions differ in their concern with particular issues, but rather one must attempt to demonstrate some direct association between social change and issues on a comparative regional basis.

When the same plenums and conferences are controlled for social mobilization in this chapter, there is a greater convergence among regions and few percentage differences. High and low mobilized regions do not vary on all issue sectors nor do all indices of social mobilization equally distinguish the issue adaptation of regional parties. At the same time regional parties do consistently differ in the emphasis assigned to important policy areas and by particular measures of change and absolute levels. Assumptions based upon extensive decentralization in the Soviet Communist Party at the regional level are unsupported by the evidence in this chapter. But, within a limited range, issues do correspond in a logical manner to widely different regional environmental characteristics in 1970. Issue adaptation is a minor but persistent reality among regional parties in 1970.

Urbanization and Economic Issues

These general conclusions are illustrated in Table 3.1. Regions are classified as low or high urban by their position relative to the arithmetic mean for change in urbanization and the absolute percentage of the urban population in 1970. From one perspective, the most important conclusion to be drawn from the percentages by obkom plenums in Table 3.1 is a negative one. There is a remarkable similarity in the percentage of industrial and agricultural problems reviewed in both high and low urban regions. True, regions with higher rates of urban change and absolute urban population in 1970 were more likely to discuss industrial issues at obkom plenums. But, on a comparative basis, the differences are slight (only 3 and 7 percent), and the higher difference by absolute urban population could easily be discounted because of the disproportionate number of regions included in the high absolute classification (17 of 25 regions).

We would anticipate some inverse ratio between low and high urban regions in their consideration of industrial and agricultural issues. Low urban regions should have a larger number of agricultural workers and a more significant portion of their regional economy dependent upon farm productivity. Greater attention to agricultural problems in obkom plenums should follow as a consequence. By a similar logic, high urban regions should have a larger concentration of industrial enterprises and workers, and the proportional ratio of industrial to agricultural issues should be the inverse of low urban regions. Yet not only do the regions vary by small percentages in Table 3.1, but the high urban regions actually discussed 5 and 2 percent more agricultural issues than did the low urban and supposedly rural regions of the sample.

The predicted inverse correlation does appear in the Table 3.1A of total regional issue sectors. One would assume a more agricultural orientation among rural regions by the number of times specifically agricultural problems are raised at combined plenums, conferences, capital gorkom plenums, and sessions of the oblast-capital Soviets. Whereas the data failed to confirm any pattern at the level of obkom plenums, rural regions should have a larger number of agricultural specialists, collective and state farm officials, and rural Party organizations. On an overall basis, the size factor alone would warrant the more frequent convocation of agricultural forums in rural regions and industrial forums in urban regions. The percentages in Table 3.1A substantiate both the assumption and the logical distinction drawn between obkom plenums and combined regional issue sectors. Agriculture constituted one-third of all issues discussed in the regions with the highest rural population in 1970. Regions with the highest urban population, in contrast, diverted a proportionately higher

62

TABLE 3.1

Obkom Plenum Themes and Urbanization in Regions, 1939-70
(in percent)

Regions by Urbanization	Ind.	Agr.	Ind.-Agr.	Ide.	Cad. Org.	Soc. Wel.	Other	Total	
Low change[a]	25	23	(+2)	4	49	—	—	100	(53)
High change[b]	28	28	0	5	32	3	3	100	(60)
Low absolute[c]	22	24	(-2)	8	41	3	3	100	(37)
High absolute[d]	29	26	(+3)	3	39	1	1	100	(76)

TABLE 3.1A

Total Regional Party Issue Sectors and Urbanization in Regions, 1939-70
(in percent)

	Ind.	Agr.	Ind.-Agr.	Ide.	Cad. Org.	Soc. Wel.	Soc. Leg.	Other	Total	
Low change	24	19	(+5)	23	22	7	5	—	100	(258)
High change	18	25	(-7)	24	20	7	4	2	100	(249)
Low absolute	16	33	(-17)	23	20	4	5	—	100	(148)
High absolute	23	17	(+6)	24	21	8	4	1	100	(358)

Note: Tables 3.1 and 3.1A categorize all 25 regions by the two measures of urban percentage change over time (1939-70) and the absolute urban percent of population in 1970. The range of urban percent change was from 11 to 40 percent, and the arithmetic mean for all regions was 26 percent. The range of absolute urban population in 1970 was 30 to 82 percent, and the medium was 53 percent. Therefore, all regions falling at the mean or below for either of the two measures were classified as "low" urban change or "low" absolute urban regions, all falling above the means on either of the two dichotomies as "high" urban change or "high" absolute regions. This dichotomy will be used throughout all the subsequent tables, as the theoretical rationale of social mobilization stresses both rates of change and absolute levels (thresholds) as relevant indices of the environment. Rate of change was computed from the base year 1939 rather than 1959, because too many of the regions cluster between 11 and 16 percent for the period 1959-70. In later tables, the base year for change will be the earliest postwar figure, in order to control for any unaccounted distortions of World War II on population. lation.

[a]Regions with percent urban change in their total population from 11-26 percent between 1939 and 1970: (12) Kursk, Tambov, Orel, Bryansk, Trans-Carpathia, Rostov, Dnepropetrovsk, Khar'kov, Crimea, Odessa, L'vov, and Kalningrad.
[b]Regions with percent urban change in their total population from 27 to 40 percent between 1939 and 1970: (13) Belgorod, Smolensk, Kaluga, Yaroslavl', Novosibirsk, Kemerovo, Zaporozh'e, Saratov, Volgograd, Perm', Vologda, Tomsk, and Kirov.
[c]Regions with absolute percent urbanization between 30 and 53 percent in 1970 total regional population: (8) Kursk, Tambov, Orel, Bryansk, Trans-Carpathia, Belgorod, Smolensk, and Kaluga.
[d]Regions with absolute percent urbanization between 54 and 82 percent in 1970 total regional population: (17) Rostov, Dnepropetrovsk, Khar'kov, Crimea, Odessa, L'vov, Kaliningrad, Yaroslavl', Novosibirsk, Kemerovo, Zaporozh'e, Saratov, Volgograd, Perm', Vologda, Tomsk, and Kirov.

Sources: Regional press of the 25 regions, January-October 1970; Itogi vsesoiuznoi perepisi naseleniia 1959 goda: SSSR Itogi vsesoiuznoi perepisi naseleniia 1970 goda: Iom I-Chislennost' naseleniia SSSR.

percentage of conferences and plenums to industrial problems. The differences for the two issue sectors were 7 percent in industry and 16 percent in agriculture—a combined inverse ratio of 23 percent. While only 8 of the 25 regions fall in the low urban category in Table 3.1A, this inverse ratio is an important finding and will be repeated in all subsequent tables. The difference in the inverse ratio of industrial to agricultural issues between low and high urban regions ranges from 20 to 23 percent.

With few exceptions in the following tables, substantive economic problems reviewed at obkom plenums do not differ by regional environmental factors. The failure to adapt may be either because of uniform performance criteria in agriculture and industry dictated by the central officials or because of the equivalent pressures felt by the regional leadership in obkom plenums to fulfill industrial and agricultural quotas. Even the most urbanized regions devoted a large percentage of all their obkom plenums to agricultural problems. Perhaps, on substantive industrial and agricultural problems, the four or five obkom plenums convened in any one year by an oblast Party must be diffusely structured: summarizing overall regional developments with rare opportunities to set aside individual plenums to particular economic sectors. In the previous chapter, as an example, the lower specificity of obkom plenums was indicated by the fact that capital gorkom plenums considered industrial issues at a much higher ratio than did obkom plenums. Even those obkom plenums with a theme specifically on agriculture or industry in 1970 quite often would find reporters and participants in the same plenum theme emphasizing the reciprocal impact of agricultural and industrial production or the mutual responsibility of rural and urban construction sites to increase production capacities in the region. To increase farm production, obkom first secretaries at obkom plenums would argue that more tractors and combines must be supplied by the industrial sector of the region to the rural districts. To convert the livestock sector to "industrial principles" of production, not only must the slaughterhouses and animal collection centers be completed, but there must be a correlative expansion in the construction of plants that service the agricultural sector with building materials.

Yet, whatever the limitations on initiative or time and the close relationship of industrial and agricultural problems, the regional leadership still can selectively respond to the varied size and dimensions of the occupational sectors and the economy in the oblast. The obkom leadership is provided an alternative channel at the subsystemic level of specialized conferences, capital gorkom plenums, and sessions of the oblast-capital soviets. Here, advice can be solicited, troublesome sectors can be singled out, and strategic occupational groups at least can be symbolically reassured of their importance.

The fact that the combined issue sectors of industry and agriculture will vary widely according to the absolute level of urbanization testifies to a limited but sustained pattern of issue adaptation among regional parties in 1970.

Cadre-Organizational Problems

From a second perspective, not absolute levels but change over time explains the wide variance in one important issue sector of obkom plenums in Table 3.1. By change in urbanization, regions varied by 17 percent in the number of plenum themes addressed to cadre-organizational problems. Almost half (49 percent) of the total plenum issues in the low urban change regions concerned either a review of cadre performance at lower Party levels or directly enacted personnel changes among obkom bureau or department officials themselves. The significance of this finding cannot be overlooked. For, as argued in the first chapter, the theory of social mobilization proposes a direct relationship between levels of social change in an environment and their impact upon the political system. As hypothesized, regions with higher levels of social mobilization in a comparable time period should be subject to greater internal Party stresses than regions of less rapid change. Unsocialized individuals, uprooted from previous social and psychological moorings, would now be entering the Party at higher rates, their demands for promotion would be more pronounced, and the regional parties would be confronted with increased internal morale problems in enlisting the support and enthusiasm of lower Party officials. If the regional leadership attempted to respond to these internal problems, basic indicators of the adaptive response would be an increasing number of new assignments to major obkom bureau and department positions and a greater than normal preoccupation at obkom plenums with the quality and morale of lower Party cadres. Surprisingly, we now find variation along the dimension of urbanization, as predicted in the theory of social mobilization, but in a direction opposite to that hypothesized. Low-urban-change regions, those with less change in their total population base and with a smaller percentage of their population moving from rural to urban settings, actually demonstrate a much greater concern with internal obkom and lower cadre problems than do those regions above the mean of urban change. The variation on cadre-organizational issues is not repeated on the total regional issue subdimension. As shown in Table 3.1A, either by change or absolute percentage levels, the cadre-organizational sector consistently accounted for a ratio between 20 and 22 percent.

While the cadres themes of obkom plenums varied by titles, the general tenor of the speeches by obkom first secretaries and the expressed need for raising Party effectiveness were quite similar in 1970. Several reporters on the cadre issue structured their speeches in response to the Central Committee Resolution of November 1969, which had condemned the practice of conducting Party meetings among lower organizations in the city of Yaroslavl'.[1] The resolution had been particularly critical of the passivity and rigidity displayed in primary Party organizations. Meetings were ill-prepared and badly conducted, the same individuals dominated the discussion of problems, and the meetings were unlikely to inspire worker morale and enthusiasm as the workers returned to their shops and work benches in the industrial enterprises. The last point was probably the real intent behind the issue of conducting primary Party meetings. For, as obkom first secretaries were to note quite frequently, the true effectiveness of Party meetings could only be judged by a single criterion: how the enterprises of the Party organization fulfilled the state plans and socialist obligations for production. To oblast parties, a decline in production, openly admitted by Brezhnev for the entire economy at the mysterious December Plenum of 1969, logically meant an equivalent failure in responsibility on the part of primary Party organizations. More lively meetings and the general improvement of Party organizations would therefore also be evaluated by the same criterion.

In Yaroslavl' itself, the resolution had a very direct and immediate impact on primary Party organizations in the city. Report-election meetings in Yaroslavl' had followed the publication of the Central Committee resolution. The turnover in officials at the primary level was dramatic. By January 24, the regional newspaper reported that more than 200 secretaries of primary Party organizations had been elected for the first time in the Yaroslavl' urban party.[2]

The resolution was not specifically discussed at the obkom level of Yaroslavl' during 1970, but several regions were to consider the criticisms significant enough to set aside an entire obkom plenum to a review of the problem in their own regions. The May 15 obkom plenum in the Tambov oblast illustrates this practice and the general conclusions drawn from the resolution by regional leaders.[3] As the first secretary of Tambov implied in his report, the criticism of badly prepared meetings had consciously influenced even the preparation of this obkom plenum. Subsequent to the publication of the Yaroslavl' resolution in November, the oblast Party in Tambov had carefully gathered information on the typical practices of conducting Party meetings from 250 primary Party organizations in the Tambov region. Members and candidate members of the obkom bureau had spent many hours in the field studying the local situation, and a large portion of First Secretary Chernyi's remarks were set aside to a laudatory evaluation of the Nikiforovsk raikom, which he had personally visited.

Still, as Chernyi admitted, "shortcomings" had been uncovered in the review of Party organizations by the bureau members. The requirement that Party meetings should be convened on a regular basis was still widely ignored by local secretaries, the same individuals delivered the principal speeches at the meetings, rank and file Party members were often excluded from contributing to the discussions, and other local secretaries refused to allow criticism of themselves or plant directors by the assembled members. The underlying problem remained delimiting the specific role of the Party organization from the broad administrative rights (edinonachalnie) of enterprise directors and the agitation prerogatives of other mass organizations in the plants. No longer should local Party organizations become overly involved in the technical aspects of industrial production, as Khrushchev had previously attempted to redefine the primary role of the Party:

> While reviewing at the meetings the basic questions of developing production, many Party organizations omit from view a specification of Party work; they forget that these very same questions are frequently discussed at trade-union, workers meetings, and production conferences. The Party meeting as such—although expressing a common aim with these other meetings (i.e., the improvement of the situation)—has to be distinguished from them not only by the presentation of problems, but by the nature of the discussion and the content of decisions undertaken . . . (after commenting on examples from primary Party organizations) Communists frequently concentrate all their attention on the technical side of production, and extensively discuss minute defects in the technological processes or in material-technical supply. At the same time the questions of work with people, upraising a conscious relationship to one's assignment, raising responsibility and assignment of Communists are omitted. . . .4

How was the situation to be rectified in Tambov? Not by a broad shake-up of lower secretaries as in Yaroslavl', but departments of the obkom, gorkoms, and raikoms would now regularly conduct seminars for Party secretaries in industry, agriculture, and the scientific institutions. Local secretaries would be instructed at these seminars on the proper functioning of meetings. Implicit in Chernyi's remarks, though, was the primary criterion for judging the success of these seminars: an increase in total industrial production and labor productivity.

While not all regions framed their cadre reports in direct response to the Yaroslavl' resolution, they too were principally concerned with the quality of lower Party organizations and cadres. For some obkom plenums, such as those in Kaliningrad and Dnepropetrovsk, the lower cadre problem was one more basic to the very nature of general Party membership and recruitment into the regional Party as a whole. The effectiveness of lower Party organizations and Party meetings depended upon the makeup of Party membership at the lower level. At the June 19 obkom plenum in Dnepropetrovsk, the report stressed a review of recent Party recruitment during the first half of 1970 in reaction to criticism that had been made in Brezhnev's December Plenum report.[5] In his report, obkom Second Secretary Pichuzhkin noted that, in the first six months of 1970, the oblast Party had recruited 70.2 percent of its new members from the ranks of workers and kolkhozniki. This percentage was 4 percent higher than the total for 1969, but there was still an inadequate Party representation among the workers in agriculture, construction, and the coal enterprises of the region.* At the Kaliningrad oblast, the January 8 plenum reviewed Party admissions since the 23d Congress.[7] As in Dnepropetrovsk, the number of workers and kolkhozniki admitted into the Party had increased, but the problem of quantitative expansion was evaluated quite differently. Since 1966, several Party organizations in Kaliningrad had been lax in their standards for admitting new members. Sounding a theme first announced in a 1965 resolution critical of the Khar'kov region,[8] the Kaliningrad secretary scored the "liberal" admission policies of several lower Party organizations and their ill-conceived emphasis on quantitative expansion over carefully reviewed qualitative additions to their Party ranks. Importantly, the second plenum report for both Kaliningrad and Dnepropetrovsk at this time closely tied the cadre problem to increased labor turnover, transportation delays, and a general decline in industrial productivity in the two regions.

------

*Although Dnepropetrovsk has numerous scientific and educational establishments with large Party membership, a low level of Party saturation in the oblasts of the Southeast Ukraine has been traditional. The ratio of Party membership has always been particularly low in the mining industries of the Donbass Region, as Pichuzhkin's comments at the plenum would affirm.[6]

The relationship between cadres and economic problems was even more explicitly drawn at the June 18 obkom plenum in Volgograd.9 While the stated theme of the obkom first secretary's report was cadres (entitled "raising the 'avant-garde' role of Communists"), in reality he set aside most of the printed report to reviewing industrial, construction, and agricultural sectors in the region. First Secretary Kulichenko pointed out the particular failures that each sector had experienced during the preceding year. Cadres were the key to solving these diverse failures; for, as Kulichenko underlined, "most often, the shortcomings in the work of economic units are nurtured because Party organizations have under-evaluated the significance of correctly assigning Communists." As a counterpoint, Kulichenko deliberately singled out several highly qualified enterprise directors and collective farm chairmen, who were natives of Volgograd and who had risen up through the ranks to assume leadership positions in the Volgograd economy. Kulichenko's message was explicit. In order to raise production, their examples had to be repeated, and greater attention would have to be given to promoting skilled natives from the regional work force. During a later report to the regional Party conference in January 1971, Kulichenko reiterated his concern in providing a wider stratum of cadres the opportunity to advance into higher positions. Many young and skilled workers or collective farmers had recently been promoted to directing positions in the regional organs of the Party, the state, and the economy.10

We will have occasion to comment on the significance of Kulichenko's remarks in later chapters, particularly as they bear upon the phenomenon more common since 1964 of native recruitment from lower ranks into the obkom bureaus. Suffice it to say at this time, though, that Kulichenko's remarks should be considered a conscious statement of one major premise in the present study. Production and Party effectiveness itself at lower levels are directly affected by the perceived opportunities for advancement by lower cadres. In lieu of these perceived opportunities, Party effectiveness suffers from what Kulichenko described in the plenum as the "poor morale problem" at the lower levels of the Party. Although Volgograd is a high urban region, the higher percentage for less rapidly changing regions in Table 3.1 suggests that Party morale was perceived to be a greater problem for rural than urban oblasts of the Soviet Union by 1970.

Urban Density

Basic methodological objections could be raised, however, to the manner in which the index of urbanization was operationalized in Table 3.1. Soviet statisticians themselves define regional urbanization in the Russian and Ukrainian republics from different population base criteria. The minimal population base that can be considered an urban settlement (poselok) is 10,000 in the Russian Republic and 15,000 in the Ukrainian Republic. The index in Table 3.1, which includes both Russian and Ukrainian regions, thus errs in combining noncomparable units of measure. Secondly, Soviet demographers who have studied the impact of urbanization in the Soviet Union have stressed the importance of large urban centers within any one regional nexus. According to these demographers, the concentrated size of urban settlements over 50,000 or over 100,000 people more realistically distinguishes regions by urbanization than do the statistical base standards adopted for census definitions of urbanization.[11]

These Soviet demographers are principally concerned with the economic and social problems posed by varying levels of large urban concentrations, but the underlying logic of their argument could obviously be extended to our own analysis of social and political change in regions. It is only from varying levels of the total regional population residing in settlements of 100,000 or more that we would anticipate some related impact on political participation in a region. The actual social change for individuals whose life situation has only been redefined from a rural settlement of 5,000 to a statistical urban settlement of 10,000 would be insignificant, whereas the change in lifeways forced upon an individual who migrates from a village to a large city of 100,000 population would follow the pattern of major psychological and social dislocation proposed by the theory of social mobilization.

Even statistically defined "urban" settlements of 10,000 and 15,000 in the Soviet Union appear to serve for the most part as agricultural market and distribution centers for the surrounding collective and state farms. For anyone who has traveled through the Russian countryside, the sight of rural unpaved roads, abandoned combines alongside houses, and chickens running freely through the square of these small urban settlements belies their statistical inclusion as urban. Very likely, in these regions large numbers of the population are still engaged in agriculturally related occupations, the regional Party is composed predominantly of rural Party organizations, and the specialists are drawn up primarily of agronomists and agricultural technicians with higher education. Such regions may appear on a general statistical scale to have a high level of urbanization, but it is the density of the urban population that actually distinguishes the degree of urbanization in the Soviet context. In highly dense regions, in particular those with large metropolitan centers over 100,000 population, the regional work force would be more limited to the industrial branches for employment; the urban, district, and primary Party organizations would balance the rural Party dominance; and a greater proportion of specialists would be recruited into industrial rather than agricultural professions. The density of a population, not the statistical base for an urban population in the census, accurately distinguishes urbanization on a comparative regional scale.

A comparison of the percent differences in Tables 3.2 and 3.1 would substantiate these arguments. To correct for the methodological limitations in Table 3.1, regions in Table 3.2 were classified urban in terms of the percent change and the absolute percent of total regional population by 1970 residing in cities of a minimal 100,000 individuals. In Table 3.1, low and high urban regions did not appear to adapt in obkom plenums to substantive agricultural and industrial issues, which should correspond to varying economic requirements of regions. When urbanization is operationalized by percent of the population in cities of 100,000 or more, we can note a limited but important pattern variation on these two issue sectors between low and high regions. Thus, in Table 3.2, high change regions devoted one-third of their obkom plenums in 1970 strictly to industrial problems, 11 percent more than low change regions. No inverse relationship between agricultural and industrial themes appears in Table 3.2 (the relative percentages of 24 and 28 percent for agriculture were actually higher in the more urban regions), but when we consider the variation again by absolute-level urbanization in Table 3.2A, we see that not only did high and low regions adhere to the predicted inverse concern with agriculture and industry but also the percent differences between sectors in both regions is exactly equal (10 percent). The total inverse ratio between agricultural and industrial issue sectors was 20 percent, slightly less than the 23 percent in Table 3.1A, but more significant in that the number of low and high regions in Table 3.2A are equal.

The Kaluga oblast in the Russian Republic typified this high policy concern with agricultural problems among the more rural regions in the sample. Kaluga is classified as a low urban region in both Tables 3.1A and 3.2A. Only 52 percent of the region was statistically classified as urban in the 1970 census; and 21 percent of the regional population is located in the capital of Kaluga, the sole metropolitan center with a population core greater than 100,000. As a consequence of its extreme rural base, 13 of the total 20 issues raised in Kaluga during the nine and a half months of 1970 were directly related to the agricultural sector. In addition to a June 4 obkom plenum and a July 10 joint oblast-capital Party atktiv on agriculture, 11 distinct oblast-wide agricultural conferences were held in the nine months from January through September. From January through April alone, conferences in Kaluga brought together oblast livestock

TABLE 3.2

Obkom Plenum Themes and Urban Density (100,000), 1939-70
(in percent)

Regions			Plenum Issue Sectors						
			Ind.-		Cad.	Soc.			
100,000	Ind.	Agr.	Agr.	Ide.	Org.	Wel.	Other	Total	
Low change[a]	22	24	(-2)	6	45	—	3	100	(67)
High change[b]	33	28	(+5)	2	33	4	—	100	(46)
Low absolute[c]	24	25	(-1)	7	39	2	3	100	(59)
High absolute[d]	30	26	(+4)	2	41	1	—	100	(54)

TABLE 3.2A

Total Regional Party Issue Sectors and
Urban Density (100,000), 1939-70
(in percent)

			Total Regional Issue Sectors							
			Ind.-		Cad.	Soc.	Soc.			
	Ind.	Agr.	Agr.	Ide.	Org.	Wel.	Leg.	Other	Total	
Low change	21	20	(+1)	21	25	7	5	1	100	(295)
High change	21	24	(-3)	27	18	6	4	1	100	(218)
Low absolute	18	28	(-10)	20	24	5	4	1	100	(261)
High absolute	25	15	(+10)	27	19	9	5	1	100	(252)

Note: The range of percent change in urban density was 0 to 31 percent, and the mean was 15 percent. The range of percent urban density in 1970 was 0 to 56 percent, and the mean was 34 percent. The year 1939 was selected as the base year, because there was little variance among the regions for the period 1959-70.

[a]Regions with percent change of 0 to 15 percent in their total regional population living in cities of 100,000 or more between 1939 and 1970: (14) Belgorod, Kursk, Tambov, Bryansk, Smolensk, Crimea, L'vov, Trans-Carpathia, Kirov, Rostov, Dnepropetrovsk, Khar'kov, Odessa, and Kaliningrad. The population for Kaliningrad in 1939 was not cited, but it was estimated that the total population living in cities of 100,000 or more in Kaliningrad had not increased by more than 15 percent in the interim.
[b]Regions with percent change of 16 to 31 percent in their total regional population living in cities of 100,000 or more between 1939 and 1970: (11) Orel, Kaluga, Perm', Vologda, Yaroslavl', Novosibirsk, Kemerovo, Tomsk, Saratov, Volgograd, and Zaporozh'e.
[c]Regions with percent of total population in cities of 100,000 or more in 1970 between 0 and 34 percent: (13) Belgorod, Kursk, Tambov, Bryansk, Smolensk, Crimea, L'vov, Trans-Carpathia, Kirov, Orel, Kaluga, Perm', and Vologda.
[d]Regions with percent of total population in cities of 100,000 or more in 1970 between 35 and 56 percent: (12) Rostov, Dnepropetrovsk, Khar'kov, Zaporozh'e, Odessa, Kaliningrad, Yaroslavl', Novosibirsk, Kemerovo, Tomsk, Saratov, and Volgograd.

Sources: Regional press of the 25 regions; Itogi-1959 goda (SSSR); Itogi-1970 goda (Tom I).

72

specialists (January 28), oblast agronomists (February 4), the first secretaries of rural gorkoms and raikoms (March 4), oblast swine-growers (March 18), directing oblast agricultural leaders (March 31), and the collective and state farm leaders (April 5-8). Principal reporters and participants at these conferences typically included the chairman of the oblast executive committee, the oblast director of agriculture, the obkom secretary specializing in agriculture, and, not infrequently, obkom First Secretary Kandrenkov himself. At the March 31 conference of directing agricultural workers, the real emphasis on agriculture in Kaluga was highlighted by the personal participation of Minister of Agriculture for the RSFSR Floren'tev and First Deputy Chairman of Agriculture for the USSR Pysin.12

While agricultural policy was the overriding priority of Party leaders in Kaluga during 1970, a primary concern with agriculture was repeated in the other 12 regions with a low urban density in 1970, as the total of 28 percent in Table 3.2A shows. Specific problems reviewed at agricultural plenums and conferences of these 13 regions often followed an identical format. Rural regions were particularly alarmed by unsatisfactory livestock production and the need to provide housing and other material incentives in the rural areas to stem the growing migration of youth to the cities. Both problems, of course, had been singled out in Brezhnev's July Plenum report on agriculture, and regional parties made the necessary"'conclusions" in seeing the logical relationship between them. As an example, the themes directly overlapped in the discussions at the June 4 agricultural plenum in Kaluga. As First Secretary Kandrenkov admitted in his report, the problem of livestock productivity for Kaluga could only be partially resolved with increased technical innovation and an expanded feed base developed in the collective and state farms. Greater attention would also have to be directed toward providing better housing and more cultural and everyday (bytovoi) facilities for the rural population. Otherwise, the positive benefit from increased technical or feed base capacities would be cancelled by a diminishing rural labor force to oversee their implementation. The second theme of the plenum was specifically devoted to the problems of housing and cultural infrastructure in the rural areas; and, reflective of the perceived gravity of the situation defined for regional Party leaders, the minister of everyday facilities for the RSFSR, A. N. Gandurin, participated directly in the discussions.13

Even for high urban regions in Table 3.2A, those in which agriculture was less frequently discussed during 1970, the direct relationship of livestock productivity to material incentives was paramount in consideration. At the July 10 plenum on agriculture in Novosibirsk, obkom First Secretary Goriachev warned the expanded plenum of the harmful effect produced by the high turnover of young rural workers on the quality of agricultural specialists and the stability of Party organizations in the Novosibirsk countryside. Livestock accounts for more than 50 percent of the total agricultural production in the region, but a primary drawback to even more productivity has been the evaluation made by several collective farmers that livestock is not as profitable as staple crops to invest additional amounts of their time and resources. To raise the profitability margin of livestock, more technical innovations would have to be introduced. Yet, as Goriachev argued, if the profitability of livestock production depended on increased mechanization, so, too, did the effect of mechanization depend upon a stable and trained core of rural specialists to drive the new machinery and supervise the implementation of new technical innovations. The leadership core of rural Party organizations would have to be strengthened with increased incentives for members to remain in the rural areas and direct the agricultural specialists. Stability in rural specialists and the guidance of rural Party organizations, of course, presumed additional material benefits for collective farms in order to break the vicious downward cycle of diminishing work forces, lower profitability margins, and unfulfilled livestock quotas. These same agricultural specialists must be persuaded at an earlier age that they would have a vested material interest not to migrate into the capital city of Novosibirsk. More higher educational institutions and agricultural teknikums must be located directly in the rural locales, and qualified teenagers who would otherwise leave the countryside to train as industrial technicians in the cities must be convinced that an occupation as a mechanizer or a livestock grower was more desirable.[14]

Both All-Union and regional Party leaders in 1970 were constantly urging what they termed "sober" and "businesslike" approaches to agricultural failures. As they would argue, recently enacted agricultural reforms in the Soviet Union had been based on a realistic assessment of problems, and the low productivity levels were being raised as a result. A prominent Western expert on Soviet agriculture has reviewed Soviet agricultural reforms between 1965 and 1970 and has concluded that, in spite of this lofty rhetoric, the policy innovations of Brezhnev and Kosygin have fallen short of dealing with basic systemic problems in the agricultural sector.[15] In order truly to stimulate agriculture, in which average productivity per worker is still only one-tenth the comparable productivity level in the United States,[16] Soviet leaders would have to commit themselves realistically to far-reaching changes in investment priorities and administrative structures for the countryside, which the leadership seems unwilling or unable to consider.

This disparity between the pronounced intentions of reforms and their reality was particularly evident in the most recent policy innovation, regional kolkhoz councils, formed at the oblast level and reported upon in the regional press during 1970. Historically, the concept of independent kolkhoz councils, linking up to an All-Union Inter-Kolkhoz Federation, had been considered and debated since the abolition of the Machine-Tractor Stations in 1958. During the period when Khrushchev was particularly identified with restructuring agricultural relations, a conflict had evolved over his support for kolkhoz councils as independent representative forums for the collective farmers.[17] The intention of the kolkhoz council, while often lost sight of during the policy-power conflict of the Khrushchev period, was to stimulate the morale and enthusiasm of collective farmers. The locally based kolkhoz councils would represent farmers' views and provide them with something of a counterbalance to traditional Party-state hegemony in agricultural quotas and pricing.

By December 1969, the Soviet leadership had apparently been won over to the concept and to the necessity of uplifting the work enthusiasm and productivity of collective farmers. In December, the Third All-Union Kolkhoz Congress had convened and adopted a Kolkhoz Charter of Rights and Responsibilities. In addition, the Congress announced true "kolkhoz democracy" was to follow with the formation of subordinate regional kolkhoz councils on the regional level during 1970. In contrast, the vacuity of the heralded kolkhoz councils was immediately witnessed by the fact that every chairman of the regional kolkhoz council announced in the regional press was simultaneously the regional director of the state agricultural administration.* With traditional state officials conspicuously assigned to head the new kolkhoz councils, regional leaders were not even using the councils for the minimal symbolic accommodation of collective farmers. Whatever the professed concern with a "business-like" approach to failures and solutions and whatever the difference on agricultural issues between urban and rural regions, issue adaptation in agriculture by 1970 still meant adjustment within the strictures of orthodox Party-state dominance.

Agricultural and Cadre Policies: Kursk Oblast

A second important finding in Table 3.2 is the 12 percent difference between low and high change regions in cadre-organizational

---

*Examples in 1970 included the directors of oblast agriculture and chairmen of the regional kolkhoz councils in Smolensk (I. K. Slabkovskii), Orel (S. S. Nikishin), Kirov (V. P. Semenovich), and Trans-Carpathia (I. M. Roman).

problems. As in Table 3.1, therefore, the rural regions of the sample were more concerned with internal Party affairs than were the more rapidly urbanizing regions. The direction is opposite to that hypothesized by the theory of social mobilization. We might bear in mind that in Table 3.2A the rural regions by absolute percentage in 1970 also considered agricultural issues at a much higher ratio than did urban regions. While no explanation could be universally offered for all rural regions, the high concern with both agricultural and cadre-organizational problems in several rural regions was directly related. Agricultural failures, at least those experienced during the period of 1969 and 1970, appeared to account for much of the turnover in Party leadership and the preoccupation with internal cadre matters in these rural regions.

These findings seem to bear out an assumption drawn by Western scholars in studies of local Party organizations. Western scholars argue that regional Party officials have traditionally devoted a large proportion of their efforts to agricultural production.[18] The reasons are both a logical division of labor and a calculated concern for their own political careers. The responsibility of the regional Party officials for industrial performance at the local level is shared with industrial enterprise directors and the central industrial ministries. It has been found that Party leaders are likely to defer to the opinions of these more knowledgeable industrial specialists in resolving industrial delays and production crises. Conversely, Party officials benefit from this shared task responsibility. Party officials can logically shift the onus for industrial failures to the same industrial specialists.

In contrast, Party officials alone are likely to be held accountable for failing to meet agricultural quotas. The assignment and performance of lower agricultural officials and Party cadres are the direct responsibility of regional Party leaders. The pressures for quota fulfillment can only increase in direct relation to the predominance of agriculture in the economy of a region. In more urban and industrialized regions, regional officials can point to industrial successes to offset any agricultural failures. Therefore, as we could conclude from Table 3.2, regional parties experienced greater internal Party changes, measured by the percentage of cadre-organizational questions reviewed at obkom plenums, in those regions that were more prominently agricultural in profile and that had serious crop or livestock failures in 1969-70.

The direct bearing of agricultural performance on cadre-organizational problems in rural regions would be illustrated best by the rural oblast of Kursk during 1970. Of the 21 issue themes considered in Kursk, agriculture and cadre-organizational problems each merited the equal attention of five separate discussions at obkom plenums, gorkom plenums, and oblast conferences. The reciprocity of both sectors was even greater than the mere figures would suggest.

Indications of grave agricultural problems were apparent from the very beginning of the year, when the obkom plenum on the December Plenum report was convened on January 6 in Kursk. Rather than printing abridged versions of the main report and the addresses of the participants (a practice followed in all subsequent obkom and gorkom plenums in the newspaper), the regional newspaper merely summarized the plenum report in two ambiguous sentences.19 In retrospect, the failure of the regional leadership to have an extensive summary report of the plenum published at this time could not have been unintentional but probably reflected the intensity of discussions at the plenum during which very serious agricultural problems were openly admitted and criticized. The gravity of the perceived situation, in contrast to the neutral statement from the official newspaper report, was hinted at only one week later. The obkom bureau reprimanded the first secretary, the chairman, and the director of district agriculture in the Konyshev raion of Kursk for failing to secure adequate protection of livestock during the preceding winter months.20 The reprimand was printed as the lead front page story, and the more general significance of the report was implied in the last paragraphs in which all districts were warned to apply suitable agrotechnical measures in protecting their livestock or suffer a fate similar to the officials in the Konyshev raion.

During the next two weeks, front page lead stories emphasized the rural raikom plenums that had followed subsequent to the mysterious obkom plenum on January 6. Failures in livestock production had apparently been the principal target of the obkom plenum, for several raikom first secretaries had been confronted with correcting their "blunders" and "shortcomings" or being replaced. As examples, the local first secretaries of the Korenev and Suzhansk raikoms engaged in acts of self-criticism before their raikom plenums and admitted that the criticism leveled against them at the obkom plenum had been justified.21 At the same time, with lightly veiled threats against their fellow raikom committee members, the raikom first secretaries proposed that, unless the situation in livestock production improved, many lower agricultural officials and farm directors would be immediately replaced. The problem of livestock was explicitly redefined as one of lower cadre performance. As later events were to suggest, the obkom first secretary, Monashev, was being held responsible by the center for the agricultural failures; Monashev, for his part, was attempting to shift the blame to other lower and less politically protected officials within the region. From the obkom first secretary downward to the raikom first secretaries and then to lower agricultural officials, the political process in Kursk had settled into the traditional Soviet bureaucratic pattern of shifting responsibility for failures to ever lower cadre levels in the hierarchy.

Monashev continued the political ploy of shifting the blame downward, as he personally addressed another rural raikom plenum on January 23. Monashev's comments were quoted extensively on the front page of the newspaper, as he singled out and severely attacked a local kolkhoz chairman for the total failure of livestock production in the district:

> . . . These shortcomings (arrogance, immodesty, the shunning of public assignments) had been pointed out to him earlier. It would seem, Communist Alekseev has to take the remarks into account and be corrected. However, judging by his performance at the plenum, he has not made the Party conclusions; instead of recognizing his mistakes, he pursued demagogic discourses or attempted to present the criticism as unmerited. In his declaration there was not anything in common with Party moral responsibility. Is this accidental? . . . The misfortune lies in that the raikom lowered its high standards to its cadres . . .22

The final settling of political scores was not to be decided for the next two months. In other regions, such as Vologda, where equally severe problems in livestock were admitted, the obkom first secretary was able to control the political outcome, and a major turnover of raikom secretaries followed as a consequence in February and March.23 In contrast, Leonid Gavrilovich Monashev had been first secretary of Kursk since 1958. Having survived the crop and livestock failures of the past, Monashev now may have reached the end of his political career and been considered expendable by the central leadership. For whatever reason, no changes of raikom officials were announced in the regional newspaper, despite the campaign under way by Monashev to establish their culpability for agricultural failures.

The deus ex machina came directly in the person of Premier Alexei Kosygin, who arrived in Kursk on April 16 ostensibly for a major ceremony in which the oblast was to be awarded the Order of Lenin. It soon became obvious that Kosygin's visit was intended as more than a goodwill visit. The relationship of Kosygin's visit to an impending personnel shakeup was ironically hinted at in the very cover story on the ceremony that welcomed him. According to the regional newspaper, among those accompanying Kosygin was the "former" obkom first secretary, P. I. Doronin, and among those who welcomed the Kosygin entourage was the first secretary of the oblast

Komsomol, A. I. Danshin, this despite the fact that the oblast Komsomol first secretary through March 27 had been one V. Ye. Tomashkevich and no official announcement of a change had ever been reported.[24] Four days later, Monashev was conspicuous by his absence at the Lenin Memorial Ceremony in Kursk to commemorate the Lenin Centenary.[25] Finally, on April 29, the regional newspaper announced that an obkom plenum held the previous day had relieved Monashev of his duties as first secretary in relation to his confirmation as councilor in the Council of Ministers of the RSFSR.[26] To add insult to injury, the Order of Lenin, the official rationale for Kosygin's visit to the region, had apparently been withdrawn.*

Surprisingly, Monashev was replaced as first secretary by the former agricultural secretary of the obkom, A. F. Gudkov. Gudkov's appointment is significant in several ways. Gudkov at this time was promoted over three other bureau officials who by natural seniority in the region and by the rank order of signers on oblast obituaries had continually outranked him prior to the change. One, I. A. Sechkov, a logical successor to Monashev, had been second secretary since the 23d Congress in 1966 and by total length of service in the obkom leadership had been at least an obkom secretary in Kursk since 1954.[27] Another potential successor to Monashev, the chairman of the oblispolkom, I. I. Dudkin, had been obkom agricultural secretary, obkom second secretary, or oblispolkom chairman since 1954.[28] Also outranking Gudkov, T. I. Arkhipova, the obkom ideology secretary, would have been an unlikely replacement to correct the agricultural problems of the region as first secretary. Yet she too had accumulated long service in the region and had been a member of the obkom bureau since 1954.[29] Indeed, even G. M. Korotaev, the oblast director of commerce in 1970, could claim extensive prior political experience in major regional Party positions. Prior to his current assignment, Korotaev had been in succession obkom second secretary in the regions of Riazan, Belgorod, and Kostroma.[30] In contrast, 40 years old at the time of his election as first secretary, Gudkov had actually been a member of the obkom bureau for only two years, when in late 1967 he had proceeded rapidly from a brief appointment as obkom Party organizational director to the position as obkom agricultural secretary.

At the same time Gudkov would be especially qualified to fill a position of the Kursk oblast, which required a major revamping of

---

*In the 1971 Yearbook of the Soviet Encyclopedia, there is no reference to the Kursk oblast in the summary list of oblasts in the Russian Republic that received the Order of Lenin during 1970. See Ezhegodnik (1971), p. 156.

agricultural leadership. A regional native who had spent a lengthy portion of his early career at minor agricultural positions in the oblast, Gudkov had graduated from the Voronezh Agricultural Institute in 1953 and returned to work in the very same rural district in which he had been born, serving subsequently as kolkhoz agronomist, director of the local machine-tractor station, and then raion agricultural inspector of the Koronev and Medvensk raions.[31] In August 1961, he was assigned to Party work for the first time as first secretary of the Khomutovsk and then Dmitriev raions. Gudkov was apparently being groomed for even higher political responsibilities; for, in 1965, he was selected to attend the Higher Party School of the Central Committee for the two-year postgraduate Party training and degree. Young, with higher degrees in agriculture and political leadership and with extensive personal knowledge of agricultural problems in the locales from his own early work experience, Gudkov signified rejuvenation and a changing of the guard in the obkom leadership by his election as first secretary.

Gudkov's election established the pattern for other changes in the obkom leadership. The former director of the obkom agricultural department, who had been first appointed at the same time Gudkov had been elected agricultural secretary in 1968, was now promoted to replace Gudkov as the new agricultural secretary on the obkom. The new obkom agricultural department director was the former raion director of agriculture (or deputy chairman of the raiispolkom) in the Dmitriev rural district. As Gudkov had served as secretary of the Dmitriev district through 1965, one could easily surmise that he was personally acquainted with the former raion director, who would also figure as a political client of Gudkov's.

Formally, Gudkov's criticisms of agricultural production and cadre performance after his election appear identical to those made by Monashev at the beginning of 1970. There is one subtle difference, though, which is telling in regard to the political outcome of assigning responsibility for errors. Raikom and lower agricultural officials are indeed criticized by Gudkov, but he is also careful to single out for equal or greater blame the obkom departments and (by inference) the obkom secretaries and other regional officials responsible for supervising the policy implementation of the departments. If there was any weakening in the selection process of cadres over the last few years, as Gudkov was reported to have said at an oblast Party aktiv in June on agriculture, primary responsibility for this situation must fall upon the officials in the obkom departments.[32] By subtle redirection, the political blame for agricultural failures was shifted to the aging and long-entrenched regional leadership, and personnel changes in the two years after 1970 appeared to confirm the pattern

of leadership renewal initiated by Gudkov's election.* As for the
lower officials who had been threatened in January and February with
severe penalties by Monashev, Gudkov's appointment for them was
symbolized by the participants who addressed a May obkom plenum
on cadre problems and the same June oblast Party aktiv on agriculture.
The chairman of the raiispolkom and the raikom first secretary of
Konyshev, who both had been reprimanded by the obkom bureau (that
is, Monashev) for cadre and agriculture shortcomings, had now returned to favor to the extent that they were selected to address the
May plenum and June Party aktiv.[33] As Gudkov himself was a very
recent lower agricultural official in Kursk, his election as first
secretary represented the victory of the lower officials over the
established oblast leadership.†

Social Welfare Policy

Social welfare is a third important theme to be considered by
regional parties. Even given the preponderant concern of most rural
parties with the impact of material incentives and cultural facilities
upon agricultural productivity, the broadly defined policy area of
social welfare was only a minor preoccupation for most regional
parties in 1970. In Tables 3.1A and 3.2A, conferences and plenums
on consumer facilities and urban development (categorized as "social
welfare") made up no more than 9 percent of all regional issues in
1970. Nevertheless, although the variation between low and high urban
regions is only 4 percent, this same percent difference of 4 to 5

---

*I. I. Dudkin, the oblispolkom chairman, was singled out and
criticized by the Russian Council of Ministers for violating state
discipline in meat shipments in March 1971 (SRos, March 18, 1971,
p. 2). He was subsequently replaced as chairman by D. V. Kamynin,
who had only been elected to the bureau as agricultural secretary,
in the month following Gudkov's election as first secretary (see
deputies elected to the Russian Supreme Soviet in SRos, June 17,
1971). Ironically, the individual selected to replace Kamynin as
agricultural secretary was I. Ye. Boiko, formerly an instructor of
the Central Committee, who had first appeared in Kursk at the same
June oblast Party aktiv at which Gudkov had soundly criticised the
obkom leadership for failures in agriculture and cadre selection
(KuP, June 20, 1971 and article by Boiko in SRos, January 4, 1972).
†Despite the leadership turnover in Kursk, the region has still
failed to meet quotas in livestock production after 1970. See "Why
Livestock Sections Are Unprofitable," P, June 27, 1972.

percent and the same 9 to 10 percent level for high regions will consistently hold for all five indices of social mobilization and apparently distinguish some common threshold of policy emphasis along which regions adapted to internal consumer demands.

Regional Party leaders would deny that rural or low mobilized regions are in any way discriminated against in the expenditure of resources or time for social welfare development. After all, they could point to several agricultural plenums and conferences in 1970 at which cultural facilities and housing for the rural population had been stressed. Yet one would logically anticipate that, as cities and urban settlements in a region reach a certain population size and density, more attention and economic resources will have to be diverted by the regional leadership into providing minimal housing for the larger number of industrial workers, mass transit systems to connect the newly built workers' dormitories and factories, commercial food and clothing outlets to service the work force and their families, and other related consumer services more typical of a highly urban environment. Of course, it is generally conceded that real policy initiative in these social welfare sectors quite often lies outside the actual scope of the regional Party or the regional government. As a recent study of Soviet social welfare policies has argued, basic decisions on the location and size of housing or consumer facilities have often been independently determined by industrial enterprises. The very economic autonomy of regions in social welfare is undermined by the fact that budgets for these sectors are allocated to the central industrial ministries, which have dual control with the regional parties over the plants and factories in the regions.[34] With each industrial ministry pursuing its own bureaucratic requirements for housing and consumer facilities, the lack of any kind of regional coordination or rationale in urban and consumer sectors is a constant complaint of regional leaders.

Even conceding the limited ability of regional parties to affect social welfare policy, the very scale of urban development and consumer facilities in higher urban regions should be such as to require the regions to employ a greater number of workers and administrative personnel with primary responsibility in this policy domain. As suggested for the substantive issues of agriculture and industry, issue adaptation connotes a varying response not only to the real magnitude of a regional problem but also to the considered size and importance of the work force and officials employed in the policy area. Therefore, the very size of the work force and administrative personnel in the social welfare area would cause higher urban regions to convene specialized oblast conferences of these workers more frequently and would (more likely) lead regional leaders to perceive that social welfare issues merit a review before official Party plenums or sessions of the oblast soviet. One can assume, then, that the percent differences by absolute levels in Tables 3.1A, and 3.2A, repeated in the subsequent tables, at least substantiate a varying adaptive response to the work sectors employed in social welfare activities by region. Whether regional leaders can actually influence social welfare policy is no less important than the demonstrated recognition on their part that the problems themselves deserve greater than normal attention.

At the same time these percent differences may be misleading. For one reason, the social welfare theme was only considered important enough to be brought before the assembled obkom in two of the total 68 obkom plenums. One was the previously noted June 4 obkom plenum in Kaluga. While careful to frame his discussion of everyday services as a general regional problem, the second secretary of Kaluga in his report cautioned the obkom that particular attention would have to be directed to the extremely inadequate cultural facilities and consumer outlets in the rural areas.[35] The only other plenum at which the issue was even tangentially raised was the January 12 plenum in the Saratov region. The director of the obkom financial department presented the draft for the 1970 regional budget, as other reporters in turn discussed the December Plenum report by Brezhnev and the development plan for local industry in 1970.[36] Regions thus either failed to consider social welfare problems at obkom plenums or, when they did infrequently as in Kaluga and Saratov, considered them only as subordinate themes to the broader issues of agricultural and industrial productivity in the region. Even capital gorkom plenums only considered social welfare issues five times. Rather, social welfare issues in 28 of the total 35 times were relegated to mere specialized oblast conferences or to sessions of the capital-oblast soviets.

It could be argued that direct responsibility for social welfare sectors actually resides in the capital and regional governments of a region and that, because of this distinct administrative responsibility, the regional capital and obkom Party plenums should be less directly identified with consumer problems. Yet the Party plenums in a region are not only the highest decisional arenas in a region but the key forums at which attention on particular issue sectors can be mobilized for the entire region. Not to downgrade the potential role of the oblast and capital governments, but, as a policy takes on increasing significance for the regional leadership, there should be some correlative spillover of issue concern from lower decisional levels upward into the capital gorkoms and obkom plenums. The dominant level at which an issue is discussed most assuredly bears some direct relationship to its perceived intensity of importance for the regional Party leadership, as they cue lower Party cadres and oblast state officials to redirect their priorities. If so, by gradation of intensity, social welfare only marginally concerned the regional Party leadership in 1970.

Moreover, if regions were truly concerned with social welfare problems at any level really comparable to the 9 percent total for high urban oblasts, a reflection of that concern would be the turnover of officials with direct responsibility for administering the urban development and consumer sectors. The oblast party would thereby signal a conscious awareness of social welfare by bringing new and supposedly more qualified personnel to these positions under a mandate to improve performance. Because of the highly political context in which policy is acted upon in the Soviet Union, positions associated with issue sector responsibility of suddenly increased priority are more likely to experience rapid turnover.

In contrast, only six personnel changes of a total 163 during 1970 can be directly linked to positions with ascribed responsibilities in the social welfare area for the region or oblast capital. Indeed, when social welfare figured prominently as an issue or was highly correlated with personnel changes in 1970, the oblast appeared to be responding not so much to local environmental pressures but to a threatened sanction from the central Party level. As an example, only in one highly urban region of 1970 did there appear to be any real demonstrated relationship between social welfare as a major policy priority and personnel changes.

With over 1.5 million or 40 percent of its total population residing in urban centers of a minimum 100,000 concentration, the region of Rostov by 1970 ranked as one of the most urban regions among the 25 in the sample. In addition to the regional capital, Rostov also includes urban boom towns that have grown up suddenly around the location of large industrial complexes since World War II. In addition to normal frustrations over housing and consumer services to be expected in rapidly industrializing areas like Rostov, the region was widely reported in the West to have experienced a violent 1962 riot over consumer demands in the urban boom town of Novocherkassk, a city of 100,000 population with 16,000 students alone housed together in cramped workers dormitories.[37] The riot, which directly stemmed from the protests of housewives and particularly embittered student-workers over the announced price rise in foods, resulted not only in the temporary isolation of the region and hurried visits by center officials like the Praesidium member A. P. Kirilenko, but the apparent dismissal or demotion of the entire obkom secretariat before the beginning of 1963.* With its recent tradition of violence

---

*Among those in the obkom secretariat at the beginning of 1962 and gone by the end of the year were A. V. Basov (first secretary),

associated with consumer discontent and the political consequences for the obkom secretariat in 1962, it is thus probably not surprising to find that even in 1970 one-sixth of all policy issues (6 of 36) for the Rostov regional leadership specifically addressed social welfare problems, and articles by Rostov officials in the central organs were frank in their concern over the current inadequate housing and consumer facilities of the expanding urban centers of the region.*

Yet the high priority assigned to social welfare policy may also have been decided for the regional leadership by the publication of a Central Committee resolution on February 3.[38] The resolution warned unspecified oblasts, krais, and cities to correct their violations of state discipline in urban construction and communal economy. Particular criticism in the resolution was directed against the unlawful misallocation of building materials away from housing and communal needs like child day-care centers to the construction of superfluous administrative sites, sport centers, and other places of public entertainment.[39] The only region of the 25 that even reviewed this resolution at any official policy forum during 1970 was Rostov, when the resolution served as the theme for the main report at the Rostov city soviet session on September 16.[40] Evidence that Rostov may well have been included in the unspecified list of miscreant regions, however, can be surmised well before the official review of the problem before the regional capital government.

Indeed, the significance of the Central Committee resolution for Rostov officials was apparently decided by the time the 5th session of the oblast soviet convened three months earlier on June 17.[41] The three separate themes presented at this extensively reported session were all closely interdependent as they bore on the social welfare sector in Rostov. The principal report discussed the work of the communal economy administration of the oblast. Delivered

---

L. I. Maiakov (second secretary), P. I. Shchelkunov (ideology secretary), V. Ye. Kimkhlov (industry-consumer secretary), and Rudenko (?) (agriculture secretary). Interestingly, Kimkhlov, who apparently had a dual responsibility for industry and social welfare policy in 1962 (see article in Meditsinskaia gazeta, November 16, 1962) still has a major role in social welfare policy as obkom director of the department of light, food, and commercial establishments (see M, August 9, 1967 and VR, June 5, 1970).

*According to an interview in Pravda with S. N. Sabaneev, the capital gorkom first secretary of Rostov, even with newly constructed consumer establishments, the city of Rostov was still 30 percent below present consumer demand. See "Vyros novyi raion" (A new district has formed), P, June 18, 1970.

by the oblast director of the communal economy administration, the report was more notable for the personal participation in the discussions of the Minister of Everyday Services in the RSFSR, A. N. Gandurin. Gandurin was apparently on a junket of Russian regions, for he had also participated in the June 5 Kaluga plenum, which, as previously noted, had discussed living conditions in the rural areas of the oblast. Yet, except for Kaluga, the only other policy forum at which such a high official from the domestic services ministries had appeared at a region during 1970 was the participation of the Russian Republic deputy minister of Commerce in a February 19 oblast public nourishment conference in Novosibirsk.[42] The Novosibirsk conference followed the dismissal of the director of Novosibirsk's industrial-construction department only two days after the February 3 resolution tion[43] and other less direct signs that Novosibirsk also may have been one of the unspecified oblasts criticized by the Central Committee. The anomaly of participation from high domestic ministerial officials like Gandurin in Rostov at least suggests that central authorities were particularly desirous of gaining firsthand information on the state of affairs in the regions of Rostov and Novosibirsk. Only the Central Committee resolution would have likely prompted such a direct mission.

The second report at the Rostov oblast soviet was delivered by the oblispolkom chairman Mazovka and followed a logical sequence in demanding a greater response on the part of oblast officials and deputies to citizens' complaints and suggestions. Consider that among the complaints and suggestions from citizens must have been those signals to the center that probably disclosed the misallocation of construction funds in Rostov in the first place. The third theme ominously discussed the responsibility for violating social order in the Rostov oblast. As a consequence, two organizational changes were announced after the reports. The deputy chairman of the oblispolkom was transferred to an undesignated position, and the director of the oblast MVD was placed on pension. Part of the responsibility for allowing the misallocation to go unnoticed in the first place was thus assigned to the principal police official in the region. Both of these officials were allowed to transfer or retire without any apparent further legal actions taken against them, but the full circle of responsibility had still not been drawn, for the next month was to witness the replacement (without explanation) of the directors of the Rostov city commerce and public housing administrations, the director of the obkom construction department, and the second secretary of the capital gorkom.[44] Finally, the oblispolkom chairman of Rostov was allowed to retire for reasons of "health" in late September.[45] The extensive personnel shakeup of those directly or indirectly responsible for social welfare could not have been unintentional.

Although the example of Rostov may typify at one extreme the reluctance of regional officials to act seriously upon social welfare policy unless threatened by the center, a few prominent officials in the social welfare area were being replaced in other regions, and not all of these new assignments could be solely attributed to illegal activities as in Rostov. Little if any biographical information on these new replacements is available. Few of their positions are important enough to merit the individual's attending the Ukrainian or All-Union Party Congresses in 1971 as a Party delegate, so not even date of Party entry listed for all Party delegates could be obtained. Even given the limited biographical sources, the example of one new official for whom an extensive biography was printed in the regional press is particularly enlightening. If he is typical of the new personnel assigned to social welfare responsibilities in 1970, the higher urban regions were indeed attempting to upgrade the quality of leadership in the consumer sector.

On August 24, Victor Boiko was elected chairman of the Dnepropetrovsk city government.[46] The sequence of personnel changes that eventually led to Boiko's election actually began with the capital gorkom plenum on August 14. A. A. Ulanov, the gorkom first secretary, was released in relation to his transfer to the apparat of the Ukrainian Central Committee and was replaced by Ye. V. Kachalovskii, who moved laterally from his previous post as chairman of the Dnepropetrovsk gorispolkom.[47] Neither Ulanov nor Kachalovskii suffered any real demotion in their new positions, as both were to appear as delegates to the 24th Party Congress the next year in Moscow. Ulanov entered the Party in 1950 and Kachalovskii in 1947, so both also reflect a postwar recruitment pattern into the obkom bureaus since 1965, a phenomenon discussed at greater length in Chapter 6.

More importantly, however, is the significance of Boiko's appointment as new chairman to replace Kachalovskii in a region like Dnepropetrovsk. As the participation and speeches of the Dnepropetrovsk chairman continually show during the period between January and October 1970, the chairman has primary responsibility for supervising the local domestic and consumer problems in the large urban center. Indicative of this specific administrative responsibility, the new chairman Boiko was elected at the same session of the city soviet in which he discussed new commission reports on the state of road construction, urban development, health, and social security in the city. The region of Dnepropetrovsk has a population density above 100,000 of 53 percent and a total capital population of 863,000 in 1970. The city is therefore quite representative of the large urban centers in the Soviet Union. Because of the direct identification of the gorispolkom chairman with social welfare supervision, the background of this official would then be an important indicator of how really concerned with domestic problems the large urban centers were by 1970. The region of Dnepropetrovsk is also reputed to be a principal patronage source for General Secretary Brezhnev, who has a direct hand over major personnel shifts in the oblast. With greater than normal reliability, the background of a new official in a specified issue area for Dnepropetrovsk could be interpreted as a general reflection of central leadership concern with that specific issue area. From a Kremlinological perspective, personnel shifts in a politically sensitive region like Dnepropetrovsk serve as a barometer of real policy emphasis for the overall political system in Moscow.

Only 39 at the time of his appointment, Boiko is a native of Dnepropetrovsk with a higher degree in engineering from the region's Krivoi-Rog Coal Institute in 1960.[48] He entered the Party in 1954, so he typifies the recruitment pattern of native post-Stalin officials whose educational training is quite contemporary. Not only does Boiko have an extensive technical background to fit his responsibilities in urban development as chairman, but, after graduating from the regional Institute in 1970, he spent the next five years employed directly in construction work assignments within the region. He was first assigned as a work superintendent in a local construction site, was then transferred to become an assistant faculty member at the same Krivoi-Rog Coal Institute, and later was placed in Party work as instructor and director of the Construction and Industrial Construction Materials Department of the Krivoi-Rog gorkom. From 1964, Boiko was promoted to comparable Party assignments on the obkom level. From 1964 through 1966, he was deputy director of the obkom Construction and Urban Economy Department and, after 1966, was promoted to director of the Department. At the time of his appointment as gorispolkom chairman, he was still serving in that capacity. Indeed, up to a week before his election as chairman, Boiko was not even a deputy in the city soviet of Dnepropetrovsk.[49]

Consequently, three background factors are particularly impressive for Boiko and argue that his appointment was intended to upgrade the domestic sectors of the city. For one, consider his extensive educational and practical experience in construction work. Boiko will now be supervising large construction sites for urban development, housing, and communal facilities in the city and would be highly qualified to provide technical leadership in this new capacity. Secondly, by assigning the former Party construction head to the gorispolkom leadership, the Party in Dnepropetrovsk has politically elevated the state position with an individual who matches high political credits and potential in the region with the required administrative background to coordinate urban construction projects. Boiko has accumulated long service in the obkom department, from which he has probably appointed and supervised lower construction officials in the region and capital. Supposedly, with his political background, he should now be better able to defend the consumer sector against encroachment by central ministries and other regional bureaucracies competing for scarce construction materials from the oblast leadership.* A technical background in itself is not sufficient for a gorispolkom chairman, if he is to carry off politically the task of raising the priority of social welfare projects in the city. Thirdly, and not totally unimportant, Boiko is a regional native whose life experiences have been formed solely in Dnepropetrovsk. As he formerly worked with or appointed many of his lower subordinate construction officials in the city, he would be quite familiar with them. Boiko would also be well acquainted with the typical administrative routines for construction work in the region, and he could more easily expedite the completion of urban construction sites by knowing where and how to reassign men and construction materials.

If Boiko exemplifies a more recent and typical personnel pattern in large urban centers, the 9 percent level for social welfare policy in the high urban regions of Tables 3.1A and 3.2A may accurately reflect an increasing real concern with consumer demands. Moreover, if Brezhnev was somehow personally responsible for Boiko's appointment, one could assume from Boiko's background a very real commitment on the part of central Party leadership (at least, the Brezhnev faction) to rationalize and strengthen the consumer sector at local levels in 1970.[50]

Ideological and Cadre Policies

If social welfare issues were in the forefront of attention for several oblast parties in 1970, ideological problems should not have been any less important. The year 1970 was the centenary anniversary of Lenin's birth, and the central leadership in Moscow had marked the occasion by mounting an extensive mobilization campaign. Presumably, the very prominence given to the campaign at the center

---

*Of course, Boiko's real political potential in the region depends upon his personal ties and position relative to the present oblast leaders. There is no evidence during 1970 that Boiko as construction head or gorispolkom chairman was either a candidate or full member of the obkom bureau. On the other hand, even the deputy director of the Construction Department in the Volgograd oblast was reported in her obituary of June 19 to have been a member of the Volgograd obkom bureau. See obituary to Ye. S. Shurygina in VP, June 19, 1970.

would have carried over into local parties and influenced them to consider ideological problems at a much higher than normal rate.

Yet Western scholars of local parties have stressed the minor role traditionally occupied by ideology and indoctrination cadres in the general priority schedule of regional Party leaders.51 When officials and cadres responsible for indoctrination affairs in a region are not deliberately shunted aside by Party leaders, all too often their university academic training and background prove incompatible with the specialist economic orientation and practical mentality of many regional Party leaders. The antagonism between indoctrination officials (that is, agitprop and ideological officials) and Party leaders has been compared to the traditional role conflict between the "man of words" and the "man of deeds." Plenums devoted entirely to ideology are an unlikely occurrence in most regional parties, for Party policy-makers can only look upon ideological problems as annoying intrusions upon their limited time better spent in meeting agricultural and industrial quotas.

In turn, the possible sexual bias in the regional party may be a significant contributing factor to the traditional antagonism and to the reinforcement of group identity among indoctrination officials. As a rule, women rising to positions as prominent as obkom bureau members were still a rarity in 1970. Although 5 of the obkom ideology secretaries identifiable by sex in 1970 were women, these exceptions do not necessarily contradict a subtle pattern of sexual discrimination in Party-state leadership positions evident from another perspective. Most officials with primary indoctrination responsibilities in the 25 regions appear to be women. In 12 of the regions, women dominated the formation of ideology policy in 1970 by holding the key positions of obkom ideology secretary, gorkom ideology secretary in the regional capital, or director of the obkom propaganda-agitation and science-educational institutions departments. Only 25 of 763 obkom bureau members who have served in the 25 regions from 1955 through 1973 have been women; and, of these 25, 11 were elected to the bureau as the obkom ideology secretary, the last and sole position that they have held on the obkom bureau. Of 111 other women who attained regional Party-state positions below the obkom bureau from 1958 through 1973, 46 percent (51) could be positively categorized as indoctrination specialists by the nature of their official positions.*

---

*That is, director of the obkom or gorkom departments of propaganda-agitation and science-educational institutions; director of the oblast administration of culture or schools; deputy chairman of the oblast executive committee responsible for ideological problems; director of the oblast division of Znanie (mass organization for creative intelligentsia), and so on.

As such, given the narrow specialization in their skills and training, once such an official commits herself to a Party career, she probably has less of an opportunity for career advancement within or beyond the regional hierarchy than would officials who specialized in agricultural or industrial problems at the regional level. Few women have ever been elected to the All-Union Central Committee,[52] only one of 72 secretaries elected to the Union-republic secretariats by the end of 1972 was a woman,[53] only six women in the 45 regions have been elected to the obkom bureaus for the first time since 1965, and only two female regional bureau members were promoted to positions at the All-Union or Union-republic levels from the 25 regions between 1955 and 1973.[54] As indoctrination specialists, women will lack the technical and political leadership background considered more essential to qualify them as members of the political elite in the Central Committee. Indoctrination appears to be a sex-typed profession and status reserved for women within the regional Party organizations.[55] As they attempt to advance in the regional hierarchy, perceived sexual discrimination among the many female indoctrination officials may add to normal career frustrations. The traditional role antagonism would thus be intensified between the "man of deeds" and the "woman of words."

Despite the Lenin Centenary celebration at the central level, the evidence in the tables on obkom plenums tends to support the conclusion that 1970 was not an atypical response to ideological problems at the regional level. Specific ideological questions were considered at only five obkom plenums during 1970. Even these five were more often exceptional plenums, as the lightly veiled attack on Jewish intellectuals in Odessa and the criticism of the press in Smolensk would have suggested from the discussion in the previous chapter. With only a total of five plenums, oblast leaders had not stressed any more formal emphasis to ideological policy than would have been expected from previous studies of local parties.

On the other hand, the proportion of total ideological issues should logically bear some direct relationship to important indices of social change in regions. Among the 25 regions in the sample are highly modern educational and cultural centers like Novosibirsk, Odessa, Rostov, and Khar'kov. Indicative of their high stage of development, all have a large number of students attending higher educational institutions, technical specialists with completed higher education active in their work force, and citizens with completed higher education. If regional parties adapt to their environments, the convergence of these three factors should necessitate a directly related response in ideological policy for two reasons.

First, as a response to work sectors, with the perceived demands upon regional parties for virtual representation, the number

of specialized conferences on ideological problems should increase
in proportion to the growing size of students and skilled specialists
in a region. More students in a region should necessitate an expansion in the regional party's network of educational cadres and
Party organizations supervising these same higher educational institutions. Similarly, cadres and personnel in the broad category of
skilled regional specialists in most regions parallel the relative
size of the creative intelligentsia employed in the region. With an
increase of students or skilled specialists in a region, specialized
conferences would be more frequently convened to deal with the problems of educational curriculum and administration or to oversee the
agenda for cultural productivity. These conferences would occur
more frequently if for no other reason than that these problems now
occupy a larger percentage of the total regional Party cadres and
oblast officials.

This thesis of virtual representation seems to be borne out by
the examples of the four regions that considered ideological problems
most frequently in 1970 and simultaneously had the largest number
of students, skilled specialists with completed higher education, and
citizens with completed higher education. By 1970 the number of
students in higher educational institutions had reached a total of
73,000 in Novosibirsk, 87,000 in Odessa, 94,000 in Rostov, and 127,-
000 in Khar'kov; skilled specialists with completed higher education,
77,000 in Novosibirsk, 84,000 in Odessa, 116,000 in Rostov, and 125,-
000 in Khar'kov; and citizens with completed higher education, 89,000
in Novosibirsk, 109,000 in Odessa, 137,000 in Rostov, and 153,000
in Khar'kov. The number of times ideological problems were separately considered in the four regions during 1970 parallels these high
educational group levels: 8 of the total 22 issue sectors in Novosibirsk;
11 of 36 issue sectors in Rostov; 8 of 27 issue sectors in Odessa;
and 5 of 15 issue sectors in Khar'kov. Although some of these conferences and plenums were limited in composition solely to Party
indoctrination officials, even greater selective response to particular
cultural subgroups of the intelligentsia was apparent in several cases.
Thus, in Khar'kov, four of the five conferences in 1970 singled out
the perceived importance of cultural and educational officials in the
region by bringing together oblast theater workers, the cultural intelligentsia, directors of general educational schools, and social
science teachers at the level of teknikums and higher educational
institutions.[56] In Rostov, 4 of the 11 ideological conferences convened
either specifically defined oblast cultural or educational officials.
In Novosibirsk, a region in which 20 percent of the total work force
just in the capital is employed in education, participation in four of
the eight ideological conferences was specifically limited to specialized educational officials and cadres, ranging in responsibilities from

the social science teachers in higher educational institutions to the scientists and Party personnel of scientific-research and design institutes in the capital. And, in Odessa, the March 20 obkom plenum, whatever its underlying intent for the Jews in the cultural intelligentsia, at least on its surface demonstrated the perceived importance attributed to this particular work sector by regional authorities.

Yet the March plenum in Odessa and the 1962 student riots in the Rostov city of Novocherkassk should also make us wary in interpreting the emphasis assigned to ideological policy solely as a response dictated by the size dimension of educational and cultural work forces in a region. Secondly, as a problem area, a highly trained and educated population may well have a more subtle indirect environmental influence upon regional parties, for increases in all three factors could pose greater difficulties of political socialization and social control. Concepts like political culture are probably needed to appreciate the real impact of a highly educated stratum upon a regional environment; but it is enough to assume that increases in university students, highly skilled specialists, and educational attainment levels of the population could impart a higher level of political sophistication and possible resistance among strategic occupational sectors in a regional work force. There need not even be an open challenge through intellectual dissent to arouse the concern of the regional Party leadership. In recent years, Party leaders have come to recognize a growing problem less of militant resistance than of passivity in eliciting the enthusiasm of work forces in the factories and farms through the traditional agitprop mobilizing techniques. As the proportion of highly trained and educated workers has expanded in agriculture and industry, the conventional oral appeals and simplistic arguments have proven less effective in stimulating labor productivity.[57] Therefore, the issue of ideologically "upraising" and "steeling" the intellectual stratum in the universities and skilled labor force should more likely become recognized as a high priority as increasing numbers of students are educated, enter the regional workforce, and have a greater sustained importance for the regional economy. In this sense, the resolution of the ideological problem becomes basic to resolving the economic problem of labor productivity.

In order to test the environmental impact and policy response to the levels of university students, skilled specialists, and highly educated citizenry in a region, the issue sectors in Tables 3.3-3.5 are compared along a median range of increases in all three factors over time and their absolute levels in 1970. As a first hypothesis, ideological issues should have a higher percentage in regions that have undergone greater change in all three factors or in which the absolute levels of all three factors are greater in 1970. In contrast, the policy response to ideological problems in all three tables fails to follow any consistent pattern of variation. In Table 3.3A, the variation between low and high regions is only 5 and 4 percent; in Table 3.4A, only 3 percent; and, in Table 3.5A, only 2 and 1 percent. In short, ideological concerns were as likely to be expressed by regional parties in which the three factors were insignificant as in those regional parties in which their environmental impact should have necessitated a more rational allocation of attention and priority.

Why, then, did low and high mobilized regions arrive at such identical ratios on the ideological issue sector in 1970? Three tentative explanations could be proposed. Either the regional parties do not as a rule respond to ideological problems in any logical manner, or the period under study was atypical, or the category of ideological issues itself obscures very important qualitative differences in the kinds of ideological conferences.

First, as already suggested, ideology holds a traditionally minor place in the overall priority schedule of regional Party leaders. Given the sharp differences by professional background, outlook, and sex between indoctrination officials and regional Party leaders, regional Party leaders are probably less concerned with demands from the ideological work sector for virtual representation of their group interests in conferences. That the proportion of educational cadres and agitprop officials increases with more students and skilled specialists in a region may be true, but what may be more important is that these same cadres and officials are predominantly women and perform meaningless, time-consuming tasks in the policy hierarchy of the many male and practice-oriented Party leaders. With the low priority given to ideology and indoctrination officials in a regional party, specific ideological conferences in all regions are fairly routinized events, have little policy consequence, and are unlikely to fluctuate in any rational sequence, even with an increase in the proportion of Party cadres occupied primarily in educational and cultural responsibilities.

Second, the number of ideological conferences convened in low mobilized regions may be abnormally high and may actually reflect the impact of the All-Union Lenin Centenary campaign. Although very few obkom ideological plenums were convened in 1970, it is impossible to dismiss the very great likelihood that the total number of ideological issues was indeed atypically high because of the great stress placed upon ideological conformity at the All-Union level. If so, the discussion of ideological problems, particularly in low mobilized regions was not a response to local environmental factors but was keyed by a standardizing impulse generated by the All-Union event. Ideology was leveled up as an issue sector in low mobilized regions by the exogenous factor of the Lenin Centenary. In more

TABLE 3.3

Obkom Plenum Themes and Students in Higher Education per
10,000 Population, 1959-70
(in percent)

| Students/ 10,000 | Plenum Issue Sectors | | | | | | | |
	Ind.	Agr.	Ind.-Agr.	Ide.	Cad. Org.	Soc. Wel.	Other	Total
Low change[a]	25	23	(+2)	8	39	2	4	100 (52)
High change[b]	28	28	0	2	41	2	—	100 (61)
Low absolute[c]	26	26	0	6	37	2	3	100 (65)
High absolute[d]	27	25	(+2)	2	44	2	—	100 (48)

TABLE 3.3A

Total Regional Party Issue Sectors and Students in
Higher Education per 10,000 Population, 1959-70
(in percent)

| | Total Regional Issue Sectors | | | | | | | | |
	Ind.	Agr.	Ind.-Agr.	Ide.	Cad. Org.	Soc. Wel.	Soc. Leg.	Other	Total
Low change	18	29	(-11)	21	23	4	4	1	100 (220)
High change	24	16	(+8)	26	19	9	5	—	100 (286)
Low absolute	20	28	(-8)	22	21	5	4	1	100 (282)
High absolute	24	15	(+9)	26	22	9	4	—	100 (225)

Note: "Students" include all those in day, evening, and correspondence faculty of higher educational institutions and universities. Unfortunately, data only on "full-time" day students in the higher educational network were not consistently defined or available for all 25 regions after 1965. The figures for 1965 do show, however, that the rank order of regions by all students is exactly identical to the rank order by full-time students. Change in the absolute number of students between 1959 and 1970 ranged from 28 to 266 per 10,000 population, and the mean for all regions was 69 per 10,000 population. The absolute number of students per 10,000 population in 1970 ranged from 41 to 576, and the mean for all regions was 150 per 10,000 population.

[a]Regions with absolute change in students per 10,000 population from 28 to 69 between 1959 and 1970: (11) Belgorod, Yaroslavl', Kaluga, Bryansk, Kursk, Tambov, Orel, Smolensk, Vologda, Kirov, and Trans-Carpathia.

[b]Regions with absolute change in students per 10,000 population from 70 to 266 between 1959 and 1970: (14) Novosibirsk, Tomsk, Kaliningrad, Khar'kov, Odessa, L'vov, Rostov, Kemerovo, Saratov, Volgograd, Perm', Dnepropetrovsk, Zaporozh'e, and Crimea.

[c]Regions with absolute number of students per 10,000 population in 1970 from 41 to 150: (15) Belgorod, Orel, Kaluga, Bryansk, Vologda, Kirov, Kursk, Tambov, Yaroslavl', Smolensk, Kemerovo, Volgograd, Perm', Crimea, and Trans-Carpathia.

[d]Regions with absolute number of students per 10,000 population in 1970 from 151 to 576: (10) Rostov, Saratov, Kaliningrad, Dnepropetrovsk, Zaporozhe'e, Novosibirsk, Tomsk, Khar'kov, Odessa, and L'vov.

Sources: Regional press of the 25 regions; Narodnoe Khoziaistvo RSFSR (1961, 1969); Narodne Gospodarstvo UKR SSR (1961, 1969).

95

TABLE 3.4

Obkom Plenum Themes and Specialists (Completed Higher
Education) per 10,000 Population, 1955-70
(in percent)

Specialists/ 10,000			Plenum Issue Sectors						
	Ind.	Agr.	Ind.-Agr.	Ide.	Cad. Org.	Soc. Wel.	Other	Total	
Low change[a]	26	28	(-2)	6	38	1	1	100	(69)
High change[b]	27	23	(+4)	2	45	2	—	100	(44)
Low absolute[c]	27	27	(0)	7	35	3	2	100	(60)
High absolute[d]	26	25	(+1)	2	47	—	—	100	(53)

TABLE 3.4A

Total Regional Party Issue Sectors and Specialists (Completed
Higher Education) per 10,000 Population, 1955-70
(in percent)

			Total Regional Issue Sectors							
	Ind.	Agr.	Ind.-Agr.	Ide.	Cad. Org.	Soc. Wel.	Soc. Leg.	Other	Total	
Low change	20	23	(-3)	25	21	6	4	1	100	(301)
High change	23	21	(+2)	22	20	9	4	—	100	(206)
Low absolute	19	28	(-9)	22	20	5	4	2	100	(251)
High absolute	24	16	(+8)	25	21	9	5	—	100	(256)

Note: Change in the absolute number of specialists between 1955 and 1970 ranged from 102 to 267 per 10,000 population, and the mean for all regions was 159 per 10,000 population. The absolute number of specialists in 1970 ranged from 177 to 442 per 10,000 population, and the mean for all regions was 261 per 10,000 population. The year 1955 was the earliest date for which data were available against a population base in all regions. The population was estimated for 1955, but it was assumed any error would be random for all regions included in the estimate.

aRegions with absolute change in specialists (completed higher education) per 10,000 population from 102 to 159 between 1955 and 1970: (15) Belgorod, Kursk, Tambov, Orel, Bryansk, Smolensk, Rostov, Yaroslavl', Kemerovo, Saratov, Perm', Vologda, L'vov, Trans-Carpathia, and Kirov.

bRegions with absolute change in specialists (completed higher education) per 10,000 population from 160 to 267 between 1955 and 1970: (10) Kaluga, Novosibirsk, Tomsk, Volgograd, Kaliningrad, Dnepropetrovsk, Zaporozh'e, Khar'kov, Crimea, and Odessa.

cRegions with absolute number of specialists (completed higher education) per 10,000 population from 177 to 261 in 1970: (13) Belgorod, Kursk, Tambov, Orel, Kaluga, Yaroslavl', Bryansk, Smolensk, Kemerovo, Perm', Vologda, Trans-Carpathia, and Kirov.

dRegions with absolute number of specialists (completed higher education) per 10,000 population from 262 to 442 in 1970: (12) Rostov, Novosibirsk, Tomsk, Saratov, Volgograd, Kaliningrad, Dnepropetrovsk, Zaporozh'e, Khar'kov, Crimea, Odessa, and L'vov.

Sources: Narodnoe Khoziaistvo RSFSR (1956-70); Narodne gospodarstvo Ukr SSR (1957-70); regional press of the 25 regions.

TABLE 3.5

Obkom Plenum Themes and Proportion of Population with
Completed Higher Education, 1939-70
(in percent)

Higher Education/ 10,000	Plenum Issue Sectors								
	Ind.	Agr.	Ind.-Agr.	Ide.	Cad. Org.	Soc. Wel.	Other	Total	
Low change[a]	28	26	(+2)	8	36	—	2	100	(53)
High change[b]	24	24	(0)	2	45	4	—	100	(49)
Low absolute[c]	27	27	(0)	7	36	—	2	100	(55)
High absolute[d]	26	24	(+2)	2	45	3	—	100	(58)

TABLE 3.5A

Total Regional Party Issue Sectors and Proportion of
Population with Completed Higher Education, 1939-70
(in percent)

	Total Regional Issue Sectors								
	Ind.	Agr.	Ind.-Agr.	Ide.	Cad. Org.	Soc. Wel.	Soc. Leg.	Other	Total
Low change	19	26	(-7)	23	21	4	4	2	100 (213)
High change	21	20	(+1)	25	20	10	5	—	100 (229)
Low absolute	20	26	(-6)	23	21	4	4	2	100 (232)
High absolute	22	19	(+3)	24	21	9	5	—	100 (275)

Note: Change in the absolute proportion of population with completed higher education (in age group over 10) between 1939 and 1970 ranged from 200 to 450 per 10,000; the mean was 281. Change in the absolute proportion of population with completed higher education (in age group over 10) in 1970 ranged from 230 to 630; the mean was 366. Figures are not cited for the regions of L'vov, Trans-Carpathia, and Kaliningrad in 1939, all three incorporated into the Soviet Union after 1939.

aRegions with absolute change in proportion of population with completed higher education (in age group over 10) per 10,000 from 200 to 281 between 1939 and 1970: (11) Belgorod, Kursk, Tambov, Orel, Bryansk, Vologda, Smolensk, Yaroslavl', Kirov, Perm', and Kemerovo.

bRegions with absolute change in proportion of population with completed higher education (in age group over 10) per 10,000 from 282 to 450 between 1939 and 1970: (11) Kaluga, Volgograd, Saratov, Rostov, Novosibirsk, Tomsk, Crimea, Odessa, Khar'kov, Dnepropetrovsk, and Zaporozh'e.

cRegions with absolute proportion of population with completed higher education (in age group over 10) per 10,000 from 230 to 366 in 1970: (12) Belgorod, Kursk, Tambov, Orel, Bryansk, Vologda, Smolensk, Yaroslavl', Kirov, Perm', Kemerovo, and Trans-Carpathia.

dRegions with absolute proportion of population with completed higher education (in age group over 10) per 10,000 from 367 to 630 in 1970: (13) Kaluga, Volgograd, Saratov, Rostov, Novosibirsk, Tomsk, Kaliningrad, Crimea, L'vov, Odessa, Khar'kov, Dnepropetrovsk, and Zaporozh'e.

Sources: Itogi-1959 goda (SSSR); Itogi vsesoiuznoi perepisi naseleniia 1970 goda: Tom III-Uroven' obrazovaniia naseleniia SSSR; regional press of the 25 regions.

normal circumstances, there would have been a greater percent difference between low and high regions, as their relative concern with ideological problems would be more immediately reflective of local environmental pressures.

Third, the category of ideological issues in reality encompasses qualitatively different kinds of conferences among the regions. As previously outlined, conferences in the four regions with the highest educational-cultural levels in most cases brought together very selective groups of educators or cultural officials from within the region. Ideological conferences in Rostov, Novosibirsk, Khar'kov, and Odessa were highly adaptive forums to the levels of educational and cultural personnel employed in these regions. In contrast, while convening as many ideological conferences as the highly mobilized regions in 1970, low mobilized regions like Smolensk and Orel organized conferences almost solely for oblast agitprop cadres or ideological secretaries from the urban and district parties of the regions. In our trial analysis, specialized educational and cultural conferences had been distinguished as a separate issue sector from these more loosely defined ideological conferences of agitprop department heads and secretaries. Yet, because of the small absolute number of educational-cultural conferences for all regions during 1970, both subcategories were later merged into the single ideological sector.

The real difference in policy emphasis may have been lost in combination. For regions like Novosibirsk and Khar'kov with high concentrations of students and skilled specialists were indeed convening very specialized conferences in 1970 and, by this fact, demonstrating their ability to selectively respond to these same occupational sectors. Ideological conferences in the low mobilized regions (a group that to some extent is identical to the regions included as low urban in Tables 3.1 and 3.2) were mostly a considered follow-up to the general problem of ideological disenchantment among rural youth, a prevalent subtheme discussed at agricultural plenums of rural regions during 1970. While the percent ratios on ideology were fairly identical between low and high mobilized regions in Tables 3.3A-3.5A, the significance of an ideological conference as an issue response in both regional categories was generally quite different. High mobilized regions were reacting more to the pressure of the intellectual stratum in their environment, while low mobilized regions reacted to falling agricultural production, linked in the minds of many regional leaders to rapid turnover of rural youth and the decline of ideological commitment in the countryside.

As a second hypothesis to test against the three tables, we would hypothesize that the policy concern with cadre-organizational problems in regional parties should parallel the rates of change or absolute levels of these three factors in their environment. From the theory of social mobilization, it should be anticipated that the acclimation of increased numbers of more highly educated specialists into a political system represents a major cadre problem for regional parties. As more lower level cadres in a region are recruited into the Party from educated skilled elites and from the students in higher educational institutions, the average educational level and technical training will soon be higher among lower cadres than among the senior Party and state officials in a region. Normal career frustration will be spurred by resentment among lower cadres that they must take orders from senior officials less qualified than they to understand the technical details of work assignments. Even a recent laudatory essay on the continuity of generations in the Soviet Union written by a Soviet sociologist hints at a possible strain or "misunderstanding" between the generations brought on by the much higher educational and cultural background of the current younger generation. Because of their higher educational and cultural background, the present younger Soviet generation has become "incomparably more demanding both to its seniors and to those who are presented with the goals of upraising and educating it as its successor."[58]

In turn, the older and less educated senior officials are likely to feel threatened by their younger, more highly trained, and "more demanding" lower cadres. As defensive mechanisms, senior officials will project the importance of such leadership attributes as long-time practical experience in the field or proven political reliability in order to counter the higher educational training and technical knowledge of their rival younger subordinates in the bureaucracies. The conflict can only become more acute as the number of students and specialists increases in a region, as they enter the lower ranks of the Party at a higher rate, and as the potential threat to senior officials becomes more real.

Between 1969 and 1972, articles alluding to this internal struggle over leadership positions on the regional level (with possible Kremlinological applications to the aging Politburo) have appeared more frequently in the central Party journals. On one hand, some articles have cautioned the younger subordinates that assignments to directing posts must still be granted on the basis of "political maturity" and to those "who have displayed their worth over a long period of 'practical work' in their present positions."[59] On the other hand, the problem of leadership cannot be ignored at the regional level, where agricultural and industrial productivity have failed to meet expected levels during the last few years. Gudkov's sudden rise to the position of first secretary in Kursk, following a poor agricultural showing in the region, illustrates in one sense the process by which younger, more educated subordinates were being rapidly promoted to leadership positions. Rare candor about the potential extent of the cadre problem was recently displayed by the obkom first secretary of the Sakhalin oblast:

> . . . Still frequently, however, knowledgeable and capable young workers are retained in secondary positions. In the Sakhalin oblast, for example, as verification has proven, many directing sectors of the enterprises in the forestry industry are headed by people who do not have specialist education, although many who work in the rank and file positions in the industry have graduated from higher educational institutions and teknikums. It should be borne in mind that it would be incorrect not to value and retain the directing-practical workers . . . But many directing-practical workers clearly lack sufficient educational knowledge and theoretical preparation; it is more difficult for them to work in contemporary conditions with each passing year, and productivity has begun to suffer as a consequence . . .60

The slight difference in implication between this article and others that have cautioned gradualism and a "continuity" of old and new leaders suggests that the problem has been contested at the regional level during 1970. The figures in Tables 3.3-3.5 would permit a partial testing of the extent to which the conflict had been resolved by the end of 1970. If regional parties adapted to this internal cadre problem in 1970, regions with increased numbers of students and skilled specialists should have been more concerned with cadre morale at obkom plenums and more likely to assign new personnel to the obkom bureau and departments. A pattern should emerge in which the proportion of cadre-organizational issues increases in proportion to the absolute level or rate of change in the three environmental indices of mobilization.

The percent variation between low and high regions by all three indices would tend to support this hypothesis. In Table 3.3, regions in 1970 with a total number of students per 10,000 greater than 150 considered cadre policy at a 7 percent higher ratio than did regions below the mean of 150. In Tables 3.4 and 3.5, both the rate of change and the absolute level of skilled specialists and regional population with completed higher education differentiate regional parties above and below the mean by 7, 12, and 9 percent.

Such minor differences must be carefully interpreted, so that we do not infer too much from them. A variation between 7 and 12 percent is still not as significant as the 12 to 17 percent previously shown for cadre policy in Tables 3.1 and 3.2. The rate of change in urbanization still differentiates all regions more widely in 1970. Small percent differences would also signify that the three indices in themselves cannot account for the relative concern of regional parties with internal cadre policy in 1970. If anything, the limited variation points up the obvious fact that the intense career and leadership conflict in regional parties has still not been resolved. True, more skilled and highly educated cadres are filling lower ranks in the Party and regional work forces. But, at the same time, a real concern with lower cadre morale or a significant turnover in obkom leadership are unlikely to follow until the old regional leadership is saddled with a poor economic performance in industrial and agricultural production, one that it can neither deny nor blame on any factors other than the oblast officials themselves.

In turn, the very level of economic success in a region, as the obkom first secretary of Volgograd has emphasized, also reflects the level of morale among lower cadres and officials, a factor equally dependent upon their perceptions of possible career advancement in a regional hierarchy. The pressure for acceding to the demands of lower cadres and officials will not be voluntarily resolved in many regional parties. Oblast bureau officials, too, have their political careers at stake. A rapid turnover initially directed against second-level officials in the region could easily extend up to bureau officials. As graphically illustrated by Monashev's unsuccessful attacks on lower officials in Kursk and the changes subsequent to Kosygin's arrival in 1970, it will be up to the outside center leadership to initiate the process of adaptation to lower cadre demands in regions. The lower cadres are most likely to find their allies in the center against the status quo interests of intermediate obkom bureau leadership in any region. Yet, as we shall see in Chapter 5, the center since 1965 has been a dubious and actually retrogressive base of political support for lower cadres in regional parties.

Conclusions

Having considered the impact of each independent environmental variable upon issue sectors in 1970, we might review in total the relative differences on all issue sectors and indices of social mobilization in 1970. Have regional parties been granted sufficient autonomy from the center by which to orchestrate central policy guidelines to demands and problems arising from their own particular environments? If so, how extensive was policy adaptation, and did it correspond to any consistent and logical pattern of regional differences, and for what particular issue sectors in 1970? The percent differences by issue sectors and social mobilization from the previous five tables are compared in Table 3.6

TABLE 3.6

Plenum Issue Sectors—Ratios by Indices of Social Mobilization (High/Low)[a]

	Ind.	Agr.	Ind.-Agr.	Ide.	Cad. Org.	Highest Percentage Difference
Change—urban	+3	+5	(+2)	+1	-17	17
Absolute—urban	+7	+2	(+5)	-5	-2	7
Change—100,000	+11	+4	(+7)	-4	-12	12
Absolute—100,00	+6	+1	(+5)	-5	+2	6
Change—specialists	+1	-5	(+6)	-4	+7	7
Absolute—specialists	-1	+2	(-3)	-5	+12	12
Change—students	+3	+5	(-2)	-6	+2	6
Absolute—students	+1	-1	0	-4	+7	7
Change—higher ed.	-4	-2	(-2)	-6	+9	9
Absolute—higher ed.	-1	-3	(+2)	-5	+9	9
Highest percentage difference	11	5	(7)	6	17	—
Total plenums[b]	27	26	(1)	4	40	—

TABLE 3.6A

Total Issue Sectors—Ratios by Indices of Social Mobilization (High/Low)[a]

	Ind.	Agr.	Ind.-Agr.	Ide.	Cad. Org.	Soc. Wel.	Soc. Leg.	Highest Percentage Difference
Change—urb.	-6	+6	0	+1	-2	0	-1	6
Absolute—urb.	+7	-16	(+23)	+1	+1	+4	-1	23
Change—100,000	0	+4	(-4)	+6	-8	-1	-1	8
Absolute—100,000	+7	-13	(+20)	+7	-5	+4	+1	20
Change—specialists	+3	-2	+5	-3	-1	+3	0	5
Absolute—specialists	+5	-12	(+17)	+3	+1	+4	+1	17
Change—students	+6	-13	(+19)	+5	-4	+5	+1	19
Absolute—students	+4	-13	(+17)	+4	+1	+4	0	17
Change—higher ed.	+2	-6	(+8)	+2	-1	+6	+1	8
Absolute—higher ed.	+2	-7	(+9)	+1	0	+5	+1	9
Highest percentage difference	7	16	(23)	7	8	6	1	—
Total Issue sectors[b]	21	22	(1)	24	21	7	4	—

[a]The percent variation between high and low regions, along the mean of each index. A plus sign indicates a higher percentage in high mobilized regions; a minus sign, a higher percentage in low mobilized regions.

[b]Percentages for all 25 regions.

Source: Compiled by the author.

If useful benchmarks to define issue adaptation at the regional level are a minimal 10 percent variation or consistent differences on almost all indices of social mobilization, we could make the following conclusions on the basis of Table 3.6:

(1) The themes at obkom plenums are less likely to vary among regions than are the total range of regional issue sectors (Table 3.6A).

(2) While demonstrating little policy autonomy at obkom plenums, regional parties were able to respond to substantive agricultural and industrial issues through the alternative channels of oblast conferences, capital gorkom plenums, and sessions of the oblast-capital soviets. Absolute levels of social mobilization distinguished substantive issues more than did rates of change.

(3) Problems of social welfare drew consistently higher attention in regions of more rapid change or higher absolute levels of social mobilization. In contrast, problems of criminal behavior (socialist legality) evidence no logical pattern by environmental differences.

(4) Issue adaptation in obkom plenums signified a varied concern with the demands of lower level cadres in the parties. Both rates of change (urbanization) and absolute levels of social mobilization (educational levels) must be considered in explaining the emphasis upon cadre policy in a region.

(5) Urbanization is the single most important factor in distinguishing both substantive and nonsubstantive issues among regional parties in 1970.

Yet a careful scrutiny of Table 3.6 must also reveal the very limited range of opportunities vested in oblast parties to consider problems on a selective basis. As should have been made apparent to the reader, the issue sectors themselves are as much artifical distinctions. All issues in some manner bore directly on the same problems of industrial and agricultural production in the regions. These two problems of industry or agriculture are the predominant issue domains from which the other subthemes take on significance for regional policy-makers. Social welfare as material incentives for workers or ideology as induced moral incentives for rural workers should more realistically be included as industry and agriculture in the tables. Similarly, cadre problems are not considered in the abstract by regional policy-makers but only as the "poor morale problem" affects production goals. While regions may differ in how they apprehend and respond to problems, the common source for all regional parties is their economic orientation and the realization that their performance will be evaluated primarily by the criteria of production.

PARTICIPATION IN OBKOM PLENUMS

The second policy dimension by which regional parties will be compared is participation in obkom plenums. The 25 regions will be ranged along the same five indices of change and absolute social mobilization to test any patterns of adaptation on this second organizational dimension.

Before presenting our findings, though, it would be useful to consider the meaning of participation in plenums and its close bearing upon issues. For, although conceptualized as a second and independent dimension, group participation in obkom plenums cannot be realistically understood apart from the nature of issues, or issue adaptation. If issues have to be defined selectively in different regions, this means regional parties must also open channels of participation on those same issues from groups commensurate to their size and importance in the regions.

Participation as a Regional Issue

There seem to be two very logical reasons for this close linkage between the nature of issues and group participation. For one, as we stressed in evaluating total regional issue sectors in the previous section, issue adaptation means not only a relative concern with an indirect environmental pressure,but also a direct response to varying occupational group levels. In particular, the diverse specialized conferences and seminars often appear to be commonly employed by regional leaders in order to provide a sense of virtual representation for specialized work sectors and Party cadres in a region. As the size or considered importance of particular occupational groups increases with environmental change, regional Party leaders will attempt to retain their enthusiasm and support through these specialized conferences and seminars identified with their work responsibilities.

Admittedly, such conferences and seminars at times may provide important information for regional Party leaders and function as an input channel from lower cadres or officials to regional decision-makers in the obkom bureau. Among several examples that could be cited from the regional newspaper during 1970, the Party-economic aktiv in the oblast of Dnepropetrovsk appeared to serve as an open forum for transmitting the group perspective of industrial officials to regional Party leaders.61 Decisional inputs, though, are probably the exceptional and unintended consequence of such conferences. More likely, the regional Party leaders, reluctant to yield their prerogatives in final decision-making, derive very positive symbolic consequences and diffuse support for themselves at these forums.

Occupational sectors consistently called together by the regional leaders will come away from the conferences and seminars with an increased sense of self-esteem and morale. The real influence of particular groups in policy-making may not be any less important than the perception and belief on their part that they can participate and influence policies. Such subjective factors are heavily influenced by virtual representation of groups in conferences and seminars. Regional Party leaders showed themselves very sensitive to the symbolic import of these forums in 1970. From the tables in the previous section, specialized conferences and seminars for agricultural Party cadres, agronomists and mechanizers, and farm directors were a more frequent occurrence in the same rural regions in which agricultural work sectors also constitute a higher proportion of the total regional work force and in which their demands for symbolic encouragement should be correspondingly greater. Social welfare conferences were also convened more frequently in the same urban regions in which the proportion of cadres and workers in domestic service and urban development were higher.

As important as the total number of regional conferences and seminars are in themselves, the real salience of any issue depends upon the policy level at which it is formally considered. In particular, we found that social welfare and ideological problems in 1970 were discussed almost solely at oblast conferences or sessions of the oblast-capital soviets. This finding signified, among other things, that these policy concerns still occupied a low independent priority to most regional leaders in 1970. Consistent with this interpretation, the dominant level at which occupational groups are called upon to participate also will affect their eventual enthusiasm and morale. To be effective, virtual representation of group interests must appear credible to the very reference groups in the environment it is intended to influence. If relegated to mere specialized conferences with little obvious impact on policy, occupational sectors are less likely to perceive their interests have been seriously taken into account by regional Party leaders. Only if representatives from occupational groups can gain direct access to the highest political platforms in a region will the political system have credibly adapted to their demands for symbolic or virtual representation.

With the exception of the obkom bureaus (whose membership we shall analyze in later chapters), the highest policy platform at which occupational group participation can be distinguished in regional political systems is the oblast committee and the official plenums of that committee. Of course, participation in obkom plenums cannot be equated with actual membership on the oblast committee. Regional parties in 1970 often convened "expanded" plenums in which noncommittee members were specifically requested to participate;

participation even in regular plenums is often opened to noncommittee members;62 and only a selected number of discussants can ever participate in discussing one topic in any obkom plenum. On the other hand, the very selective process for participants in a plenum makes the distributive character of the participants all the more significant. If participants must be chosen from many alternative groups and work sectors in an environment, a comparison of group participants would provide important indicators of their perceived relevance and importance on issues by different regional leaders. If the size of occupational groups should correspond to the level and rate of social mobilization among regions, then the ratio of occupational group participation in obkom plenums should also vary directly with the same indices of social mobilization.

There is even a more direct second reason that participation and issues should be closely linked in regional parties. The impact of participation upon policy has become a very real concern for many regional parties during the last three years. It should be remembered that the Yaroslavl' resolution in November of 1969 had criticized meetings of lower Party organizations not only for their inflexibility in discussing the same topics but also for their failure to draw upon the backgrounds and expertise of a more varied cross-section of the total Party aktiv at meetings. Meetings had become not only un-responsive in their rigid focus on identical themes for all Party or-ganizations, but participation in these meetings had been traditionally limited to the same leadership group of so-called "state orators," who alone decided all major alternatives and remedies for every issue. As a response to these criticisms, regional leaders have be-come particularly aware of the need to broaden the representativeness of groups in the region who participate in meetings and plenums. Regional parties will now enumerate the occupational backgrounds and skills of committee members at all levels of the regional party, especially the oblast committee itself, as graphic indicators of the extent to which the leadership has adapted to group interests in the total environment.63

More than the pro forma preoccupation with virtual representa-tion may be involved in these attempts to broaden group membership on Party committees. Again, the significance in any discussion of cadre problems must be viewed against the background of falling productivity and a stagnant economic growth level, both of which prob-ably have become recognized since Brezhnev's blunt appraisal de-livered at the December Plenum in 1969. As a result, regional Party leaders now appear to be emphasizing the group changes in Party committees from the standpoint of increased Party effectiveness to production. Party leaders contend that, as the elected Party members become more representative of occupational groups in the regional environment, a greater diversity of opinions and alternatives will be brought to bear on the issue under consideration. A greater diversity of opinions and views extends the overall scope of alternative remedies to the same industrial and agricultural issues. Greater participation is thus explicitly linked with a heightened effectiveness of the party in dealing with production problems—that is, issue adaptation. The group views or alternatives taken into account by regional parties define the total range of viable alternatives from which leaders will adopt corresponding solutions. The more alternatives that are perceived for any issue, the greater the likelihood for a comprehensive and realistic solution of production problems. Both issue adaptation and participation from more varied groups would characterize a single process of more rational problem-solving and a strengthening of the regional parties.

We have already witnessed how the same issues of agriculture or industry can be interpreted quite differently among regions. Industrial and agricultural problems were interchangeably explained as an ideological problem of worker commitment, a cadre problem due to the inability of lower Party officials to advance their careers, or, more rarely, as a social welfare problem due to inadequate consumer facilities and material goods. Very obviously, cause and remedy are directly dependent upon the level of analysis at which the problem is perceived in any obkom plenum and what alternative group views are then deemed relevant to the problem by the regional policy-makers. The various alternatives regional leaders comprehend will in turn reflect the range of group views they allow to be expressed at obkom plenums.

Every Party plenum during 1970 in some manner demonstrated this varying impact of group participation on the eventual definition of issues in regions. Two industrial plenums in the regions of Vologda and Tomsk could be offered as particularly obvious examples. In Vologda, the chief doctor at the city hospital was among those who were requested to participate in the capital gorkom plenum on April 28.[64] The participation of a doctor at a defined industrial plenum seems out of place at first, until one observes the potential significance of his presence for the definition of the issue under review by the Party committee. The doctor attributed the general difficulties in completing a major ball-bearing plant not to typical technical conditions and remedies but to the poor health environment under which many construction crews at the plant had been compelled to work. At its more fundamental level of causality, industry was a health problem. According to the doctor, unsanitary conditions and uncontrolled alcoholism at the plant site had led to illness among the construction crews, subsequent rising absenteeism, and the inevitable staggering in the completion of work on the new industrial facility.

The consequences went beyond just a consideration of the plant itself. For many subsidiary enterprises in the region are dependent on parts from the ball-bearing plant, and delays in its full operations have undermined the ability of regional industry to meet its quotas. Therefore, by the contribution of the group view represented by the doctor (that is, the medical profession), the narrow industrial issue for Party leaders has now been closely identified with the general problem of health and social welfare in the region.

In the region of Tomsk, two obkom plenums during 1970 discussed the varied problems associated with the expanding oil-extraction industry in West Siberia and the reasons for delay in its full-scale operations in Tomsk.[65] On one hand, the plenums as reported in the press could not better have typified the technical ideal critics of the Communist Party have found wanting in Party decision-making. Several of the participants were geologists, transportation specialists, academicians from technical research-design institutes, or industrial officials from the All-Union level of the government. From the printed remarks and suggestions of the participants, the discussion occurred at a very complex and technical level, as the specialists offered remedies from their professional orientations and knowledge.

On the other hand, Party leaders were not bound solely to narrow technical alternatives on the issue of the oil industry. At the March 5 plenum, the oblast first secretary of the Komsomol was also requested to participate. He offered the interpretation that many of the "shock" construction sites on oil riggings had fallen behind schedule not because of technical deficiencies but because the majority of the workers in these construction crews were teenagers. The youth factor was particularly important because the regional government had failed to provide any movies, dances, and other recreational activities to maintain the morale and enthusiasm of the predominantly teenage construction workers. That the Komsomol secretary was defining the problem in terms of his own nominal youth constituency is true. The secretary may also have been looking for a reasonable excuse to protect himself and the Komsomol organization against charges from the Party for failing to mobilize the construction sites more effectively. Moreover, if the Komsomol secretary is a spokesman for a group interest in this sense, he is also a candidate member of the obkom bureau with access to policy-making and would not exemplify any broadening in the representative group base of the regional party in obkom plenums. Yet one should also bear in mind that the Komsomol secretary, as the doctor in Vologda, has now reinterpreted the industrial issue and offered an alternative solution for Party leaders. His particular group viewpoint may have broken down or at least "humanized" the narrow technical bias from which industrial policy would have been traditionally defined. With the addition of this group interest (albeit, from one already on the oblast committee and bureau), industry has become something of a social welfare problem for Party leaders, requiring a more comprehensive understanding and sensitivity to the human motivational factor of production policy.

Consequently, as issue adaptation, occupational participation in obkom plenums should be interpreted as a relative response both to direct and indirect environmental pressures. As a response to direct pressures, through virtual representation of group sectors in obkom plenums, the regional party can hope to generate symbolic support from those same group sectors in the environment. Differences in the absolute and relative rates of change in the environment would necessitate a rebalancing of symbolic support commensurate to the changing size and importance of occupational sectors. At a minimum, farm officials should participate at a higher ratio in more rural regions, enterprise officials at a higher ratio in industrialized urban regions. Moreover, criticism of the Communist Party, both in the West and more recently in the Soviet Union itself, has centered upon the absence of technical and scientific representation in Party decision-making. Logically, the proportion of scientists, technical elites, and industrial officials in any region will correspond to the level of modernization achieved by the region. If regional parties demonstrate organizational adaptation to sectors, this should be evidenced in part by a direct relationship between increasing levels of social mobilization among regions and the percentage of times that members from the total scientific-technical community participate in obkom plenums.

Virtual representation is the only finding one could derive from a comparative analysis of participation in obkom plenums. For, as a response to indirect environmental pressures, participation could also be interpreted as interest articulation on issues. Any variation in participation among regions would reflect upon the very ability of regional parties to resolve mounting production difficulties. Participation from a more varied cross-section of the work forces and lower Party aktiv increases awareness of alternative approaches and solutions during the consideration of plenary themes.

At the same time, individuals as obkom participants cannot be correlated with environmental characteristics. Unlike virtual representation, such subtle interest articulation would not by logical necessity have any direct causal relationship to changes in a social environment. The reason for this should be apparent. Contributions at obkom plenums can only be classified by the title or elected position of the group participant. Such tentative classifications really fail to allow for the considerable variation of interpretation from participants who may be classified within the same nominal group category. For instance, the doctor in Vologda had stressed the health factor as a source of industrial problems. While he would be classified as a member of the scientific-technical elite in a region, his stress on the human motivation factor differs sharply from the conventional technical focus one would expect from the industrial officials who make up the majority of the defined scientific-technical elite. The doctor and the oblast Komsomol first secretary in Tomsk, although they would be classified in different occupational sectors, were actually quite similar in their common concern with the broad human motivational source of industrial problems. It is impossible to evaluate variation within or across any occupational group categories, unless the printed comments of each participant are analyzed by their content and coded separately (the dubious reliability of printed newspaper reports was discussed in the previous chapter). The unit of analysis for group participation as interest articulation would have to be the orientation of the actor, not his occupational role.* All this is to state the obvious but often overlooked fact that in the Soviet Union attitudes cannot be imputed to an individual from the occupational position he holds.66

While relatively the same percentage of plenum themes were considered by low and high mobilized regions in 1970,† regional parties called upon different occupations to discuss what were otherwise equivalent plenary issues. Occupational sectors were not always limited to participating in issue areas for which they had a direct

---

*Nor would the nature of a defined group be limited to the occupational sector of a participant. The ethnic origins of individuals, especially in the multinational Ukrainian oblasts, may be as equally an important consideration when participants are asked to address an obkom plenum. Regional parties may deliberately draw their levels of participation in terms of an ethnic balance, intended to reflect the corresponding size of ethnic minorities in the region. Were the ethnic origins of all participants in Ukrainian plenums available, as an example, it would be interesting to classify participants by ethnic background and compare their percentages to the total ethnic distribution in the region. Nor, given our previous discussion of sexual discrimination against female indoctrination officials, can one minimize the possible significance of some token female participation in obkom plenums intended to balance the percentage of women in the lower ranks of the regional party.

†The only issue area with significant variation was cadre-organizational problems. No participants are ever cited, however, when the obkom removes personnel in the obkom bureau or departments during the organizational phase of discussing cadre policy in plenums.

administrative or political responsibility. Industrial enterprise directors in several regions participated as frequently at agricultural as at industrial plenums. As regional parties have the option to select any discussants on the same nominal issue, the relative proportion by which different occupational sectors participated in all obkom plenums should evidence their overall symbolic importance in a region. If the party has adapted organizationally, the proportion of groups in plenums should be related to their size and importance in a regional environment. The group classification of an individual may be arbitrarily factored out from several alternative categories in which he could be placed, and participation may tell little of his actual approach to a problem at an obkom plenum. Yet his ascribed role as a member of an occupational group can still be assumed to have a direct symbolic effect upon occupational reference groups with whom he is nominally identified in a region.

Components of Plenum Participation

To test the response of regional parties to participation, occupational groups for all obkom plenums have been correlated with the five indices of social mobilization in Tables 3.7-3.11. As in Tables 3.1-3.5, the five tables range occupational sectors along a typology of absolute levels and rates of change in urbanization, urban density, skilled specialists, students in higher educational institutions, and regional population with completed higher education. As Table 3.6, Table 3.12 then compares the highest percent differences by occupational sectors and the 10 measures of social mobilization.

Generally, the findings show very little political adaptation among regions and almost the same duplicated ratio of occupational groups, despite inherent environmental differences among regions. Environment, even though it should be causally linked, has a negligible relationship to the proportion of times that individuals from occupational sectors participated in obkom plenums.

The reader can confirm this conclusion by contrasting the percentages for all 10 measures of social mobilization in the tables. As shown, none of the occupational sectors varied by any consistent pattern between low and high mobilized regions. As an example, oblast officials as a group participated most frequently in agricultural plenums during 1970. One might then have expected that the same oblast officials should appear more frequently in rural or low mobilized regions. Quite the opposite is proven in Tables 3.7 and 3.8. Oblast officials never vary by more than 2 percent between low and high urban regions.

111

TABLE 3.7

Participants in Obkom Plenums and Urbanization, 1939-70
(in percent)

Regions by Urbanization	Gorrai Secs.	Obl. Off.	Obl. Mass	Occupational Sectors Farm	Ind. Off.	Tech. Eng.	Total (Sci.-Tech.)	Other	Total
Low change	40	14	5	13	8	4	(12)	15	100 (385)
High change	33	15	4	12	9	6	(15)	19	100 (447)
Low absolute	38	15	6	14	10	4	(14)	14	100 (280)
High absolute	36	15	5	11	8	6	(14)	19	100 (552)

Note: For the description of regional categories, see Table 3.1. For the definition of occupational sectors, see Table 2.4.

Source: Regional press of the 25 regions, January-October 1970.

TABLE 3.8

Participants in Obkom Plenums and Urban Density (100,000), 1939-70
(in percent)

Regions/ 100,000	Gorrai Secs.	Obl. Off.	Obl. Mass	Occupational Sectors Farm	Ind. Off.	Tech. Eng.	Total (Sci.-Tech.)	Other	Total
Low change	38	15	5	14	7	4	(11)	17	100 (454)
High change	34	14	5	10	10	7	(17)	20	100 (378)
Low absolute	38	16	5	12	8	4	(12)	17	100 (441)
High absolute	35	14	4	11	9	7	(16)	20	100 (391)

Note: For the description of regional categories, see Table 3.2. For the definition of occupational sectors, see Table 2.4.

Source: Regional press of the 25 regions, January-October 1970.

Participants in Obkom Plenums and Students in Higher Education per 10,000 Population, 1959-70
(in percent)

Students/10,000	Gorrai Secs.	Obl. Off.	Obl. Mass	Farm	Occupational Sectors		Total (Sci.-Tech.)	Other	Total
					Ind. Off.	Tech. Eng.			
Low Change	37	15	6	14	10	4	(14)	14	100 (371)
High change	36	15	4	11	8	6	(14)	20	100 (461)
Low absolute	37	16	5	12	10	4	(14)	16	100 (497)
High absolute	36	13	4	13	7	7	(14)	20	100 (335)

Note: For description of regional categories, see Table 3.3. For definition of occupational categories, see Table 2.4.

Source: Regional press of the 25 regions, January-October 1970.

TABLE 3.10

Participants in Obkom Plenums and Specialists (Completed Higher Education) per 10,000 Population, (1955-70)
(in percent)

Specialists/10,000	Gorrai Secs.	Obl. Off.	Obl. Mass	Farm	Occupational Sectors		Total (Sci.-Tech.)	Other	Total
					Ind. Off.	Tech. Eng.			
Low change	38	15	5	12	10	5	(15)	15	100 (497)
High change	35	13	6	12	7	7	(14)	21	100 (335)
Low absolute	37	15	6	12	10	5	(15)	16	100 (445)
High absolute	36	14	5	12	7	6	(13)	19	100 (387)

Note: For description of regional categories, see Table 3.4. For definition of occupational categories, see Table 2.4.

Source: Regional press of the 25 regions, January-October 1970.

TABLE 3.11

Participants in Obkom Plenums and Proportion of Population with Completed Higher Education, 1939-70
(in percent)

Higher Education/10,000	Gorrai Secs.	Obl. Off.	Obl. Mass	Farm	Occupational Sectors		Total (Sci.-Tech.)	Other	Total
					Ind. Off.	Tech. Eng.			
Low change	36	14	7	11	11	4	(15)	18	100 (339)
High change	35	14	6	12	8	7	(15)	18	100 (350)
Low absolute	36	14	7	12	11	4	(15)	17	100 (364)
High absolute	36	14	5	12	7	7	(14)	18	100 (416)

Note: For description of regional categories, see Table 3.5. For definition of occupational categories, see Table 2.4.

Source: Regional press of the 25 regions, January-October 1970.

TABLE 3.12

Occupational Sectors—Ratios by Indices of Social
Mobilization (High/Low)[a]

	Gorrai Secs.	Obl. Off.	Obl. Mass	Farm	Ind. Off.	Tech. Eng.	Total (Sci.-Tech.)	Other	Highest Percentage Difference[a]
Change—urban	-7	+1	-1	-1	+1	+2	(+3)	+4	7
Absolute—urban	-2	0	-1	-3	-2	+2	0	+5	3
Change—100,000	-4	-1	0	-4	+3	+3	(+6)	+3	6
Absolute—100,000	-3	-2	-1	-1	+1	+3	(+4)	+3	4
Change—students	-1	0	-2	-3	-2	+2	0	+6	3
Absolute—students	-1	-3	-1	+1	-3	+3	0	+4	3
Change—specialists	-3	-2	+1	0	-3	+2	(-1)	+6	3
Absolute—specialists	-1	-1	-1	0	-3	+1	(-2)	+3	3
Change— higher ed.	-1	0	-1	+1	-3	+3	0	0	3
Absolute— higher ed.	0	0	-2	0	-4	+3	(-1)	+1	4
Highest percentage difference	7	3	2	4	4	3	6	6	—
Total plenum participants[b]	37	15	5	12	9	5	14	16	—

[a]The percent variation between high and low regions along the mean of each index.
[b]Percentages for all 25 regions.

Source: Regional press of the 25 regions, January-October 1970.

114

By issue area, officials of the oblast mass organizations (Komsomol, control commission, trade-union council) had participated at their highest ratio when obkom plenums discussed cadre problems in 1970 or when industrial plenums were specifically linked to the cadre dimension stressed in Brezhnev's December Plenum report. Their functionally specific identification with cadre problems is unrelated to the nature of the region. For, when regions are now classified by rate and absolute level of mobilization, there is only a 2 percent difference at best between the ratio of participation by these oblast mass officials.

The same limited association of environment and participation is evident for farm officials, an occupational sector that includes all agricultural specialists and Party-state leaders from the collective and state farms in a region. Logically, one would anticipate that farm officials as a group should participate at a higher ratio in more rural regions, where their relative size factor and overall importance for the regional economy are greater than in urban industrialized regions. In fact, as shown in Tables 3.7 and 3.8, farm officials in the rural or low mobilized regions never participated at more than 4 percent above the equivalent level for farm officials in the more urban or high mobilized regions.

Given the significance attributed to industrial and technical officials in Soviet society, perhaps the most striking findings in the tables appear for that broadly defined occupational sector considered to be the scientific-technical elite in the regional work force. In the tables, this occupational sector was defined into three categories: "industrial enterprise officials"; "technical-engineer" personnel employed in industrial enterprises or the regional government; and a total "scientific-technical" elite, which combines the previous two individual categories. As should be true for farm officials, the participation of industrial and technical elites in obkom plenums should vary with the level of environmental development in a region, although conversely to farm officials, their ratio in obkom plenums should increase with urbanization, skilled specialists, students in higher education, and regional population with completed higher education. In contrast, one can distinguish hardly any percentage differences at all between regions. Industrial officals did not participate at a higher ratio in more urban industrialized regions. Indeed, in Table 3.7, when regions are classified by absolute urbanization in 1970, enterprise officials participated at a 2 percent higher level in the more rural regions of the sample. The indices for skilled specialists, students, and regional population evidence the same marginal and often inverse pattern from that hypothesized. In Tables 3.9-3.11, the ratio between low and high regions is actually greater by 3 to 4 percent in the regions with fewer skilled specialists, students, and population with completed higher education. Some positive correlation of high to low regions does appear for the occupational sector defined as "technical-engineer" personnel. Even in this category, though, the ratio of high to low mobilized regions is only 1 to 3 percent.

When the two categories are combined as a single scientific-technical elite, the only percentage difference of even minimal significance appears in Table 3.8. The combined scientific-technical elite exceeded the corresponding level in the low urban regions by 6 and 4 percent. Yet, when the scientific-technical elite is correlated with the other three indices, the percent variation falls to a range between zero and 2 percent. Seven of the 10 measures show absolutely no difference or a minus value between high and low mobilized regions. In brief, the demands even for symbolic representation that might be expected to arise from the members of scientific-technical elite, as their ranks increase and they become more self-conscious of their common identities and problems, have not been incorporated at the obkom plenum level in 1970.

Conclusion

The ratios by occupational sectors and mobilization are shown in Table 3.12. Again, one can only be struck by the seeming absence of any selective concern with occupational groups in different regions. The clustering of occupational sectors at the same levels would almost defy any statistical test of probability for the same large number of units. Consider that the tables categorize occupational sectors for 832 obkom participants in 68 obkom plenums over 25 regions. By multiplying the 8 defined occupational sectors by the 10 measures of mobilization, we find there were 80 alternative participation ratios on which the group sectors could have varied. Yet in 14 of the 80 cells, there is absolutely no percentage difference. In 24 other cells, the difference falls within 1 percent. The stability of participation across all regions is thus evidenced by the fact that a total of 48 percent (38 of 80) of all measures for possible variation were either zero or 1 percent.

While regional parties failed to adapt organizationally to any occupational sectors in their environment, the scientific-technical elite were allowed some form of symbolic participation in policy-making, but it occurred predominantly at the lower policy levels of the regional party in 1970. As the previous tables on issue adaptation demonstrated, regions with the highest levels of social mobilization in 1970 also convened a larger percentage of industrial conferences and seminars. While full listings of speakers or participants at these conferences and seminars were inconsistently reported in the regional press, in 29 industrial conferences and seminars during 1970, the combined scientific-technical elite constituted over 22 percent of the total 352 speakers and participants listed. Substantiated by other studies of industrial managers,[67] the evidence would suggest that such industrial conferences are particularly intended for the industrial and technical elite in a region. The conferences and seminars, inter alia, function as informal working assemblies through which the industrial and technical elite can express their positions on general policy problems related to their specific administrative or professional concerns. Moreover, in the 19 capital gorkom plenums for which discussants were fully reported in the regional press, the combined scientific-technical elite accounted for 34 percent of all participants, in comparison to the total 14 percent of scientific-technical elite in all obkom plenums. In other words, the scientific-technical elite may be foreclosed from participation at any but a very standardized ratio in obkom plenums; but, in regions where their size and importance have reached a certain threshold, Party leaders can attempt to incorporate their views at lower policy levels such as industrial conferences, seminars, and capital gorkom plenums.

Yet we have also been careful to point out that the very symbolic support a regional party can hope to generate from occupational sectors in its environment may well depend upon the level at which the same groups can achieve meaningful access to policy-making. The key to virtual representation is its very credibility for the groups it is intended to influence. In 1970 the scientific-technical elite is still relegated to the less prestigious and credible level of conferences, seminars, and capital gorkom plenums. Their inability to rise above certain prescribed norms of participation in more industrialized obkom plenums could have a demoralizing impact upon their sense of efficacy over industrial policy in those very same regions where they should be playing a more significant role in policy.

Two of the regions with the highest ratio of scientific-technical participation in 1970 probably best illustrate the generally inflexible response of regional parties. During 1970, in the rural region of Belgorod, 23 percent (8 of 37) of all plenum participants were either industrial officials or technical-engineering personnel. In the highly industrialized region of Dnepropetrovsk, exactly the same 23 percent (8 of 37) of all plenum participants were drawn from the same occupational sectors in Dnepropetrovsk. In both regions, six industrial enterprise directors participated in obkom plenums over the same period of time. Soviet officials would take these percentages out of context to argue that obkom plenums throughout the Soviet Union are very open and that production issues are resolved at a very high technical level by local parties. Such an interpretation would overlook the widely differing nature of both regions. Over 65 percent of

Belgorod's population in 1970 was rural, but over 76 percent of Dnepro-petrovsk was urban, according to the same 1970 census. Further-more, in 1970, 25,000 skilled specialists with completed higher educa-tion were employed in Belgorod. In Dnepropetrovsk, the industrial linchpin of the all-important Donets-Dnepr Coal Basin, there were over 112,000 skilled specialists with completed higher education em-ployed in 1970. Had Party leaders in Dnepropetrovsk truly adapted to group levels in 1970, the ratio of scientific-technical elite who participated in obkom plenums should have far exceeded the compa-rable level for as extreme a rural agricultural region as Belgorod.[68]

Unwilling or unable to deviate almost from a prescribed level of group participation in obkom plenums, regional parties in 1970 like Belgorod and Dnepropetrovsk typified those marked tendencies of bureaucratic sclerosis known in the Soviet Union as shablonism. Perhaps it is useful to remember that shablonism in regional parties has been condemned since 1965 in the same general decentralizing drive that saw greater authority supposedly invested in the industrial enterprises. The economic reform was intended to break the rigid pattern of industrial production the collective leadership had inherited in 1965, by making production responsive to local needs and demands. Much the same intent of greater local responsiveness has underlain the attempts to make regional parties more representative of local interests in obkom plenums. The reluctance or inability of regional parties to depart from routinized participation in obkom plenums in part may be undermining the very purpose of the economic reform. For, with the greater dependency of industrial and technical person-nel upon local Party leaders, shablonism in the regional parties will only reinforce the traditional inefficient duplication at the regional level. A not inconsequential source of the economic problems, which were continually bemoaned at obkom plenums in 1970, may be sought in the limited kinds of individuals who themselves were allowed to discuss the economic problems at the same obkom plenums.

NOTES

1. "On the Practice of Conducting Party Meetings in the Yaro-slavl' Urban Party Organization," Resolution of Central Committee CPSU (November 3, 1969), in SPR, Vyp. 10, pp. 278-283.

2. SR, January 24, 1970. There are 1,500 primary and shop Party organizations in the city of Yaroslavl'. Whether deliberate or not, the turnover in secretaries was not mentioned either by the gorkom first secretary or obkom first secretary in later articles they wrote in the All-Union Party journals on changes consequent to the November resolution in the city of Yaroslavl'. See V. Barabash,

"Partiinoe sobranie: Soderzhanie i deistvennost'" (Party meeting: substance and effectiveness), PZh, no. 18 (September 1970), pp. 31-37; and F. Loshchenkov, "Partiinoe sobranie i aktivnost' kommunistov" (Party meeting and the active spirit of Communists), K, no. 13 (September 1970), pp. 22-33.

3. TP, May 17, 1970.

4. Ibid.

5. DP, June 21, 1970.

6. For a discussion of Party membership in Dnepropetrovsk, see T. H. Rigby, Communist Party Membership in the USSR: 1917-1967 (Princeton, N.J.: Princeton University Press, 1968), p. 499.

7. KaP, January 11, 1970.

8. "On Serious Shortcomings in the Work of the Khar'kov Oblast Party Organization on Accepting into the Party and Training Young Communists," Resolution of the Central Committee CPSU (July 20, 1965), in SPR, Vyp. 6, pp. 383-386. For alternative interpretations of the underlying intent behind the Khar'kov resolution, see Rigby, Communist Party Membership in the USSR, pp. 317-323, and Michel Tatu, Power in the Kremlin: From Khrushchev to Kosygin (New York: Viking Press, 1970), pp. 501-503.

9. VP, June 20, 1970.

10. "Na partiinikh konferentsiiakh Rossiiskoi Federatsii i Ukrainy" (At Party conferences of the Russian Federation and the Ukraine), PZh, no. 6 (March 6, 1971), p. 42.

11. Among the most prominent demographic studies that have emphasized the importance of regional density and absolute size factors in defining urbanization, see O. A. Konstantinov "An Experiment in Defining the Districts of Settlement in the USSR," in O. A. Konstantinov, ed., Geografiia naseleniia i naselennykh punktov SSSR (Geography of population and population centers of the USSR) (Leningrad: Nauka, 1967), pp. 5-62; V. T. Davidovich, "Cities and Settlements—Satellites in the USSR," in V. T. Davidovich, ed., Goroda-sputniki (Cities-satellites) (Moscow: Geograficheskii lit, 1961), pp. 1-39; and B. Khorev, Gorodskie poseleniia SSSR (Urban settlements of the USSR) (Moscow: Mysl', 1968).

12. Z(K), April 1, 1970.

13. Ibid., June 5, 1970.

14. VN, July 11 and 13, 1970. On the general problems of motivation among rural youth in Novosibirsk and other rural areas of the Soviet Union, see Ellen Mickiewicz, "The Urban-Rural Gap as a Source of Cleavage in Soviet Society," unpublished paper presented at the International Studies Association Convention, Dallas, Texas, March 17, 1972. On the demographic and economic problems resulting from the migration of rural youth particularly in Western European areas of the Soviet Union, see V. A. Boldyrev, "The Problem of

Generations and Demographic Changes in the Contemporary Epoch,"
in L. N. Moskvichev et al., eds., Preemstvennost' pokolenii kak
sotsiologicheskaia problema (The continuity of generations as a
sociological problem) (Moscow: Mysl', 1973), pp. 34-37.

15. Roy Laird, "Prospects for Soviet Agriculture," Problems
of Communism 21, 5 (September-October 1971): 31-40.

16. New York Times, December 24, 1972.

17. Sidney I. Ploss, Conflict and Decision-Making in Soviet
Russia: A Case Study of Agricultural Policy—1953-1963 (Princeton,
N.J.: Princeton University Press, 1965), pp. 154-183.

18. Merle Fainsod, Smolensk under Soviet Rule (New York:
Vintage Books, 1963), pp. 69-72, 80-83; Philip Stewart, Political
Power in the Soviet Union (New York: Bobbs-Merrill, 1968), pp. 101-
107; Jerry Hough, The Soviet Prefects: The Local Party Organs in
Industrial Decision-Making (Cambridge: Harvard University Press,
1969), pp. 107, 199-202, 238-239.

19. KuP, January 7, 1970. "The main task of the oblast Party
organization includes the mobilization of Communists and all toilers
for the further realization of decisions emanating from the 23rd
Congress of the Party, for the securing of the glorious commemoration
of the 100th Centennial Anniversary of Vladimir Il'ich Lenin, and in
order to fulfill the quotas during the 1970 Jubilee Year and the present
Five-Year Plan before the required deadline. The obligation of Party
committees consists in concentrating the forces of Soviet, Komsomol,
trade-union organizations, and economic leaders upon educating
workers, kolkhozniki, employees, and engineer-technical workers
into a conscious relationship to their labor and the strictest observ-
ance of state and labor discipline and the norms of Communist moral-
ity."

20. Ibid., January 15, 1970.

21. Ibid., January 20 and 22, 1970.

22. Ibid., January 23, 1970.

23. From January through March, 13 secretaries of rural
gorkoms or raikoms in Vologda were either retired on pension or
transferred to undesignated new positions. See KS: January 7, January 22, February 7, February 15, March 13-15, and April 3, 1970.

24. KuP, April 18, 1970. The last apparent reference to Tomashkevich as first secretary of the oblast Komsomol may have been
inadvertent. On March 27, his name appears 14th from the top in
the nonalphabetical order of signatures on an obituary to an obkom
member; the order of full and candidate members of the obkom bureau
followed in several preceding obituaries.

25. Ibid., April 23, 1970. Furthermore, the opening address
was delivered by the obkom ideology secretary, T. I. Arkhipova.
For all other regions, the opening remarks and main address at the

Lenin Memorial ceremonies on April 22 were personally delivered by the obkom first secretaries. Monashev had met Kosygin at the airport as first secretary on April 17, according to the front-page picture of the newspaper on April 18.

26. Ibid., April 29, 1970. The transfer meant an obvious demotion for Monashev, who was dropped from the Central Committee at the 24th Congress and fails to appear even as a delegate at the Congress in April of 1971.

27. See references to Sechkov as obkom secretary in Kursk during unveiling of memorial to Soviet tank drivers in Belgorod (P, August 9, 1954) and delegates at XXIII KPSS.

28. For references to Dudkin and his official positions, see article on agriculture by Dudkin (SRos, October 3, 1958), deputies from Kursk to Russian Supreme Soviet (SRos, March 6, 1959), award for agricultural achievement (P, December 30, 1959), and biography in 1966 Deputaty.

29. For references to Arkhipova and her indoctrination responsibilities, see deputies from Kursk to Supreme Soviet (I, March 18, 1954); PZh, January 1955, p. 29; Narodnoe obrazovanie, no. 2, 1956, p. 75; conference of journalists (Sovetskaia pechat', no. 4, 1959); theoretical conference (P, January 23, 1963); and ideological conference (P, October 18, 1966, p. 2).

30. See article by Korotaev in P, August 17, 1950; deputies from Belgorod to Russian Supreme Soviet (I, March 3, 1955); delegates at XXI KPSS; and article as Kostroma secretary in Lesnaia promyshlennost', January 21, 1960. For position in Kursk, KuP, January 7, 1970.

31. From the biography of Gudkov on his nomination to the Supreme Soviet in KuP, May 21, 1970.

32. Ibid., June 20-21, 1970.

33. Ibid., June 20-21, 1970 (V. M. Zhil'tsov) and May 16-17, 1970 (A. D. Gridin).

34. Robert Osborn, Social Social Policies (Homewood, Ill.: Dorsey Press, 1970), pp. 187-231. Osborn's concern with the possible growth of local policy diversity in various areas of Soviet public welfare dovetails with the major thesis of this study.

35. Z (K), June 5, 1970.

36. K(S), January 14, 1970.

37. Michel Tatu, Power in the Kremlin, p. 219; Albert Boiter, "The Truth about Novocherkassk," Radio Liberty Research Dispatch, No. 1359, September 24, 1962. The growth of Novocherkassk coincided with the decision to relocate a large chemical complex shipped intact there from East Germany after the war.

38. "On Serious Violations of State Discipline in Urban Construstruction and the Communal Economy," Resolution of the Central

Committee CPSU and the Council of Ministers USSR (February 3, 1970), in SPR, Vyp. 10, pp. 201-204.

39. The particular relevance of the February 3 resolution for communal services to support working mothers is considered in Helen Desfosses Cohn, "Population Policy in the USSR," Problems of Communism 22, 4 (July-August 1973): 50-51.

40. VR, September 18, 1970.

41. Ibid., June 18, 1970.

42. VN, February 19, 1970.

43. Ibid., February 5, 1970.

44. VR, June 26, July 3, and July 21, 1970. At least one of the transferred officials, V. K. Lazarev, director of the Rostov city commerce administration, had already been strictly criticized two years before for his collusion in a scandal involving the Rostov Fish Cooperative, the oblast MVD, and the oblast procuracy. See "Posle togo, kak vystupili izvestiia" (After Izvestiia had reported), I, February 27, 1968.

45. VR, September 25, 1970.

46. DP, August 25, 1970.

47. Ibid., August 15, 1970.

48. Biographical information on Boiko was obtained from an extended biography published the same day as his election as gorispolkom chairman (mayor). See DP, August 25, 1970.

49. A small insert appeared on the front page of Dneprovskaia pravda on August 18, announcing that one V. G. Boiko had been registered for the first time as a candidate for deputy to the city soviet. Boiko's rapid rise from nomination to a deputy seat in the city soviet to chairman of the city executive committee took all of seven days!

50. An increase in the technical preparedness of mayors (that is, gorispolkom chairmen) in major Soviet cities may reflect a general policy in personnel assignment. As Boiko, the last three mayors of Moscow have all been appointed after long careers in housing construction and administration. See B. Michael Frolic, "Decision-Making in Soviet Cities," American Political Science Review 64, 1 (March 1972): 46.

51. John A. Armstrong, The Soviet Bureaucratic Elite: A Case Study of the Ukrainian Apparatus (New York: Praeger Publishers, 1959), pp. 95-101; Jerry Hough, The Soviet Prefects, pp. 144-48; Philip Stewart, Political Power in the Soviet Union, pp. 75-78; Frederick A. Fleron, "System Attributes and Career Attributes: The Soviet Political Leadership System, 1952 to 1965," in Carl Beck et al., Comparative Communist Political Leadership (New York: David McKay Company, 1973), pp. 69-77.

52. As an example, only six women were elected full members of the All-Union Central Committee at the 24th Congress in 1971.

See Robert Donaldson, "The 1971 Soviet Central Committee: An Assessment of the New Elite," World Politics 24, 3 (April 1972): 386.

53. Herwig Kraus, "The Present Composition of the Secretariats of the Union Republic CP Central Committees," Radio Liberty Research Bulletin, 31/73, February 5, 1973, p. 1.

54. D. P. Komarova, the present minister of Social Security of the Russian Republic, was formerly the chairman of the oblast executive committee in the Briansk region between 1960 and 1966 (see biographies in 1962 and 1966 Deputaty, 1966 and 1971 Ezhegodniki). L. P. Lykova, minister of Social Security prior to Komarova and presently deputy chairman of the Russian Republic Council of Ministers, was formerly obkom second secretary of the Smolensk region between 1959 and 1961 (see biographies in 1966 and 1971 Ezhegodniki, announcement of changes on Radio Smolensk, January 13, 1962 and in P, July 2, 1969, p. 4). Lykova, born in 1913, is probably close to retirement. While seven years younger than Lykova, Komarova is unlikely to rise any higher than her in career, probably succeeding Lykova as deputy minister upon her retirement.

55. That women are typically limited to defined lower status and "female" occupations or professions is emphasized in Cynthia Fuchs Epstein's Woman's Place: Options and Limits in Professional Careers (Berkeley and Los Angeles: University of California Press, 1971), pp. 151-166. The particular institutional, cultural, and social constraints on the female political role in the Soviet Union are discussed in Barbara W. Jancar, "Women and Soviet Politics," unpublished paper presented at the American Political Science Association Convention, Washington, D.C., September 5, 1972, pp. 29-38.

56. A considerably large proportion of the population in the capital city of Khar'kov is composed of students in higher educational institutions and associated educators, scientists, and cultural officials. For an extended and detailed statistical analysis of the social composition of Khar'kov by these group characteristics, see M. V. Kurman and I. V. Lebedinskii, Naseleniia bol-shogo sotsialisticheskogo goroda (The population of a large socialist city) (Moscow: Statistika, 1968), pp. 129-152 and 177-192.

57. Reflective of this concern are two resolutions of the Central Committee highly critical of the passivity displayed in socialist competition campaigns and the growing indifference of the more highly educated workers and specialists in the Soviet economy: "On Further Improving the Organization of Socialist Competition" (August 31, 1971), SPR, Vyp. 12, pp. 128-136; and "On the Participation of Directing and Engineer-Technical Workers of the Cherepovets Metallurgical Plant in the Ideological-Political Upraising of Members of the Collective" (December 21, 1971), SPR, Vyp. 12, pp. 186-191. On

the political dispute among indoctrination officials as to the best means of mobilizing this more sophisticated work force, see Aryeh L. Unger, "Politinformator or Agitator: A Decision Blocked," Problems of Communism 19, 5 (September-October 1970): 30-43.

58. V. I. Volovik, "The Continuity of Generations and the Traditions of Socialist Society," in Moskvichev et al., Preemstvennost' pokolenii, p. 231.

59. Volovik, "The Continuity of Generations," pp. 226-227; A. Vodolazskii, "Leninskie printsipy partiinogo rukovodstva v deistvii" (The Leninist principles of party direction in action), K, no. 2 (January 1971), p. 46; and I. Koval, "Ulushat' podbor, podnimat' otvetstvennost' kadrov" (To improve the selection and to upraise the sense of responsibility of cadres), PZh, no. 11 (July 1970), pp. 32-33.

60. P. A. Leonov, "Razvitie XXIV sezdom KPSS Leninskikh printsipov raboty s kadrami" (The development by the 24th Congress CPSU of the Leninist principles of work with cadres), K, no. 18 (December 1971), p. 52.

61. DP, April 4, 1970. The principal report was delivered at the Party-economic aktiv by Obkom First Secretary Vatchenko, who criticized the failure on the part of Party organizations and plant directors in exerting the required push for the completion of capital development in several industrial enterprises. Eight of the cited discussants on the report were either enterprise directors or directors of scientific-research institutes in Dnepropetrovsk. In addition, 12 All-Union or Union-republic industrial ministers and industrial Party officials participated in the meeting of the aktiv.

62. In his study of the Stalingrad obkom, Stewart found that noncommittee members made up 48 percent of all participants in obkom plenums over a seven-year span of time. See Stewart, Political Power in the Soviet Union, p. 82.

63. Among several examples that could be cited, see A. Skochilov (Obkom First Secretary of the Ul'ianovsk Oblast), "Sobliudaia Leninskie printsipy podbora i vospitaniia kadrov" (Observing the Leninist principles of the selection and upraising of cadres), PZh, no. 3 (February 1971), pp. 16-24; N. Kirichenko, "Povyshaetsia rol' organov kollektivnogo rukovodstva" (The role of collective leadership organs is raised), PZh, no. 19 (October 1971), pp. 29-35; P. A. Leonov, "Razvitie XXIV s"ezdom," pp. 46-57.

64. KS, April 29, 1970.

65. KrZ(T), March 6-7, June 20-21, 1970.

66. The significant differences of attitudes, which often appear in the same institutional or professional groups, are discussed in several of the case studies in H. Gordon Skilling and Franklyn Griffiths, eds., Interest Groups in Soviet Politics (Princeton, N.J.: Princeton University Press, 1971). Rather than static and predetermined interest positions, the alliances and cleavages that form around

policy are likely to reflect how the issue has been defined in terms of alternative solutions, goals, and means.

67. John P. Hardt and Theodore Frankel, "The Industrial Managers," in Skilling and Griffiths, Interest Groups in Soviet Politics, pp. 201-204.

68. None of this is to overlook the fact that industrial specialists on the regional level may not require formal participation in obkom plenums to have their demands satisfactorily met. With their superior technical knowledge and their close ties to powerful central ministries, industrial specialists in particular can ignore or overrule actions of the regional Party leader. Even the obkom first secretary, as Hough has characterized his relationship with industrial ministers, at best occupies a slightly subordinate position in dealing with influential regional industrial specialists. See Jerry Hough, The Soviet Prefects.

THE INFLUENCE
OF OBKOM FIRST SECRETARIES
UPON POLICY

Until now in our analysis, we have assumed that environmental characteristics are the primary determinants of regional policy. In reality, it is the obkom first secretary, whether he was Monashev in Kursk or Sinitsa in Odessa, who interpreted the given environmental demands and constraints on his actions. For, in studies of regional parties in the Soviet Union written by Western scholars, the obkom first secretary has consistently emerged as the dominant political figure at the regional level. Whether described as a "little Stalin" in Smolensk during the 1930s[1] or as a "prefect" in the Soviet administrative hierarchy during the 1960s[2], the obkom first secretary occupies a political position that gives him wide-ranging influence over all political, cultural, and economic activities of a region. The obkom first secretary must interpret and implement central policy guidelines within the context of local conditions, coordinate regional planning, resolve distribution squabbles among industrial enterprises, bargain for regional interests with All-Union Party and State officials, and bear ultimate responsibility for the successes and failures of the region. As Stewart concluded on the role of the first secretary in Volgograd, the first secretary sets the "style of obkom policy-making": the consideration of information on issues, the range of acceptable proposals, and the relative performance of political-administrative personnel on issues.[3] It is in particular his ultimate accountability to central leaders for regional performance that gives the first secretary his dominant role in policy-making and in the selection of subordinate officials for his region.

The impact of the obkom first secretary in regional policy-making and personnel selection is not without very real constraints and limitations. His influence is checked by the dual authority invested in the regional representatives of state and police bureaucracies. Central All-Union leaders of these regional bureaucracies will contest personnel assignments that fall under their local administrative domain; and the policies carried out by their regional subordinates (especially, the KBG security police) are not always accountable either to the regional party or to the obkom first secretary. We need only recall that, in social welfare policy, industrial enterprises in a region are responsible to their central ministries in planning the location and size of housing and consumer-related services for their own work forces. A large proportion of the regional budget for urban development is actually allocated to the central ministries, not to the regional government through which the first secretary could exert influence over final decisions. With each industrial ministry pursuing its own bureaucratic requirements for housing and consumer facilities, the lack of any regional coordination or rationale in urban planning is a typical complaint of regional leaders. The most that a consumer-oriented first secretary can hope for is a technically competent specialist like Victor Boiko in Dnepropetrovsk, who can potentially counter the divisive tendencies in social welfare allocations. Furthermore—with their superior technical knowledge and their close ties with powerful central ministries—industrial specialists and officials in a region, while dependent upon the support of the obkom first secretary, can also overrule or ignore actions initiated by him with which they disagree.[4]

At best, the first secretary may hope informally to influence the selection process of lower officials by appealing undesired assignments to central officials on the premise that particular individuals would irreparably harm the regional economic performance by which both his (the first secretary's) career and those of the central officials will be evaluated.[5] Or he can select the directors of lower cadre departments in regional bureaucracies; and they in turn will submit the lists of prospective candidates to central economic ministries.[6] Yet, most importantly, obkom first secretaries will have little influence in the selection of their fellow obkom secretaries or gorkom first secretaries for major industrial centers in their regions, all of whom will vitally affect regional policy but will fall under the selection authority (nomenklatura) of the central Party secretariat in Moscow.

Even with these uncertain constraints and limitations, Western scholars have still proceeded from the assumption that obkom first secretaries have a dominant influential role over Party policy and personnel selection in their regions. The logical corollary to this assumption is that policy and personnel assignments in a region will come to reflect the particular political style and attitudes of obkom first secretaries. By political style and attitudes, Western scholars refer to the formative characteristics of background and career. As true of any political elites, these characteristics will shape the eventual personality and outlook of the first secretary. To the extent his actions as political leader are determined by the manner in which he apprehends, defines, and responds to problems in his region, the range of policy-making within a regional party could be interpreted as a direct consequence of the first secretary and his particular style and attitudes. Differences at a similar period of time in the nature of issues emphasized by regional parties and in the nature of individuals who participate in regional policy-making could thus be directly attributed to differences in the background and career characteristics of regional first secretaries.

While hypothesizing such a relationship, Western scholars have yet to test it in any systematic fashion. At best, studies of regional parties have alluded to the impact of first secretaries in general without any comparative evidence of that impact.[7] Other studies have found a direct relationship between the particular nature of the first secretary and a regional party, but their analysis is based upon a single regional party for a particular time period. Fainsod's description of the autocratic first secretary Rumiantsev in Smolensk during the 1930s serves as an obvious example in this regard.

At worst, Western scholars have admitted their inability to prove that personality does influence political behavior but then proceeded to detail the social background and career characteristics typical of all obkom first secretaries in the Soviet Union.[8] Variance in background and career factors is assumed to affect differences in policy-making among regions. As yet, however, Western scholars have failed to establish what exact impact the varying attitudes and styles of first secretaries have upon regional policy nor even how such an impact could be studied and specified. We know there are differences and similarities among first secretaries both at any comparable time period and longitudinally, but have those differences actually affected the relative performance of regional parties? The answer to this question would obviously have a decisive bearing not only on the capabilities of the regional parties to resolve policy problems, but on the actual willingness of the Soviet leadership to allow greater diversity or political pluralism in the system.

METHODOLOGICAL PROBLEMS

Three very difficult methodological pitfalls have confronted Western scholars who have attempted until now to examine the supposed impact of first secretaries in regional policy. For one reason, the supposed linkage between background and attitudes has failed to distinguish exactly which characteristics will have the greatest formative influence upon the first secretary in his later career. From many studies that have been written on the socialization of political elites, one could anticipate a number of noncumulative, unpredictable, and often contradictory influences upon the personality of elites like obkom first secretaries. While all individuals reflect the total sum of their socializing experiences, certain background and career factors may have a greater influence upon later attitudes and behavior than other factors.[9] Western scholars have avoided this key theoretical problem by attributing the process of political socialization to the total range of career-background factors for first secretaries. While generally valid, such analysis still begs the essential question of which factor or related characteristics have the highest direct association with what patterns of elite behavior response among first secretaries.

This failure to distinguish among a total set of background-career characteristics is particularly significant for a second reason. Studies of political elites have also commonly shown a high association between current leadership roles and political behaviors.[10] Role expectations are uniform for certain identical positions. Elites recruited to these identical positions may be cued to perceive and act in a similar manner by the nature of their prescribed roles, irrespective of any inherent differences in their prior careers and social backgrounds. The current role dramatically affects the attitude formation and style of the political elites. Rather than characteristics like age and education, it may be more important to identify common role expectations for similar political leadership positions in order to account for resultant attitudes and behavior responses. Thus, even though all obkom first secretaries have different backgrounds, a congruency in their attitudes and behaviors may result because of a similarity in the more salient role demands made upon them as regional "prefects."

Thirdly, Western scholars have yet to prove that background and career characteristics actually do affect later attitudes and behaviors. The obvious problem in this regard is the lack of any information either on the political attitudes or behaviors of Party leaders in the Soviet Union. In order to test the linkage of background-attitudes-behavior, the researcher would first require data that could be reasonably defined as dimensions of regional policy-making directly attributable to several obkom first secretaries. As dependent variables, the data could then be correlated with differences among prior background-career characteristics of the obkom first secretaries. To avoid the other two methodological stumbling blocks, the association of several alternative background-career characteristics would have to be determined independently with the same policy responses. The intervening variable of elite role would be held constant, as long as one assumes that first secretaries act out the same roles as regional prefects in the Soviet Union. Therefore, with equivalent role expectations and demands upon all obkom first secretaries, any variance in their behaviors would be logically explained only by differences in their prior background and career.

With these considerations in mind, we are presented with the unique opportunity of testing the supposed differential impact of first secretaries on regional policy-making by comparing the responses of the first secretaries who served in the 25 regions of our sample during 1970. The policy responses of the obkom first secretary could be operationally defined as the same three policy dimensions of issue adaptation and participation that we have already analyzed. For, as already emphasized, the influence of obkom first secretaries lies in their ability to shape policy concerns and to select political-administrative personnel for their regions. In this sense, their concerns could be interpreted in part from the themes discussed at obkom plenums and from the relative emphasis assigned to policy problems through the diverse obkom and capital gorkom plenums, conferences, and soviets. These political forums may only constitute a highly formalized and secondary level of regional policy-making to mobilize support for decisions initiated by central Party organs and already debated and approved within the obkom bureau of the regional party. Yet these same political forums, all either directly organized or indirectly authorized by the regional party under the leadership of the obkom first secretary, at least should reveal the outer context of policy concerns that have been defined by first secretaries in different regional parties. Any variation among regional parties in the frequency that local problems such as criminal behavior, ideology, consumer welfare, or internal changes in the ranks of the Party-state bureaucracies are raised at these political forums would evidence the ability of the obkom first secretary to structure a regional agenda in terms of his own perceived understanding of those problems.

Similarly, the policy-making process includes those occupational sectors selected to participate as contributors to themes reviewed at regional obkom plenums. Whether participants function as interest groups or merely serve to reassure symbolically other individuals in the same occupational sectors of the region, their very presence can be directly attributed to the obkom first secretary. Dependent upon his own estimation of their particular relevance and the manner in which he has defined the nature of regional policy, the first secretary can select individuals from several alternative occupational sectors in the region to participate in obkom plenums. Differences in occupational group participation for several regional plenums would suggest variance in the importance and administrative competence of occupational groups as perceived by obkom first secretaries.

The three policy dimensions are correlated in the following tables with four background and career variables of first secretaries who served in the 25 regions during 1970. The independent unit of analysis for each dimension is still the region, but, rather than by environmental characteristics, it is operationally defined by the variable of the obkom first secretary in each table. Regions in which two obkom first secretaries served during 1970 were excluded from any table in which the two first secretaries differed by any background or career variable. The four variables of age, year of Party entry, career background, and recruitment origins were selected and delineated to reflect three general working hypotheses:

1. Younger obkom first secretaries or those who entered the Party after 1941 should be more sensitive to regional demands and less fearful of change than older first secretaries or those whose attitudes were formed by entering the Party before the War.

2. Obkom first secretaries with extensive specialized careers outside the Party bureaucracy should take a less doctrinaire approach to local problems than those first secretaries whose careers have been almost solely limited to Party or political offices.

3. Obkom first secretaries born, educated, and with lengthy careers in the same regions to which they are assigned should be more responsive to regional needs and cadre demands than outsiders designated from the center with no ties to the region.

DATA AND ANALYSIS

Age Cohorts and Party Generations

Age and year of Party entry are consistently singled out by Western scholars as important indications of leadership change in the Soviet Union. Many of the leadership changes during the last half-century can be usefully understood from the traditional Russian dichotomy between "fathers" and "sons." The similar age of political leaders may predict individuals whose attitudes and dominant values were formed as a consequence of common socializing experiences particular to that generation. In this regard, Western scholars have described the differences in attitudes and experiences between the generation of the "Old Bolsheviks," typified by intellectuals like Bukharin whose personalities evolved in the Russian underground before 1917 and those younger "Stalinists" who replaced them during the purges of the 1930s, the practical-minded and ruthless administrators like Khrushchev and Malenkov whose commitments and ideals evolved under Stalin and a Communist government in power.[11]

The same generational differences could be drawn for the obkom first secretaries who served as political leaders of the 25 regions in 1970. Nine of the obkom first secretaries were born in the decade

of the 1920s or later. They reached political maturity and self-awareness during World War II. Several of them were still relatively young
when Stalin died in 1953. A review of their political careers reveals
that most only began their advancement in the Party hierarchy under
the regimes of Khrushchev and Brezhnev-Kosygin. They only emerged
as a distinct leadership group after the death of Stalin, and their value
premises likely have been influenced by their primary association
with the Soviet scientific and space achievements since the late 1950s.
In contrast to them stand those 19 first secretaries in 1970 who were
products and often direct beneficiaries of the Stalin era. Fourteen
of the first secretaries were born in the decade between 1905 and
1914. As a consequence, they were old enough to have experienced
the purges as adults, and their early political apprenticeships were
served under Stalin in the 1940s and early 1950s. We could assume
that their memory of the Stalin era is more direct than that of the
younger first secretaries. As self-justification for their participation
in the Stalin era, they may have a fonder and more positive sense of
commitment to Stalinist priorities like heavy industry, social control
through the police apparatus, and a distrust of material aspirations
among the Soviet population.

As age, the year in which an obkom first secretary began his
political career by entering the Party could also be used to predict
generations in attitudes and styles. The dominant circumstances and
motivating factors inducing an individual to join the Party have probably varied sharply throughout Soviet history. It is at least possible
that those initial circumstances and factors would later reappear in
terms of personality types particular to Party recruits in different
generations of the current Party leadership. One Western scholar
has stressed particular importance to those recruits who entered the
Party during the ideologically relaxed period of World War II.[12] As
Hough argues, during the war, military pride and discipline, esprit
de corps, and patriotism were the dominant values of Soviet society.
Soviet leaders attempted to mobilize resistance against Nazi Germany
by direct appeals to nationalism and the fatherland. During the war,
there was a relatively greater openness and flexibility to others, a
closer affinity of Party and society. Individuals who first joined the
Party during this era of genuine enthusiasm were more likely to have
been motivated from a common sense in which Party membership,
mass initiative against the invading Germans, and defense of the
fatherland were all positively associated.

If one were to extend Hough's interpretation, postwar recruits
would tend to share attitudes and values more similar to those from
the war period than before 1942. Between 1946 and 1952, Party membership became closely identified with leadership of the national effort
to reconstruct the devastated economy. Those who entered the Party

in the post-Stalin era after 1952 would be even less ideological and more committed to the Party as an agent of economic transformation. More pragmatic, the post-Stalin generation would be more likely to identify their Party membership even more with participation in the post-Sputnik technological and space achievements.

As such, obkom first secretaries who entered the Party during or after the war would be expected to project those initial motivations and value premises in their later political attitudes and styles.* Because of the dominant influence of early socializing experiences upon an individual, they would constitute a distinguishable leadership group by their concerns and conduct of their offices. They would differ significantly from the generation of first secretaries who joined the Party prior to 1942, in an era typified by ideological rigidity, opportunism, and a callous cynicism toward popular aspirations. Those who entered the Party after 1941 would be less preoccupied with ideological discipline and more receptive to material demands among the Soviet poulation. More practically oriented, they should also be less fearful and resentful of outside expertise drawn into Party policy making. Scientific-technical elites would be more openly courted to participate in Party plenums. Older obkom first secretaries are more likely to suspect any intrusion upon Party integrity from competitive outsiders who lack the essential commitment and perspective of Party apparatchiki. Older and more sectarian, such obkom first secretaries are also more likely than younger first secretaries to be out of touch with recent technical innovations and knowledge. Because of their greater real ignorance, they would feel personally threatened by the new expertise identified with scientific-technical elites and would be more reluctant to allow outside specialists even nominally to influence Party decisions as participants in obkom plenums.

---

*With justification, Western scholars might object to categorizing Party entrants from the 1942-45 period with those who entered the Party after 1945. For one, they could point out that the 1946-52 era in the Soviet Union saw a return to ideological rigidity (Zhdanovshchina) and a tightening of internal Party discipline, not the expansive moral upsurge and nationalism identified with Party membership during the war. Whether this objectification is valid or not, it is rendered moot by the fact that 9 of the 12 first secretaries categorized as post-1941 in Table 4.2 entered the Party in the 1942-45 period; three in the 1946-52 period. As to the post-Stalin era, the only first secretary who entered the Party after 1953 is A. F. Gudkov of Kursk, which with two first secretaries from different Party generations in 1970 is excluded in Table 4.2.

Tables 4.1 and 4.2 allow us to evaluate the immediate impact of age cohorts and Party generations among first secretaries in 1970. While there are minor percentage differences for particular occupational or issue sectors, both tables evidence little general significance to the period in which an obkom first secretary was born or entered the Party. The findings are particularly enlightening for the similarity in regional issues emphasized by different first secretaries. Consider, for example, the total regional response to ideological problems, a policy area that should have declined among younger and post-1941 first secretaries. Yet, in Table 4.1B, the youngest first secretaries actually convened 2 to 3 percent more ideological conferences and plenums than the two older generations of first secretaries. In Table 4.1B, regions with first secretaries who entered the Party after 1941, an era characterized as one of ideological relaxation, convened 3 percent more ideological conferences and plenums than regions with first secretaries from the prewar period.

Similarly, first secretaries should have differed in their formal concern with consumer welfare and criminal sanctions. Younger first secretaries would have been expected to project the value premises of their early careers, more receptive to material demands of the regional population and less preoccupied with defined antisocial behavior. The tables fail to bear out these assumptions. As the reader can see, neither younger first secretaries nor those who entered the Party at a later period differed at all from other first secretaries. Regions in both Tables 4.1B and 4.2B show the same approximate 7 percent level of response to social welfare policy. Nor were younger first secretaries less likely to downplay the importance of social control. Indeed, in both subtables, the total regional response to the policy area of socialist legality was 2 to 3 percent higher in regions led by the youngest and post-1941 first secretaries.

It would have been anticipated that younger first secretaries at least should be more responsive to the demands for promotion and recognition among lower cadres and officials in the Party-state bureaucracies. Younger first secretaries would make up a group closer in age and values to the same lower cadres and officials. More practically oriented, they should have been more sensitive to the need for advancing younger skilled experts into policy-making ranks of the regional bureaucracies. Indications of that sensitivity would have been a greater concern with cadre policy in regions with younger first secretaries.

The only support for this assumption can be found in Table 4.1A, in which the youngest cohort of first secretaries did convene 6 and 18 percent more cadre-organizational plenums than the two older cohorts. The generational response is most apparent for regions with first secretaries born between 1915 and 1919. Only 29

TABLE 4.1

Regional Policy Dimensions by Age of First Secretaries
in 1970
(in percent)

4.1 A
Plenum Issue Sectors

Age	Ind.	Agr.	Ind.-Agr.	Ide.	Cad. Org.	Soc. Wel.	Other	Total (N)
56-65 (11)[a]	28	24	(+4)	6	41	—	2	100 (54)
51-55 (5)[b]	29	29	0	4	29	8	—	100 (24)
41-49 (8)[c]	23	27	(-4)	3	47	—	—	100 (30)

4.1 B
Regional Issue Sectors

	Ind.	Agr.	Ind.-Agr.	Ide.	Cad. Org.	Soc. Wel.	Soc. Leg.	Other	Total (N)
56-65 (11)	22	21	(+1)	24	21	7	4	2	100 (218)
51-55 (5)	18	30	(-12)	23	20	6	3	2	100 (102)
41-49 (8)	21	20	(+1)	26	21	7	5	1	100 (159)

4.1 C
Occupational Sectors

	Gorrai Secs.	Obl. Off.	Obl. Mass	Farm	Sci. Tech.	Center	Other	Total (N)
56-65 (11)	40	15	3	11	16	4	11	100 (364)
51-55 (5)	35	13	8	14	19	3	8	100 (172)
41-49 (8)	34	14	7	12	10	14	9	100 (236)

Note: The obkom first secretary in Kursk was replaced in 1970 by an individual born in different time period. The four obkom first secretaries who served in Orel and Odessa during 1970 all were born in the same time periods.

[a]Regions in which obkom first secretaries were born between 1905 and 1914: Orel, Bryansk, Vologda, Kirov, Volgograd, Kaliningrad, Novosibirsk, Kemerovo, Odessa, Tambov, Dnepropetrovsk.

[b]Regions in which obkom first secretaries were born between 1915 and 1919: Belgorod, Yaroslavl', Kaluga, Saratov, Zaporozh'e.

[c]Regions in which obkom first secretaries were born between 1921 and 1929: Smolensk, Perm', Rostov, Crimea, Trans-Carpathia, Khar'kov, L'vov.

Sources: Regional press of the 25 regions, January-October 1970; Deputaty (1962, 1966, 1970).

TABLE 4.2

Regional Policy Dimensions by Year of Party Entry
of First Secretaries in 1970
(in percent)

4.2 A
Plenum Issue Sectors

Year of Party Entry	Ind.	Agr.	Ind.-Agr.	Ide.	Cad. Org.	Soc. Wel.	Other	Total (N)
Through 1941 (11)a	26	24	(+2)	4	41	4	1	100 (53)
1942+ (12)b	27	29	(-2)	4	40	—	2	100 (48)

4.2 B
Regional Issue Sectors

	Ind.	Agr.	Ind.-Agr.	Ide.	Cad. Org.	Soc. Wel.	Soc. Leg.	Other	Total (N)
Through 1941 (11)	21	24	(-3)	22	22	7	3	1	100 (220)
1942+ (12)	21	21	0	25	20	7	5	1	100 (238)

4.2 C
Occupational Sectors

	Gorrai Secs.	Obl. Off.	Obl. Mass	Farm	Sci. Tech.	Center	Other	Total (N)
Through 1941 (11)	37	16	7	10	15	5	10	100 (397)
1942+ (12)	34	14	6	13	15	9	9	100 (368)

Note: The obkom first secretaries in Odessa and Kursk were replaced in 1970 by men who entered the Party in a different time period. The two obkom first secretaries who served in Orel during 1970 both entered the Party in the period 1939-41.

aRegions in which obkom first secretaries entered Party before 1942: Kaliningrad, Novoskibirsk, Tambov, Orel, Kaluga, Bryansk, Volgograd, Kirov, Saratov, Vologda, Dnepropertrovsk.

bRegions in which obkom first secretaries entered Party during or after 1942: Belgorod, Yaroslavl', Kemerovo, Tomsk, Crimea, L'vov, Trans-Carpathia, Zaporozh'e, Khar'kov, Smolensk, Perm', Rostov.

Sources: Regional press of the 25 regions, January-October 1970; Deputaty (1962, 1966, 1970).

percent of all obkom plenums for this intermediary age group considered cadre-organizational issues in 1970. Yet the total regional response to cadre policy is remarkably similar for all age cohorts and Party generations at a stable level of 20 to 22 percent.

Participation in obkom plenums also demonstrates little association with age or Party generations. In particular, scientific-technical elites found no greater opportunity to participate in regions with younger first secretaries. By year of Party entry, exactly the same 15 percent of scientific-technical elites participated in obkom plenums. By age, there is actually a decrease in the proportion of scientific-technical elites in regions led by the youngest first secretaries under 50. The maximum opportunity for scientific-technical elites to participate occurred in regions with first secretaries between 51 and 55 years of age in 1970. In contrast, the 10 percent level of regions with first secretaries 41 to 49 is almost one-half this 19 percent ratio for the intermediary age group regions.

Age does predict one sector of participation, but in a manner unrelated to the attitudes or style of the first secretary. Fourteen percent of all participants in plenums convened by the very youngest first secretaries in 1970 were either All-Union or Union-republic officials dispatched from the center. This high percentage of center officials (the average for all regions was only 7 percent) suggests that regions with the very youngest first secretaries as a rule may fall under closer direct scrutiny. Even in their forties, these "young" first secretaries may still be viewed by center officials as political apprentices, requiring more continuous verification of their leadership abilities and performance than other first secretaries. In itself, the percentage of center officials who participate in obkom plenums may serve as an inverse measure of trust in regional first secretaries.

Career Backgrounds

The variable of prior career background has been recognized in several career-line analyses of Soviet elites written by Western scholars. The background of Soviet elites is frequently differentiated by the number of years prior to his current elected office a leader spent in both non-Party and Party positions.[13]

Western scholars have in particular stressed a trend apparent since the early 1950s to recruit Soviet political elites with more diversified career experiences. According to these scholars, more Party leaders at all levels of the Soviet hierarchy can be identified with extensive prior occupational backgrounds as industrial managers, agricultural specialists, or other technical professionals. Supposedly, this trend is evidence of a concerted attempt to recruit a leadership stratum with better administrative and technical qualifications. As Party leaders, former non-Party specialists would be more competent to resolve the detailed industrial and agricultural problems that confront them in any geographical locale. So-called recruited Party leaders, those who have typically been found in leadership positions like obkom first secretary, usually had little prior occupational experience outside the Party bureaucracy. Most of their prior careers were spent as Party apparatchiki. Their capacity to supervise the regional economy as obkom first secretary would have been limited as a consequence. "Recruited" officials lacked the broadened technical background and insight of specialists coopted into leadership positions at a later stage of their adult careers. Even when educated in the same industrial or agricultural institutes as "coopted" officials, "recruited" Party officials more likely would still reflect the limited in-bred norms and perspectives of a full-time careerist in the Party bureaucracy.

By contrast, the new leadership stratum of "coopted" officials, with a significant portion of their former careers outside the Party bureaucracy, would be more effective administrators and political leaders. As administrators, they would have a sufficient technical breadth to understand the more demanding production techniques and procedures of the Soviet regional economy. Having served a major part of their careers as industrial or agricultural specialists, "coopted" obkom first secretaries would be more personally aware of and responsive to the daily problems of the present industrial directors and agricultural specialists under their supervision in their own regions. They would be more politically adaptive to the views of such specialists, more willing to take their advice into account in policy-making.

The infusion of diversified career expertise into leadership positions of the regions can be seen in the backgrounds of the 28 obkom first secretaries in 1970. Thirteen of the first secretaries could be considered coopted officials, if we were to classify those first secretaries with at least 45 percent of their careers in direct agricultural or industrial production outside the Party bureaucarcy before they were first elected to the present obkom bureau.* Indicative are the three first secretaries in the regions of Kemerovo, Khar'-kov, and Kursk. After graduating from the Donets Industrial Institute in 1937, A. F. Yeshtokin, the first secretary of Kemerovo in 1970,

---

*The classification of coopted officials in this chapter will differ from the criteria used in differentiating all bureau members by career backgrounds in Table 6.9. Bureau members with 45 to 55 percent of their career in specialized occupations will be distinguished as an intermediate category between recruited and coopted officials.

spent the next 21 years of his career in technical capacities as engineer
or director of coal mines and coal combines in the Donbass and Urals
coal basins.14 Not only would Yeshtokin obviously qualify in over-
seeing a region like Kemerovo in which a major proportion of industrial output is dependent upon coal extraction, but the promotion of
two Kemerovo industrial officials since 1965 indicates that administrative performance in the region is highly valued as a training ground
for future ministry officials on the All-Union level.* Before his
election as first secretary in 1963, G. I. Vashchenko, obkom first
secretary of Khar'kov in 1970, had served 20 years in engineering-
technical positions in local Khar'kov industrial enterprises.15 It is
significant that several of those years were spent in the Malyshev
Transport Machine-Building Plant, a major industrial enterprise of
the region and one on which the overall successful industrial production of the region is highly dependent.† The occupational background
of A. F. Gudkov, the current first secretary of Kursk, was described
at great length in the previous chapter in relation to the agricultural
failures experienced in the Kursk oblast during early 1970. Prior to
his first position on the obkom bureau in 1968, the coopted official
Gudkov had spent eight years in direct agricultural assignments as
an agronomist and director of a local MTS in Kursk and as raion
inspector of agriculture in two rural districts of Kursk.16

On the one hand, the backgrounds of these and other defined
coopted officials should not in itself be interpreted as a major reversal
in leadership recruitment at the regional level or the emergence of
a regional technocratic elite in the Soviet Union. Before his election
as first secretary, an individual with extensive specialized background
first will be subjected to Party indoctrination and a period of political

_____

*V. D. Nikitin, obkom industrial secretary of Kemerovo in 1961
(P, July 24, 1961) and first deputy chairman of the Kemerovo and
Kuzbass sovnarkhoz from late 1961 through 1964 (delegates at XXII
KPSS; Meditsinskii rabochii, July 31, 1964, p. 2; P, September 8,
1964) is currently deputy minister of the All-Union Coal Ministry
(Kuz, June 10, 1970; P, January 7, 1971). V. V. Listov, capital gorkom
first secretary of Kemerovo from 1966 through 1970 (delegates at
XXIII KPSS; P, July 2, 1969), was transferred to directing work in
the All-Union Chemical Ministry in late 1970 (Kuz, September 8,
1970).
†Indicative of the importance ascribed to the Malyshev Plant,
the director of the plant since December 1965, O. V. Soich, has been
elected a full member of the Ukrainian Central Committee in both
1966 and 1971 (biography of Soich in KrZ [Kh], May 24, 1970; XXIII
and XXIV KPUkr).

139

apprenticeship. Only after this initial period of testing and assimilation, in which the apprentice proves his leadership capabilities and his primary commitment to the Party bureaucracy, would he be entrusted with as politically sensitive a position as obkom first secretary. Thus, Yeshtokin was elected first secretary of Kemerovo only after having served five years from 1958 to 1962 as second secretary and chairman of the Sverdlov oblast and (for a brief period) as inspector for the coal industrial department of the Central Committee. Vashchenko was secretary of the Malyshev Plant Party Committee and second secretary of the Khar'kov obkom for six years before his election as first secretary in July 1963. Gudkov was required to demonstrate his political responsibility with eight years in Party work at the raion level and in the obkom apparat. Besides his apprenticeship in the regional Party apparat, Gudkov did not become an actual member of the obkom bureau as director of the Party-organizational department in 1967 until he had first completed a two-year political education training course at the Central Committee Higher Party School.

On the other hand, we need only recall the revitalized position of lower cadres and agricultural specialists in Kursk after Gudkov's election to appreciate the possibility of some consistent relationship between the prior careers of first secretaries and their response to policy questions. To test this association, regions in Table 4.3 are operationally defined by the career typology of first secretaries in 1970. The career types of recruited and coopted officials correspond to the level of political and nonpolitical specialized background attained by first secretaries before their first elected position on the current regional bureau.*

A scan of the table generally fails to substantiate any meaningful relationship between the prior career backgrounds of first secretaries and current regional policy-making. By obkom plenum issues,

----

*The same 13 to 15 elected positions in each of the 25 regions were assumed to confer full or candidate membership on the regional obkom bureaus from 1955 through 1973. Specific determination of bureau membership and changes in the turnover and composition of the same bureau members are analyzed in Chapters 5 and 6. The typology of coopted and recruited officials is borrowed from Frederick A. Fleron. Our criteria, however, differ from Fleron, who classifies an individual as a coopted official if he spent a minimum of seven years in a professional or technical vocation before attaining political or Party officies more or less regularly. As Fleron, we have defined Party bureaucracy positions to include a formal post in the government and Party apparatus, the Komsomol, trade unions, or police.

coopted secretaries differed from recruited first secretaries only in the percentage of agricultural plenums, a policy area with no direct bearing on the level of occupational expertise. More significant is that such politically sensitive policy areas as cadre-organizational problems demonstrate almost no consistent pattern by prior career. Both recruited and coopted first secretaries convened an equivalent 38 percent cadre-organizational plenums. The same null relationship is evidenced for the total regional response to cadre policy (Subtable 4.3B). Coopted secretaries were no more concerned with social welfare problems than those recruited and no less likely to feel an obligation to the Party indoctrination organs and the regional police apparatus. Indeed, coopted first secretaries convened fewer conferences on consumer policy and exactly the same percentage of conferences on antisocial behavior as recruited officials, who would be expected to reflect the more dogmatic and in-bred biases of full-time Party apparatchiki.

Nor did career background influence the responsiveness of first secretaries to various occupational sectors in the region. As former industrial or agricultural specialists, coopted first secretaries would have been expected to allow scientific-technical elites greater direct access to Party decision-making. The percentage of scientific-technical elites who participated in obkom plenums should have increased in regions led by coopted first secretaries in 1970. For individual regions, the association of career background with participation could be tentatively affirmed in 1970. As one pertinent example, in the Kemerovo region, led by the coal industrialist specialist Yeshtokin, 9 of the 34 obkom participants (26 percent) were scientific-technical elites from the regional work force.[17] Yet, on an overall comparative basis, very little significant difference can be proven. Of participants in coopted regions, 16 percent were scientific-technical elites, only 3 percent above the level in recruited regions. As age and year of Party entry, the career background of first secretaries does not appear to have any noticeable or consistent impact upon regional policy-making in 1970.

Recruitment Origins

One of the background variables generally overlooked until now by Western scholars has been the relative strength of the ties of the obkom first secretary with the region in which he has been elected. It is true that individual studies have described the phenomenon of native recruitment among local Party leaders at the regional or Union-republic levels. But such studies have typically been concerned with nationalism among ethnic groups in the same regions or Union-republics. Native recruitment is viewed as a calculated response to the

TABLE 4.3

Regional Policy Dimensions by Career Background
of First Secretaries in 1970
(in percent)

4.3 A
Plenum Issue Sectors

Career Background	Ind.	Agr.	Ind.-Agr.	Ide.	Cad. Org.	Soc. Wel.	Other	Total
Recruited (13)[a]	27	31	(-4)	2	38	2	—	100 (48)
Coopted (10)[b]	28	23	(+5)	6	38	2	2	100 (53)

4.3 B
Regional Issue Sectors

	Ind.	Agr.	Ind.-Agr.	Ide.	Cad. Org.	Soc. Wel.	Soc. Leg.	Other	Total
Recruited (13)	24	24	0	22	18	8	4	—	100 (233)
Coopted (10)	21	23	(-2)	24	21	6	4	2	100 (242)

4.3 C
Occupational Sectors

	Gorrai Secs.	Obl. Off.	Obl. Mass	Farm	Sci. Tech.	Center	Other	Total
Recruited (13)	36	15	6	10	13	9	11	100 (473)
Coopted (10)	39	12	9	13	16	4	7	100 (282)

Note: The career backgrounds of the two obkom secretaries in both Orel and Kursk in 1970 were different.

[a]Regions in which obkom first secretaries defined as recruited: Belgorod, Tambov, Kaluga, Bryansk, Perm', Volgograd, Kaliningrad, Novosibirsk, Tomsk, Crimea, Trans-Carpathia, Zaporozh'e, Dnepropetrovsk.
[b]Regions in which obkom first secretaries defined as coopted: Yaroslavl', Smolensk, Vologda, Kirov, Saratov, Rostov, Kemerovo, Odessa, L'vov, Khar'kov.

Sources: Regional press of the 25 regions, January-October 1970; Deputaty (1962), 1966, 1970), Ezhegodniki (1962, 1966, 1971).

larger number of non-Russian ethnic minorities in the regions and republics. Thus, Western scholars have found that the Party may deliberately attempt to balance the number of Russian leaders with local Uzbek nationals in Uzbekistan,[18] with local Tadzhiks in Tadzhikistan,[19] and with local Polish-Hungarian-Rumanian natives in Western Ukrainian regions.[20] Such native locals are often very conspicuous figureheads appointed to satisfy mass ethnic feelings of participation in their own affairs. In actuality, as Western scholars caution, real power in the regions is entrusted to nominally subordinate Party officials like the obkom second secretary. In the Western Ukrainian regions, this means that the obkom second secretary may be a Russian or Ukrainian national sent from the Eastern regions of the Ukraine or Kiev*; in Tadzhikistan or Uzbekistan, he may be a Russian or Russified native sent from Dushanbe or Tashkent.

What Western scholars may have failed to consider is that native recruitment of local obkom first secretaries could represent a general cadre policy of the Party, one independent of or at least concurrent with ethnic concerns. The assignment of local natives to the political leadership of a regional party could be defended from very sound economic reasons of Party performance and administration.

For one reason, charges of "localism" appear frequently enough in the Soviet press to indicate the intensity of regional identification among local officials in the Soviet Union. As a group identity among cadres in the same regional party, regional localism would produce reactions comparable to those felt by personnel in any defined bureaucracy. Local Party cadres and officials, whose life and political careers had been spent entirely within the same region, may resent the imposition of an outsider from the center to head their regional Party organization as obkom first secretary. An insider, a regional native who had advanced from lower levels of the regional party to become first secretary, is more likely to have the positive support and respect of lower Party cadres and officials. Lower Party cadres and officials will know him personally and can identify their own

---

*To cite relevant examples from the two Western Ukrainian regions in our own study: L'vov—Z. T. Serdyuk, secretary of the Ukrainian Central Committee (1949-51) and obkom first secretary (1951-54); Yu. N. Yel'chenko, second or first secretary of the Ukrainain Komsomol (1958-68) and obkom second secretary (1969-71). Trans-Carpathia—I. A. Mozgovoi, secretary of the Ukrainian Komsomol (1955-62) and obkom second secretary (1963-65); I. I. Skiba, secretary of the Ukrainian Komsomol (1962-71) and obkom second secretary (1972-   ).

political ambitions for advancement with his successful career.* By assigning an outsider to the highest political office in the region, central authorities, guided by a traditional Soviet bias that views natives as politically unreliable and more subject to local corrupting influences, at the same time may contribute to undermining the morale of lower Party cadres and officials. An outsider is not only a stranger and unknown political factor to lower cadres and officials, with whom he must now contend on a day-to-day basis, but he has assumed a position that might otherwise have gone to one of the same aspiring cadres and officials, whose career options will mostly be limited to the highest regional Party offices.† Resentment is likely to be further exacerbated by feelings of ethnic discrimination when the outsider is a member of an ethnic group other than that of the many lower cadres and officials.

Central authorities cannot ignore the potential disruptive consequences of resentment and declining morale among lower Party cadres and officials in a region. For, to the extent that economic production is highly dependent upon the motivation of cadres and officials who administer industrial and agricultural sectors, the imposition of an outsider as a symbolic repudiation of regionalism could well have ramifications beyond just the injured sense of pride and self-esteem among cadres and officials. As we can recall from the analysis of cadre policy in the previous chapter, at least one obkom first secretary, L. S. Kulichenko of Volgograd, implicitly called attention to this factor of local career expectations in his major economic report to a 1970 obkom plenum in Volgograd. Kulichenko went to great lengths in his reported address to link the economic problems of Volgograd during the preceding years to what he termed the "poor morale problem" among lower Party cadres and state officials. In contrast, Kulichenko pointed to several highly qualified native enterprise directors and collective farm chairmen whose achievements had been recognized with rapid promotion and whose careers should

---

*Of course, motivation and response will vary greatly among individual Party cadres and officials. Some may be more discouraged by the election of a former political cohort who has succeeded while they have failed.

† Once elected to an obkom bureau, bureau members may be transferred laterally to the leadership of another local Party organ, but very few will be promoted to minor or major positions in the center. At least, of 1,108 regional officials in the 25 oblasts from 1955 through 1973, only 100 are known to have attained a position at the center or Union-republic level after leaving the region at least equivalent in authority to what they held immediately prior to being reassigned from the region.

serve as relevant success models for other native cadres and officials. In order to correct the "poor morale problem" by motivating behavior among current lower cadres and officials, Kulichenko reasoned that more skilled and dedicated natives such as these would have to be given preference in promotion.

All this is not to deny that Kulichenko's remarks have probably become almost a standard rhetorical theme in the repertoire of speeches delivered by obkom first secretaries to their subordinates in a regional party. But what is particularly noteworthy is that Kulichenko himself is an actual native of Volgograd who worked his way up from lower ranks to his current position. Born in the Volgograd city of Tsarshchyne in 1913 and a graduate of the Volgograd Mechanical Institute in 1936, except for the war years and three years at the Higher Party School of the Central Committee, Kulichenko has never been employed in any region other than his native Volgograd.[21] His argument would thus appear more credible if for no other reason than that Kulichenko perfectly exemplifies in his own career the native success model with which he has now closely identified himself. Furthermore, when Kulichenko contends that a positive attempt has been made only in recent years to advance natives into higher positions of authority, his audience of lower cadres and officials cannot be unaware that Kulichenko's election as obkom first secretary in November 1965 was the first assignment of a native to that office at least since 1948.*

A second reason that local recruitment of first secretaries could be justified is that a native will be more personally familiar with lower officials and particular economic situations in his region than would an outsider. From studies of regional parties by Western scholars, it is obvious that a successful first secretary must be extremely knowledgeable of affairs in his region, have the dedicated loyalty and support of lower cadres and officials, and be sensitive to the decisions and operative routines carried out on an informal daily basis in his region. Knowing how to coordinate policies and to optimize the allocation of scarce materials and manpower resources among industrial enterprises and farms are key administrative skills

---

*I. T. Grishin (1948-55), I. K. Zhegalin (1955-60), and A. M. Shkol'nikov (1961-65) were the three obkom first secretaries who preceded Kulichenko. All three were born or educated outside of Volgograd; and, except for nine months Grishin spent as obkom second secretary of Volgograd in 1948, none of them had any direct career experience in Volgograd before they were elected obkom first secretary for the first time. A more detailed analysis of their backgrounds in contrast to Kulichenko is presented in Chapter 6, pp. 232-234.

of a successful obkom first secretary.[22] The apprenticeship of an outsider in these skills is likely to require a lengthy learning period during which the region may suffer economically. An insider already would have developed these capabilities through his long practical experience at lower levels of the regional hierarchy during which he became personally familiar with economic officials and was socialized into regional patterns of policy implementation and economic routines.

As Hough has pointed out in his study of industrial decision-making on the regional level, the first secretary may also be placed in a situation in which he will have to advocate particular industrial interests in his region to central ministries for lower quotas or higher budgetary allowances.[23] The bargaining skill of the first secretary in lowering quotas or raising allocations may often be the subtle difference that determines the economic success or failure of a region in any given year. Logically, the bargaining skill of an obkom first secretary is predicated upon his actual commitment to regional interests and the confidence he receives from local officials to argue their case. Neither characteristic is likely to be as typical of an outsider with no demonstrable ties or long identification with regional operations. If the level of cooperation and informal understanding between first secretaries and industrial officials normally has a decisive bearing upon regional industrial performance, the necessity could only have increased since the implementation of the 1965 economic reform, in which greater independent authority was supposedly granted to local industrial enterprises.[24] As such, any policy to recruit native first secretaries, particularly since 1965, could have been defended by proponents in the central Party apparat as a rational extension of the economic reform on the political level and as a general attempt to spur economic productivity by fostering local initiative and expertise.

Whatever weight is actually given economic considerations by central authorities in determining cadre policy, evidence of a recent formal commitment to native first secretaries was revealed by General Secretary Brezhnev himself in his report of the Central Committee to the 24th Party Congress in 1971. In his enumeration of positive changes in local elected Party organs, Brezhnev pointed to the number of "local" workers who had been deliberately assigned as first secretary of Union-republic, krai, and oblast Party committees. As Brezhnev stressed, only in "exceptional cases" had the center assigned outsiders to these positions in recent years.[25]

Brezhnev's remark could not have been unintentionally included. The importance of recruitment origins is indicated by the fact that the same two sentences Brezhnev used in the report to refer to "local" first secretaries were quoted verbatim in articles on cadre policy in the central Party journals following the Congress report.[26] More

146

importantly, local recruitment is consistently identified in both Brezhnev's report and in these later articles with regional economic advancement. Improvement in cadre policy would be measured by economic performance, and both were positively affected by the assignment of "local" workers as obkom first secretaries.

Whether the reference by Brezhnev at the 24th Congress has paralleled any real departure in cadre policy after 1964 can only be answered by comparing the origins of all obkom first secretaries over a number of years. In Chapter 6, the recruitment origins both of first secretaries and all obkom bureau members will be analyzed for the 18-year period from 1955 to 1973. At that time, the percentage of natives recruited into the obkom bureau will be considered as a dependent variable and an index of regional Party adaptation. At this point of our analysis, it is sufficient to consider only the origins of first secretaries serving in 1970 and what immediate impact the recruitment variable may have on their response to regional policies in 1970.

From biographies in the regional press and other secondary sources, 9 of the 28 first secretaries in 1970 would be classified as "natives" by very demanding criteria of prior demographic and career ties to their current regions. The term "natives" refers to those first secretaries either born or educated (secondary level or higher education) in the same region or contiguous regional area in which they held their office in 1970. Not only were "natives" tied to their regions by birth or education, but they have also served a minimum 75 percent of their total careers in the same current region. An additional four first secretaries in 1970, classified "intermediates," could also lay claim to close demographic ties to their current region by birth or education; but, unlike the nine actual "natives," the careers of "intermediate" first secretaries have been more interspersed with lengthy assignments in the central apparat or outside local Party organizations.

In addition to the previously cited cases of Gudkov in Kursk and Kulichenko in Volgograd, examples of natives in 1970 are M. N. Vsevolozhskii in Zaporozh'e, I. A. Bondarenko in Rostov, and Yu. V. Il'nitskii in Trans-Carpathia. Vsevolozhskii was born in the Zaporozh'e city of Vasil'evka in 1917 and graduated from the Zaporozh'e Machine-Building Teknikum in 1936. Except for a brief period during the occupation of Zaporozh'e in World War II, Vsevolozhskii has spent his total occupational and political career within the region.[27] A graduate of the Azov Black Sea Agricultural Institute of Rostov in 1956, Bondarenko was assigned agricultural responsibilities at the raion level of Rostov early in his career, later served as director of an agricultural experimental station and as assistant professor at the same Azov Institute, and, since 1959, held various regional

Party and state positions in Rostov until his election as obkom first secretary in November 1966.28 Although Ukrainian by nationality in a region of non-Ukrainian ethnic minorities, Il'nitskii has nevertheless been cited as a regional native in a recent one-volume study of Trans-Carpathia.29 With the exception of a brief assignment as inspector for the Ukrainian Central Committee, Il'Nitskii has spent his entire career in Trans-Carpathia, working his way up from instructor of the Volovets okrugkom in 1946 to obkom first secretary, a position he has held since 1962.30

Fifteen of the obkom first secretaries in 1970 would be classified as "outsiders." While some nominally could be considered "native" by the criterion of holding a lower position inside the region before their first election to the obkom bureau, the outsiders were neither born nor educated in the region or regional area, they entered the obkom bureau at relatively advanced stages of their political careers, and their total association with regional problems and cohorts is consequently much less than that of regional natives or intermediates. Typical of outsiders in 1970 and the recruitment policy that may have been more consistently followed before 1965 are A. I. Shibaev in Saratov, V. I. Chernyi in Tambov, and M. S. Sinitsa in Odessa. Shibaev was born and educated in the Gorkii oblast and was never assigned to any position in Saratov until he was 35, when he was appointed director of the Saratov Aviation Plant in 1950. He became a member of the obkom bureau five years later when he was elected obkom second secretary in 1955.[31] Chernyi is even more representative of the outsider. A native of the Crimea, he spent almost his entire career as an agricultural and Party official in the Crimean oblast, Kirgiziia, and the Northern Ossetian Autonomous Republic. His first position in Tambov occurred on his election to the obkom bureau as oblispolkom chairman in 1961 at the age of 48.[32] Sinitsa, dismissed as first secretary of Odessa in 1970, was actually a native of Kiev, where he was educated and spent his entire career prior to Odessa in engineering and Party work. His first appearance in Odessa occurred only in 1961, when at the age of 48 he was dispatched from the outside to be obkom first secretary.33

However important native first secretaries could figure as an indication of elite change in the Soviet Union, the primary implication in Brezhnev's reference is that native first secretaries have been assigned more frequently in recent years only because they have proven to be more capable or responsive political leaders and administrators than outsiders. In other words, it is the performance of these native first secretaries that has allowed Brezhnev to evaluate the change as a positive one. If Brezhnev's view is correct, then, native first secretaries could be assumed to approach policy at the local level quite differently than outsiders. To test this relationship, regions in Table 4.4 are grouped by the recruitment origins of first secretaries in 1970: native and intermediate regions (that is, with first secretaries born or educated in the current region or regional area) and outsider regions.

From our characterization of natives, first secretaries born or educated in their regions should have been more accessible to lower cadre demands for career advancement. After all, it was the native first secretary of Volgograd, L. S. Kulichenko, who himself had coined the term "poor morale problem" in arguing for more rapid career mobility of natives. If Kulichenko's concern would logically express a view more typical of natives, regions with native first secretaries in 1970 should have convened more cadre-organizational plenums in which lower cadres were assigned obkom leadership positions or Party cadres were sympathetically assured of their importance.

Direct evidence in Subtable 4.4A tends to support this conclusion, but only on a very limited scale. Native regions in 1970 convened 4 percent more cadre-organizational plenums than did outsider regions, hardly a significant indication of greater responsiveness. In the region of Volgograd itself, the theme of Party cadres justified two individual plenums of the obkom and capital gorkom.[34] More telling, though, is that Kulichenko's nominal concern with rapid career mobility corresponded to little actual personnel change even in Volgograd. In fact, Volgograd stands out among all 25 regions in 1970 for its particularly low turnover ratio. During 1970, only two personnel changes of officials from the region, urban, or district levels were reported in the regional newspaper. The first was a deputy director of the obkom construction department (who actually died);[35] the second, a politically insignificant director of the oblast public education department, transferred to another post in late September.[36] Furthermore, natives were not identified with more cadre-organizational changes and conferences on a total regional basis. Of regional issues in native regions, 22 percent centered on cadre policy, in comparison to the fairly equivalent 20 percent for the 12 regions with outsiders.

Nor were natives any more responsive to direct participation from lower cadres in obkom plenums. While farm officials found a slightly greater opportunity to participate in plenums with natives, secretaries from the district and urban Party organizations actually participated at a 3 percent higher level in regions with outsiders. If the policy change to more native first secretaries had been intended by central authorities to forge closer cooperation with industrial officials, again Subtable 4.4C fails to substantiate this impact in 1970. Of participants in native regions, 16 percent were scientific-technical elites, only 2 percent higher than the comparable level for outsider regions.

TABLE 4.4

Regional Policy Dimensions by Recruitment Origins
of First Secretaries in 1970
(in percent)

4.4 A

Plenum Issue Sectors

Recruitment Origins	Ind.	Agr.	Ind.-Agr.	Ide	Cad. Org.	Soc. Wel.	Other	Total
Native (11)[a]	26	28	(-2)	3	40	3	—	100 (40)
Outsider (12)[b]	31	26	(+5)	5	36	1	1	100 (61)

4.4 B

Regional Issue Sectors

	Ind.	Agr.	Ind.-Agr.	Ide.	Cad. Org.	Soc. Wel.	Soc. Leg.	Other	Total
Native (11)	22	21	(+1)	23	22	7	4	1	100 (225)
Outsider (12)	19	27	(-8)	23	19	7	4	1	100 (253)

4.4 C

Occupational Sectors

	Gorrai Secs.	Obl. Off.	Obl. Mass	Farm	Sci. Tech.	Center	Other	Total
Native (11)	34	14	7	13	16	8	8	100 (331)
Outsider (12)	37	14	12	8	14	5	10	100 (440)

Note: The origins of the two first secretaries in Orel and Kursk oblasts were different.

[a]Regions in which obkom first secretaries defined as natives: Kaluga, Smolensk, Yaroslavl', Tomsk, Rostov, Volgograd, Dnepropetrovsk, Zaporozh'e, Khar'kov, L'vov, Trans-Carpathia.

[b]Regions in which obkom first secretaries defined as outsiders: Belgorod, Tambov, Bryansk, Vologda, Kirov, Perm', Saratov, Kaliningrad, Kemerovo, Crimea, Odessa, Novogibirsk.

Sources: Regional press of the 25 regions, January-October 1970; Deputaty (1962, 1966, 1970), Ezhegodniki (1962, 1966, 1971).

Finally, the recruitment origins of obkom first secretaries evidence little relationship to such sensitive policy areas as social welfare and socialist legality. Differences in recruitment origins should have produced a varying emphasis on consumer and antisocial problems. Natives, born and educated in the same region or contiguous regional area, would have been expected as first secretaries to be more receptive to material aspirations among their own native population than outsiders, relative strangers assigned to the obkom leadership with few emotional links to the regional population. In contrast, we would have expected outsiders to be less sympathetic toward popular attitudes and mass disaffections. When faced with mounting economic failures and declining morale, outsiders would likely assume a more intolerant doctrinaire approach and attribute the source of the problems to criminal behavior. For outsiders, the region would be more just an assignment by which their political careers are evaluated; for natives, the region must be both a political assignment and a familiar, emotional context of problems and people. The percentage of social welfare and socialist legality issues raised in 1970 does not bear out these characteristics. According to Subtable 4.4B, natives and outsiders convened exactly the same percentage of conferences, plenums, and soviet sessions on both themes. If the recruitment of native first secretaries had been intended by Brezhnev to bring more imaginative leadership to the regional level, that effect cannot be demonstrated by the data on regional policy-making in 1970.

Political and Environmental Variables

The four tables on obkom first secretaries have failed to show any direct independent relationship between the background-career characteristics of regional political leadership and the Party response to regional problems and political-administrative personnel in 1970. Yet, in our analysis, we have considered environmental factors and first secretaries only as alternative rather than mutual determinants of regional policy. The theoretical problem more logically should have been conceived as the simultaneous impact of the first secretary and the regional environment upon policy. Do young obkom first secretaries respond the same in rural and urban regions? Are co-opted first secretaries as equally accessible to scientific-technical elites in industrialized and agricultural regions? Are native first secretaries more sensitive to lower cadre demands for advancement and recognition in regions that have undergone greater environmental change? Or, in contrast, is it the environment that accounts for any policy differences among regions, irrespective of the first secretary?

Tables 4.5 and 4.6 provide at least a preliminary test of this key theoretical problem by controlling for the simultaneous impact

TABLE 4.5

Cadre-Organizational Obkom Plenums by
Social Mobilization and Obkom First Secretaries
(percent; number of regions in parentheses)

| Obkom First | Change Urbanization (1939-70) | |
Secretaries	Low Change (11-26%)	High Change (27-40%)
Through 1941	29 (5)	36 (6)
1942+	59 (5)	29 (7)
Recruited	41 (6)	32 (7)
Coopted	53 (4)	31 (6)
Natives	53 (5)	30 (6)
Outsiders	42 (5)	32 (7)
Total	49 (12)	32 (13)

Sources: Regional press of the 25 regions, January-October
1970; Itogi—1959 goda (SSSR); Itogi—1970 goda (Tom I).

TABLE 4.6

Participation of Scientific-Technical Elites in
Obkom Plenums by Industrialization and
Obkom First Secretaries
(percent; number of regions in parentheses)

| Obkom First | Urban Concentration (100,000) (1970) | |
Secretaries	Low Ind. (0-34)	High Ind. (35-56)
Through 1941	14 (6)	14 (5)
1942+	12 (6)	18 (6)
Recruited	13 (7)	14 (5)
Coopted	11 (4)	20 (6)
Natives	13 (4)	17 (7)
Outsiders	12 (7)	16 (5)
Total	12 (13)	16 (12)

Sources: Regional press of the 25 regions, January-October
1970; Itogi—1959 goda (SSSR); Itogi—1970 goda (Tom I).

of environment, background, and career as determinants of two principal policy sectors in our analysis. In Table 4.5, the percentage of
cadre-organizational plenums is simultaneously controlled for Party
entry, career and recruitment origins, and the percent urban change
in regions between 1939 and 1970. Two tentative conclusions can be
derived from the table. First, environmental change has a greater
independent impact upon cadre policy than does the obkom first secretary. As we found in the previous chapter, the low mobilized and (in
most cases) more agricultural regions of the Soviet Union convened
a higher percentage of cadre-organizational plenums in 1970. Whatever the differences among first secretaries, cadre policy in high
urban change regions consistently falls within a very limited range
between 29 and 36 percent. On the other hand, the importance of the
first secretary, especially in the same agricultural and low change
regions, cannot be discounted. By year of Party entry, first secretaries who entered the Party after 1941 convened 30 percent more
cadre-organizational plenums in agricultural regions than those who
entered the Party before the war. While less significant, coopted
and native first secretaries also convened 11 and 12 percent more
cadre-organizational plenums than their counterparts. In other words,
lower cadres and officials are likely to be aware of greater opportunities for career advancement in agricultural regions with first
secretaries who entered the Party after 1941, are regional natives,
and have spent a major period of their career outside the Party bureaucracy in the same native regions. The figures thus appear to confirm
a general tendency for agricultural regions that we had previously
identified for the Kursk oblast and the young native specialist Gudkov
in 1970.

Both the regional environment and the first secretary must also
be considered in explaining the participation of scientific-technical
elites in obkom plenums. Scientific-technical elites do participate
at a higher level in the more urban industrialized regions of the Soviet
Union, but especially in industrialized regions led by a first secretary
who himself has spent much of his early career in the same specialized
occupations as the current scientific-technical elites. As shown in
Table 4.6, the actual geographical location of that former specialized
background appears less important a factor than the background itself
(native and outsider first secretaries are almost identical in the ratio
of scientific-technical elites), and the difference between recruited
and coopted first secretaries is admittedly only 6 percent. The 14
percent level for highly industrialized regions with recruited first
secretaries in 1970 only confirms that a first secretary cannot ignore
the counsel of scientific-technical elites, but the more relevant question for Soviet industrial performance may be the extent to which he
openly solicits cooperation and advice from them. The higher 20

153

percent ratio for regions with coopted first secretaries at least suggests a greater nominal attempt has been made to involve them actively in the policy-making process. Some limited support is gained for the conventional belief that first secretaries with extensive specialized backgrounds will be more inclined to technical solutions of policy problems and will feel less personally threatened by non-Party elites than first secretaries whose knowledge and career associations have been almost entirely limited to the Party bureaucracy.

CONCLUSION

The potential for decentralization and adaptive policy-making in regional parties cannot be minimized. That regional parties do have at least some discretion to define problems and formulate solutions in response to local conditions was demonstrated in the previous chapter. Indices to social mobilization consistently distinguished the relative emphasis assigned to industrial, agricultural, cadre, and social welfare policies by regional parties. Yet, despite the qualified impact of both background and environment in the preceding section, the data in this chapter would not support the contention that the obkom first secretary makes a significant independent impact upon regional policy. If obkom first secretaries make little apparent difference, does this only confirm the prevalent Western interpretation of a highly bureaucratized Party structure in which local Party leaders merely transmit central policy? And does this then refute General Secretary Brezhnev, who, in his reference to the native origins of first secretaries, has contended that leadership does have a significant bearing upon Party performance in the locales?

Part of the problem in resolving these two alternative views lies in the manner that the regional policy-making process is conceptualized. The particular attitudes and political styles of different first secretaries very likely have influenced regional policy in 1970. Yet the actual impact of the first secretary and the very nature of the regional policy-making process must be conceived in a broader and more dynamic context than we have been able to develop through comparative quantitative analysis in Chapters 3 and 4. Limiting our scope of policy to formal decisional arenas fails to account for the ongoing nature of coordination, initiative, implementation, and even deliberate restraint exercised on an informal daily basis in any region. It is only here in the continuous flow of phone calls, messages, and contacts with officials on the regional and central levels, in the subtle political bargaining and conflict with obkom bureau members and lower Party and economic officials, and in the actual investment of financial resources, time, personnel, and influence to his own perceived priorities that the role of the first secretary and the valid scope of regional policy-making can be adequately described.

A failure to discuss an issue like social welfare may signify not a lack of concern on the part of the first secretary but only that he has committed himself in a more meaningful fashion to defend appropriation requests from the regional government to central ministries in order to fund additional schools, housing, roads, and consumer services for the regional population. Even the assignment of a skilled construction specialist like Boiko in Dnepropetrovsk to the key social welfare position of a region may have a more positive impact on consumer policy than the formal emphasis placed on housing construction at obkom plenums by a first secretary. Writers and artists in a region will be concerned less with the number of times ideological conformity is urged at obkom plenums and conferences than with the relative influence of indoctrination officials under a particular first secretary, the seriousness of intent with which a first secretary attempts to enforce compliance, and the implicit understanding between themselves and a first secretary, which will define the real parameters of tolerance for their creativity. It may only be when that informal area of coexistence between the regional party and the intellectual community breaks down or is transgressed by a first secretary like Sinitsa in Odessa desperately searching for a a political scapegoat that the tendencies in regional ideological policy can be understood. Participation in obkom plenums or the number of industrial conferences convened in any quarter may be less important for scientific-technical elites than the actual extent of cooperation and nonintervention they then can derive from Party officials in the regional hierarchy. Pronouncements and plenary reports on the improving cadre situation will have little policy meaning unless that formal commitment is translated into a rapid turnover and promotion of lower cadres and officials to higher regional positions, as the pattern may have evolved in Kursk since Gudkov's election as first secretary in 1970.

Despite Brezhnev's stress on the "local" nature of first secretaries, the obkom first secretary is also obviously only one member of the total regional policy elite. A more comprehensive view of regional policy would have to take into account the characteristics and adaptive potential of several other key members in the regional leadership besides the obkom first secretary who vitally affect the determination and success of regional policies. No matter how significant his role may be, the obkom first secretary must decide and execute policy in concert with these other regional policy leaders. In order to provide this broader base to evaluate the potential for policy diversity at the regional level, it will be the task of the next two chapters to examine this potential in terms of the leadership elected to the obkom bureaus of the 25 regions from 1955 to 1973.

NOTES

1. Merle Fainsod, Smolensk under Soviet Rule (New York: Vintage Books, 1963), pp. 62-92.

2. Jerry Hough, The Soviet Prefects: The Local Party Organs in Industrial Decision-making (Cambridge: Harvard University Press, 1969).

3. Philip Stewart, Political Power in the Soviet Union (New York: Bobbs-Merrill, 1968), p. 134.

4. Hough, The Soviet Prefects.

5. This is probably one of several informal bargaining counters in personnel selection available to the obkom first secretary. For a general consideration of formal and informal bargaining in the selection of lower cadres and industrial officials by local Party organs, see Hough, The Soviet Prefects, pp. 149-177, and Bohdan Harasymiw, "Nomenklatura: The Soviet Communist Party's Leadership Recruitment System," Canadian Journal of Political Science, no. 2 (December 1969), pp. 493-512.

6. The importance to the first secretary of selecting cadre administrators in regional bureaucracies has been stressed by the obkom first secretary of the Sakhalin oblast. See P. A. Leonov, "Razvitie XXIV s"ezdom KPSS Leninskikh printsipov raboty s kadrami" (The development by the 24th Congress CPSU of the Leninist principles of work with cadres), K, no. 18 (December 1971), p. 53.

7. Hough, The Soviet Prefects; Stewart, Political Power in the Soviet Union, pp. 134-177.

8. Peter Frank, "The CPSU First Secretary: A Profile," British Journal of Policital Science 1, 2 (April 1971): 173-190; Robert Blackwell, "The Soviet Political Elite: Alternative Recruitment Policies at the Obkom Level," Comparative Politics 6, 1 (October 1973): 99-121.

9. Establishing direct linkages between social background characteristics and elite attitudes and behavior has been recognized as the principal methodological difficulty in elite analysis. See Lewis J. Edinger and Donald D. Searing, "Social Background in Elite Analysis: A Methodological Inquiry," American Political Science Review 61, 2 (June 1967): 428-445. The varying impact of demographic and career characteristics upon Communist elites is a major underlying concern in the empirical studies published by Carl Beck et al., Comparative Communist Political Leadership (New York: David McKay Company, 1973). See, in particular, William Welsh, "Introduction: The Comparative Study of Political Leadership in Communist Systems," pp. 8-22.

10. For general considerations of role theory in the social sciences, see Bruce J. Biddle and Edwin J. Thomas, eds., Role

Theory: Concepts and Research (New York: John Wiley and Sons, 1966). On the importance of roles to Party elite attitudes and behavior in the Soviet Union, see Erik P. Hoffman, "Role Conflict and Ambiguity in the Communist Party of the Soviet Union," in Roger E. Kanet, ed., The Behavioral Revolution and Communist Studies (New York: Free Press, 1971), pp. 233-258. Also, see differences in attitudes between local and center apparatchiki and elites in Milton Lodge, "Attitudinal Cleavages within the Soviet Political Leadership," in Carl Beck et al., Comparative Communist Political Leadership, pp. 202-225.

11. An interpretation emphasized among others by Leonard Schapiro, The Communist Party of the Soviet Union (rev. ed.; New York: Vintage Books, 1971), pp. 422-456.

12. Jerry Hough, "The Soviet Elite: II—In Whose Hands the Future?" Problems of Communism 16, 2 (March-April 1967): 25.

13. See, in particular, Frederick J. Fleron, "Representation of Career Types in the Soviet Leadership," in R. Barry Farrell, ed., Political Leadership in Eastern Europe and the Soviet Union (Chicago: Aldine Publishing Company, 1971), pp. 108-139 and "System Attributes and Career Attributes: The Soviet Leadership System, 1952 to 1965," in Carl Beck et al., Comparative Communist Political Leadership, pp. 43-85; Robert Blackwell, "The Soviet Political Elite"; George Fischer, The Soviet System and Modern Society (New York: Atherton Press, 1968); Robert Donaldson, "The 1971 Soviet Central Committee: An Assessment of the New Elite," World Politics 24, 3 (April 1972): 404-407. While several of these studies equate specialized careers in industrial and agricultural sectors, the latter could be questioned as a relevant indication of nonpolitical background. Among others, the Soviet biologist Zhores Medvedev (The Rise and Fall of T. D. Lysenko) has detailed the intellectual prostitution of agricultural specialists and institutes under the impact of Lysenkoism during both the Stalin and Khrushchev eras.

14. Information on Yeshtokin was drawn principally from an extensive biography that appeared in the regional press when Yeshtokin was nominated to the Supreme Soviet in 1970. Typically, biographies of Supreme Soviet candidates like Yeshtokin in the regional newspapers were much more detailed than the entry that appears in the official Deputaty Verkhovnogo Soveta SSSR. Included in the regional newspaper and absent from the official entry were place of birth, locations of early work experiences, and length of service in each position. See Kuz, May 17, 1970.

15. From a biography of Vashchenko on his nomination to the Supreme Soviet in KrZ(Kh), June 3, 1970. Vashchenko was promoted to first vice-chairman of the Ukrainian Council of Ministers in June 1972, in the aftermath of personnel changes that followed the replacement of Shelest' by Shcherbitsky as first party secretary of the Ukraine.

16. From a biography of Gudkov on his nomination to the Supreme Soviet in KuP, May 21, 1970.

17. See the published summaries of obkom plenums in Kuz, January 7, April 3, and July 10, 1970.

18. Michael Rywkin, Russia in Central Asia (New York: Collier Books, 1963), pp. 101-152,

19. Teresa Rakowska-Harmstrone, Russia and Nationalism in Central Asia: The Case of Tadzhikistan (Baltimore: Johns Hopkins Press, 1971), pp. 94-191.

20. John A. Armstrong, The Soviet Bureaucratic Elite: A Case Study of the Ukrainian Apparatus (New York: Praeger Publishers, 1959), pp. 114-122.

21. From a biography of Kulichenko on his nomination to the Supreme Soviet in VP, May 17, 1970.

22. Hough, The Soviet Prefects, pp. 214-255.

23. Ibid., pp. 256-271.

24. On the changing relationship between industrial managers and local Party organizations since 1965, see John P. Hardt and Theodore Frankel, "The Industrial Managers," in H. Gordon Skilling and Franklyn Griffiths, eds., Interest Groups in Soviet Politics (Princeton, N.J.: Princeton University Press, 1971), especially p. 203.

25. Leonid Brezhnev, XXIV KPSS, vol. 1, p. 124.

26. As an example, see article by Leonov, "Razvitie XXIV s" ezdom . . . ," p. 51.

27. From a biography of Vsevolozhskii on his nomination to the Supreme Soviet in IZ, June 5, 1970.

28. See biography of Bondarenko in 1962 and 1966 Deputaty and 1971 Ezhegodnik; also Radio Rostov, May 26, 1961 and September 26, 1962.

29. Istoriya mist i sil Ukrains'koi RSR v dvadtsiatishesti tamakh: Zakarpats'ka oblast' (History of the cities and villages of the Ukrainian Soviet Socialist Republic: Trans-Carpathia oblast') (Kiev: AN URSR, 1970), p. 683.

30. See biography in 1962 and 1966 Deputaty.

31. From a biography of Shibaev on his nomination to the Supreme Soviet in K(S), May 24, 1970.

32. From a biography of Chernyi on his nomination to the Supreme Soviet in TP, May 22, 1970.

33. See biographies of Sinitsa in 1962 Ezhegodnik and 1966 Deputaty.

34. VP, May 27 and June 18, 1970.

35. Ibid., June 19, 1970.

36. Ibid., September 25, 1970.

5

ACCESS TO
OBKOM BUREAU MEMBERSHIP,
1955-73

OBKOM BUREAUS

A realistic assessment of policy-making and political adaptation would have to consider the political leadership on the regional level. The obvious reasons for this conclusion have already been suggested at several points of our previous analysis. In policy-making, the occupational background of individuals who participate in obkom plenums or conferences tells little of their actual attitudes or impact upon decisions. Attitudes cannot be inferred from the position an individual holds in a region. Even if attitudes do bear some consistent relationship to a position, those participating in a plenum as a rule have very little impact upon the actual decision adopted by the regional party. Rather, the plenums and conferences (and therefore their participants) are secondary aspects of a policy formation process in which the basic decisions are initiated by the central and regional political leadership. As noted in discussing participation, it may often be true that plenum and conference participants can modify or redefine an issue to take into account alternative solutions, their own occupational interests in the problem, or the realities of local circumstances. Yet this reverse or feedback effect upon policy is marginal when contrasted with the determinant influence of the central authorities and the obkom bureau in the overall policy process. At most, plenum participants can be assumed to have a symbolic effect by providing lower cadres and others identified with them in the work force with a forum for virtual representation of their interests.

If participation in obkom plenums is little more than symbolic in meaning (important as symbolic consequences may be for regional commitment and political adaptation), a very real impact upon policy can be attributed to those who participate in policy formation at the preliminary stage and wield preponderant influence upon the eventual outcomes and implementation of decisions. At the regional level, those identified with this prominent role are the designated members of the regional obkom bureau. It is their attitudes and behaviors that will have a very direct bearing upon decisions enacted by the regional party. As the regional leadership, the members of the obkom bureau initiate policy (or at least mediate policy initiated by the central leadership), implement decisions, and bear ultimate responsibility for their success or failure to central officials. The bureau is able to perform these tasks because it is not only the principal policy-making organ in the region but also an integrative forum for regional administrators. As an integrative forum, the obkom bureau draws together in its membership the leaders from the dominant Party, state, mass organization, and police bureaucracies of the region.

Its purpose in integrating regional operations can be seen in the similarity of a prescribed membership in the obkom bureaus. In all 25 regions of our sample during 1970, the following 13 to 15 officials were typically found as full or candidate members on the obkom bureau: the five secretaries of the obkom committee (four in Trans-Carpathia); the chairman and first deputy chairman of the oblast executive committee; the regional leaders of the Komsomol, control commission, and the trade-union council; the editor of the oblast newspaper (more likely, the Russian-language edition of the Ukrainian regions in 1970); the director of the Party organizational department; the oblast director of the KGB (the security police); the first secretary of the capital gorkom; and, in individual regions, the first secretaries of borough, district, or urban parties with a large concentration of regional industry (Rybinsk gorkom in Yaroslavl') or with particular military-strategic significance (Sevastopol' gorkom in the Crimea).

Some adjust to local conditions in defining membership on the obkom bureau is apparent. As an example, the military have an ex officio position in at least three of the regional elites. The director of Political Administration in the Trans-Carpathia Military Okrug was a full member of the L'vov obkom bureau in 1970 and, as his predecessor in 1966, was elected a candidate member of the Ukrainian Central Committee from this position in 1971.[1] Similarly, the vice admiral of the Black Sea Fleet is at least a full member of the Sevastopol' gorkom bureau in the Crimea,[2] and the admiral of the Baltic Fleet is a full member of the Kaliningrad obkom bureau.[3] It is also interesting that the deputy director of a department in the All-Union Central Committee Secretariat of the Komsomol is for some reason simultaneously a candidate member of the Kaliningrad obkom bureau in 1970.[4] Yet the military probably has no more than a nominal participatory role on bureaus. Its official positions alone would disqualify it except in extreme circumstances from any major contribution to bureau policies, which mostly concern related industrial or agricultural production in the region.

More fundamentally, the membership of the obkom bureaus is identical for all regions and, with few exceptions,[5] has not likely varied since 1955. The individuals who hold these 13 to 15 positions at any one time can be assumed to be the identifiable regional policy elite. Excluding the director of the oblast KGB (whose identity except for 1970 could not be ascertained in most regions), knowledge of the bureau members in several regions at one comparable time period or longitudinally could provide a significant composite index of stability and change on the regional political level of the Soviet Union. A direct comparison of the careers and background characteristics among a universe of bureau members could evidence potential differences in their attitudes, their capabilities, and, most importantly, their likely behavior and responses to regional problems. Carefully interpreted, any differences in careers and backgrounds would be relevant to the question of political change in the Soviet Union.

While all members of an obkom bureau could be studied as a composite regional elite, such analysis would have to consider fundamental distinctions among the members of the bureau itself. For one reason, not all positions can be assumed to give the individual an equal weight upon policy-making or an equal ranking in the obkom bureau. If nothing else, the very distinction between full and candidate members is an obvious rank order of political status among bureau members. No position is consistently limited to candidate membership on a bureau, although in 1970 many directors of the Party organizational departments and at least one of the three mass organization leaders were candidate members in the 25 regions. Even among all full members, there is a very real hierarchy in political influence. In particular, the obkom first secretary has been found in previous studies by Western scholars to dominate bureau policy-making. By his ability to define the nature of problems and solutions, the obkom first secretary can control the eventual decision arrived at by the bureau.[6] Thus, while described as an integrative forum, the bureau may not always function as a consultative body in which divergent bureaucratic views are expressed and given equal consideration.

One would also speculate that the nature of the region itself will determine the actual status of the full bureau member. Obkom secretaries in particular who specialize in a policy area may be politically more important for a region in which those responsibilities are deemed essential to the successful functioning of the regional party. Agricultural secretaries in a predominantly agricultural region, industrial secretaries in a predominantly industrial region, or ideological secretaries in a region with many university students and cultural officials* may have a higher political status than would the equivalent position in other regions. The position of oblast Komsomol first secretary conceivably would be more crucial in regions like Rostov with a large young-adult population in the universities and factories.† And the director of the oblast KGB, while nominally only a coequal member of the bureau, cannot reasonably be considered as just another bureau member. Through his direct accountability only to central officials, his vaguely defined authority to intervene in all other regional bureaucracies, and his supervision of the coercive apparatus in the region, the oblast KGB director occupies a political role that could give him influence on certain policy areas equivalent to the rest of the combined bureau. This influence may have been particularly manifested in the regions of L'vov and Dnepropetrovsk, both centers of political dissent since 1961.[7]

Differences among bureau members may also form around the policy concerns or identifications of particular bureau members. As recently stressed by a student of local parties in the Soviet Union,[8] it may be a gross simplification to associate common policy attitudes with individuals solely on the basis of their positions as Party

---

*As an example, the region of Tomsk, with the highest proportion of students in higher educational institutions per 10,000 in 1970 (576), has delegated indoctrination responsibilities in 1970 to its obkom second secretary, A. I. Kuznetsov. Normally, the second secretary in a region would be assigned primary responsibility only for Party cadre supervision and the oblast mass organizations. Yet, given the high concentration of students in the regional environment, the obkom second secretary in Tomsk in reality functions as the obkom ideology secretary. For evidence of Kuznetsov's duties, see his reports and participation in ideological conferences reported in KrZ(T), January 20, January 23, March 4, August 12, 1970. As further evidence, Kuznetsov was the Tomsk representative at the Jubilee Session of the Siberian Academy of Sciences, held in Novosibirsk on February 25 (VN) and whose participants were said to include only the directing ideological officials from West Siberia.

†Thus, after having served as Rostov Komsomol first secretary from 1956 to 1959 (see articles in KoP, January 5, 1956, July 21, 1957, January 3, 1958, and August 3, 1958), Yu. P. Tupchenko was reassigned as oblast director of the KGB (see delegates at XXII and XXIII KPSS; deputies to Russian Supreme Soviet in I, March 7, 1963). Given the strategic importance of the KGB director, it seems unlikely that Tupchenko would have been assigned unless he had already been allocated great authority and prior experience in social control as Komsomol first secretary.

162

apparatchiki or their office in the same bureaucracy. In the obkom bureau, individuals are frequently rotated between official positions, and coalitions on particular policies probably evolve across nominal bureaucratic allegiances.

At the same time rotations in the bureau and the careers of several bureau members often appear to correspond to a very logically structured and consistent pattern of functional specialization. A former first secretary of the same major agricultural district in a region will often become the director of the obkom agricultural department and will later be found in his career as the obkom agricultural secretary.* When assigned out of the obkom apparat, the "agricultural" specialist of the bureau is likely to become chairman and first deputy chairman of the oblispolkom (positions with primary agricultural responsibilities in rural regions) or deputy chairman of the oblispolkom in charge of agriculture.[9] The bureau "cadres" specialist is frequently rotated between official positions with primary authority for supervision of the Party and oblast mass organizations: director of the obkom Party organizational department; obkom second secretary in charge of cadres; chairman of the Party control commission; Komsomol first secretary; chairman of the trade-union council; and even director of the oblast MVD.[10] The "industrial" specialist is the former first secretary of the capital gorkom or another major industrial city reassigned as obkom industrial secretary or director of the obkom industrial department.[11] It is not uncommon to find

---

*In this regard, three recent agricultural specialists in Kursk have a very similar career pattern. Prior to his election as obkom agricultural secretary in 1968, A. F. Gudkov was both first secretary of the Dmitriev raikom and chairman of the Soviet raiispolkom (biography in KuP, May 21, 1970). Succeeding Gudkov as agricultural secretary in 1970 (KuP, April 28, 1970), D. V. Kamynin had been director of the obkom agricultural department and previously first secretary of the same Soviet rural district (see his article in PZh, June 12, 1967). Kamynin, in turn, was succeeded as agricultural director by V. S. Preidunov, until that time deputy chairman of the same Dmitriev raikom in which Gudkov had been first secretary in 1964-65. Similarly, two of the current agricultural specialists in Khar'kov were both former raikom first secretaries of the Balakleia district. A. P. Bezdetko, oblispolkom chairman since 1968 and agricultural deputy chairman for 1962-68, was first secretary of Balakleia from 1950 to 1955 (biography in KrZ(Kh), May 28, 1970); I. M. Kulinich, who succeeded Bezdetko as agricultural deputy chairman, was first secretary of Balakleia at least from 1966 through 1968 (delegates at XXIII KPSS; reference as agricultural specialist in LP, May 22, 1970).

163

him in his new position in 1970 specializing on industrial problems particular to his former industrial city;* and, as "agricultural" specialists, the careers of "industrial" specialists often appear to follow almost a structured line of political succession in a regional hierarchy.† An even more limited career track appears to be followed by "indoctrination" specialists, who will be interchangeably reassigned from director of the obkom agitprop department and obkom ideological secretary to the oblast executive committee as deputy chairman of the oblispolkom in charge of indoctrination problems or even editor of the oblast newspaper.[12] Even when promoted to a position outside the region, "indoctrination" specialists often assume comparable policy responsibilities at the All-Union or Union-republic level.[13] Indeed, for certain regions in which indoctrination responsibilities could be considered of paramount importance, a successful "indoctrination" specialist may come to expect promotion to the center or Union-republic apparat almost as a natural extension of his career in the regional party.‡

---

*Thus, prior to his election to the Perm' obkom bureau as the industry secretary in 1968, L. A. Kondratov had been first secretary of the Berezniki gorkom, a major chemical industrial complex on the upper Kama River in Perm' (see lengthy article on importance of Berezniki in Z[P], April 19, 1970). At the 11th obkom plenum in 1970, Kondratov delivered the major report on industry in which he stressed development of the second potassium combine in Berezniki. For references to Kondratov, see delegates at XXIII KPSS, report on obkom apparat in PZh, no. 6 (March 1966), and obkom plenum in Z(P), May 16-17, 1970.

†Thus, as Kondratov, the last two obkom first secretaries of Perm', K. I. Galanshin (1960-68) and B. F. Korotkov (1968-72), were both first secretary of the Berezniki gorkom immediately prior to their first election to the obkom bureau as the industrial obkom secretaries. If the pattern is followed in the future, Kondratov will likely become obkom first secretary and the current first secretary of the Bereznik gorkom, R. A. Bagin, will be elected obkom industrial secretary.

‡Consider only the key educational and cultural region of Khar'kov, from which three regional "indoctrination" specialists have been promoted since 1957: (1) Yu. Yu. Kondufor, director of the obkom agitprop department through 1957 (PU citation, March 19, 1958) and director of the Ukrainian CC Department of Science and Culture from 1958 through at least 1967 (PU, June 1, 1958 and December 13, 1967, p. 1; Pravda Vostoka, May 21, 1965, p. 1); (2) A. D. Skaba, editor of the oblast Ukrainian newspaper and obkom ideology secretary (1950-59)

In a later section of this chapter, the extent of internal rotation among bureau members will be considered a potential factor blocking the entrance of new members onto the bureau itself; and, as we shall later see, bureau members have as often been appointed from the center or laterally reassigned from other regional parties in order to fill positions of policy concentration in which they are apparently deemed to be specialists. At this point it is sufficient to recognize the phenomenon of functional specialization among many bureau members and the possibility of divergent policy concerns or groups within the total bureau membership.

However aware one must be of potential differences within the bureau, elite analysis of all bureau members over time could provide an essential indication of political adaptation at the regional level. As argued in the introductory chapter, the very concept of political adaptation implies the willingness of the regional party to recruit into its leadership ranks individuals who, by background, outlook, and qualifications, harmonize and integrate the regional party with changing social forces in its environment. There are two identifiable channels by which lower cadres and officials can hope to participate meaningfully in the regional policy process: direct participation in obkom plenums and conferences; and indirect participation by recruitment into the obkom leadership itself. The first channel of access was considered in the previous three chapters, in which regional participation for plenums was correlated with characteristics particular to each region.

As stressed at several points, however, the credibility of participation as a symbolic response for lower officials may well depend upon the level at which they can perceive a direct accounting of their views or career aspirations. The second channel of participation, elite recruitment, would therefore be particularly crucial. As for any individual in an occupation or elected position, the present level of commitment and morale displayed by lower cadres and officials will depend upon the opportunities they can perceive for future career advancement as a result of performance in their present positions. Both as an effective symbolic response and as an attempt to recruit individuals who can relate to social groups and problems in the region, the regional leadership must provide a flexible enough structure of

(biographies in 1962 and 1966 Deputaty; PU, August 14, 1955 and July 28, 1957) and ideology secretary of the Ukrainian CC (1959-1970; demoted in 1971); and (3) Yu. A. Skliarov, obkom ideology secretary (1964-69) (PU, December 16, 1964, KrZ(Kh), January 16, 1970) and deputy director of propaganda in the All-Union CC (P, December 18, 1969 and May 24, 1971, p. 2)

career opportunities from which lower cadres and officials are rapidly advanced in the regional hierarchy. If the regional party forecloses the possibility of leadership change, or if the individuals recruited to leadership positions are not representative of the broader social groups in the environment, the regional Party leaders run the risk of isolating themselves from the very Party cadres and officials who are essential to the economic and political progress of the region. Two criteria are therefore basic in determining the adaptive capacity of an obkom bureau to its environment: the extent of elite turnover in the bureau, and the relative ties of bureau members to their own regions.

Realistically, the problem of adaptation and recruitment will vary between regional bureaucracies located within the same region. At the same time that trade-union and Komsomol leaders may be entrenched officials out of step with the changing mood and aspirations of lower officials in their bureaucracies, urban and district secretaries in the Party apparat may have been significantly replaced by an influx of recent Party entrants. The average age and educational background of these recent Party entrants would be more representative of the average lower Party apparatchiki in the region. The problem of political adaptation can also be resolved at lower levels of any one bureaucracy without affecting the make-up of leadership at the highest ranks. In the example of the Party apparat, a turnover in gorkom and raikom secretaries may be considered sufficient to accommodate the career aspirations of Party apparatchiki without necessitating any replacement of the major policy officials in the obkom apparat. Such, indeed, may have been one purpose of the 1969 Central Committee resolution on the failures of the Yaroslavl' urban Party organization. As recalled, the resolution directly criticized only the secretaries of primary Party organizations in Yaroslavl' for being unrepresentative of the views and composition of the Party aktiv. Over 200 new secretaries at the primary Party level in the city were elected immediately after the resolution, but no parallel turnover at all occurred among bureau members in the capital gorkom and the obkom of the Party.

Nor is there any reason to assume a priori that the member of any bureaucracy or organization elected to the bureau is necessarily representative of leadership at lower ranks of the same organization or bureaucracy. Many bureau members are Party officials, whose assignment is initiated or at least confirmed by authorities in the central apparat. In particular, the leader of a mass organization like the Komsomol and the trade-unions council is more likely to be a "cadres" specialist, a full-time Party apparatchik interchangeably reassigned to positions of cadre supervision in the region. When he has not been recruited from lower ranks of each bureaucracy or organization, his ties to the lower Komsomol or trade-union aktiv are likely to be minimal.

166

Even with these qualifications in mind, membership on the obkom bureaus within any specific time period could be seen as an approximate indication of regional adaptation. As noted, the major officials in almost all key regional bureaucracies or organizations will be represented on the obkom bureau. Given the extensive authority of the regional party in the assignment of local cadres and officials in the region (nomenklatura), personnel changes within each bureaucracy or organization would eventually be reflected in the kinds of individuals who are elected to the top leadership position. Knowledge of obkom bureau members is usually the only information available on the leadership of regional bureaucracies. With the exception of the oblast committee, the bureau would also be the only level of analysis from which to evaluate political adaptation for a total region. Therefore—whatever assumptions one must make to interpret bureau membership—turnover and recruitment on the bureau remain the only theoretically relevant indications of regional political adaptation. If regional parties attempt to adapt to their environments, evidence of that concern would be provided in the nature of changes that have occurred in leadership turnover and recruitment in several regional bureaus over an extended span of time.

EXPLANATORY FACTORS

If membership in obkom bureaus is an indication of regional adaptation, what independent factors would explain differences in the turnover level and recruitment of bureau members? In Chapter 1, two alternative explanations were offered to account for the pattern of turnover and recruitment at the regional level.

First, assuming a direct dependence of the regional bureau membership upon significant political trends at the center, we hypothesized that bureau adaptation should have been influenced by change in the central political leadership. That change was identified with the overthrow of Khrushchev in 1964. The Soviet political system since 1955 was characterized as two distinct political regimes: the Khrushchev regime between 1955 and 1964, and the Brezhnev-Kosygin regime between 1965 and 1973. The Khrushchev regime was considered distinct in its impact upon regional bureaus by the supposed greater concern of Khrushchev with personnel change in the political leadership at the local levels. Examples of this concern were the mandatory turnover ratios for elected Party organs adopted at the 22d Congress in 1961 and the bifurcation of oblast committees in 1963-64.

In contrast, the Brezhnev-Kosygin regime was typified as a conservative bureaucracy in its impact upon local leadership. The central leadership from 1965 would have been fearful of any significant personnel change at the local levels. Such change could potentially challenge the vested interests of local Party leaders who had supported the coup in the Central Committee or could bring to authoritative posts cadres with dubious loyalties and commitments to the present central regime. Turnover, understood by political opponents as an attempted departure from collectivism to one-man rule, would also disrupt the short-term stability reached in central leadership. The stability since October 1964 had been based upon a political compromise that allowed all participants to benefit in some equal measure and precluded any return to the dominance of one man in the Soviet political system.

Because of these inherent conservative features in the central leadership from 1965, a comparison of turnover and recruitment patterns for the 25 regions should evidence significant differences from the Khrushchev period and a general trend under Brezhnev-Kosygin toward less regional adaptation: (1) longer tenure of bureau officials and a subsequent reduction in bureau turnover; (2) an older regional elite by age and year of party entry; and (3) a bureau membership more isolated by background and outlook from their regions than those assigned during the Khrushchev period of dynamic Party reform.

While we assumed the same dependence of regime change upon bureau membership, a second interpretation of the Brezhnev-Kosygin regime was also drawn. Potential similarities between the two regimes were emphasized. As in the Khrushchev regime, it was assumed that any personnel changes initiated by the Brezhnev-Kosygin regime would be predicated upon the desire to optimize economic performance at the local levels. Because of its fragile collective nature, the Brezhnev-Kosygin regime is highly dependent upon a successful economy if it is to remain in power. Primarily concerned with economic performance, the leadership from 1965 has shifted greater responsibility to local Party organizations. With this responsibility, regional leaders have been compelled to draw upon the positive support and commitment of lower cadres and officials. There is a greater necessity to accommodate the career aspirations of these cadres and officials. Under the directive of central Party leaders, regional leaders have thus found it expedient to recruit bureau members knowledgeable in local economic situations and representative of the lower Party aktiv.

Therefore, by needs characteristic both of the Khrushchev and Brezhnev-Kosygin regimes, the turnover in regional bureaus should be as high in 1965-73 as in 1955-64. Even compared to the Khrushchev regime, the typical bureau official in 1965-73 should continue to be younger, highly educated, technically qualified, and tied by background and origin to the region in which he has been elected to the political

168

elite. Expressed as a null hypothesis, the second interpretation assumes no variance will be evident at the bureau level between the two regimes. The Brezhnev-Kosygin regime at the bureau level would be typified as "Khrushchevism without Khrushchev."

Logically, four alternative possibilities could be derived from the two interpretations. Turnover and recruitment in obkom bureaus could have changed or remained stable in any of four directions between the Khrushchev and the Brezhnev-Kosygin regimes: (1) change both in the rate of turnover and the types of individuals represented on the obkom bureau; (2) change in the rate of turnover but no difference in the types of individuals represented in the obkom bureau; (3) no difference in the rate of turnover but change in the types of individuals represented on the obkom bureau; or (4) no difference either in the rate of turnover or in the types of individuals represented on the obkom bureau.

The second explanatory factor to account for bureau membership is the regional environment. Rather than a dependence upon regime change, membership in obkom bureaus should have been more directly affected by the nature of the social forces and the level of change in each region. If regional parties adapt to their environment, variation in bureau characteristics should relate to socioeconomic differences among regions.

The theory of social mobilization was proposed to explain variation that should predictably appear in obkom bureaus with different regional environments. According to the theory of social mobilization, groups and strata in the society are psychologically and socially uprooted by modernization, and statistically occurring levels of change would produce heightened demands upon political systems for participation. Those demands would manifest in regional parties because a larger percentage of new Party entrants and lower officials have been recruited from the newly mobilized segments of the region. To retain its legitimacy and the support of these new lower officials, regional Party leaders in high mobilized environments would have to recruit sizable enough proportions of lower officials into higher leadership positions. If central leaders calculate in response to local circumstances, regions of high social mobilization should therefore have a higher turnover rate in the limited positions of the obkom bureau. Low-change regions would not experience as great a demand from lower officials for participation and recruitment into the obkom bureau. In addition, the background and origins of bureau officials in high-change regions should give evidence of a greater concern with political adaptation. Bureau members should be younger and more highly skilled in professional backgrounds to match the growing number of young and technically trained lower officials. A larger percentage of native officials should be recruited into the bureau in relation to the demands for local participation by lower officials.

169

As it would be true for the variable of political regime change, turnover and recruitment in obkom bureaus would logically correspond to any one of four alternatives between low and high change regions: (1) different both in the rate of turnover and the types of individuals represented on the bureau; (2) different in the rate of turnover but similar in the types of individuals represented on the bureau; (3) similar in the rate of turnover but different in the types of individuals represented on the bureau; and (4) similar both in the rate of turnover and the types of individuals represented on the bureau. If environment is the primary determinant of bureau membership, regions of high change should have a higher turnover and proportion of native, professionally trained, and younger bureau members than low change regions. This variation among regions should be confirmed over the period 1955-73 and within each of the two political regimes, 1955-64 and 1965-73.

In order to test the relative impact of the political regime change and the environment, career and biographical data have been gathered on 763 obkom bureau members elected in the 25 regions from 1955 through the first six months of 1973.* In delimiting the universe of bureau members, we have assumed that the same 13-15 positions have conferred full or candidate membership in the 25 regions over this 19-year span, and any individual could be identified as a bureau member if he was elected to one of these 13-15 positions during this period. In addition, career and biographic data were accumulated on 345 nonbureau officials to provide a representative profile of the middle political elite in regions. The "middle political elite" was

---

*The basic source in the identification and compilation of career-biographic characteristics of bureau members was personnel references and career patterns pooled together and derived from an exhaustive examination of the principal All-Union and Union-republic periodicals published between 1950 and the middle of 1973. In addition, the list of regional delegates attending the Ukrainian and All-Union Party Congresses (1956-71) and standard biographical sources such as the Deputaty, Ezhegodniki, and the State Department Biographic Directories were cross-checked, although they provided extensive information and identification only for a limited segment of the most prominent of the total 763 bureau members. Careers and references were first traced back from the complete listings of bureau members obtained from the 1970 regional newspapers; and composite bureau charts were then reconstructed for each of the 25 bureaus over the 19 years, including names, specific bureau positions held in each region, and years in each bureau position. From these charts, the 763 bureau members were separately coded in terms of 80 alternative variables on an original codebook devised by the author.

defined to include all obkom department directors (with the exception of the Party organizational director on the obkom bureau), deputy chairmen of the oblispolkom, directors of oblast and capital departments and administrations, and gorkom-raikom first Party secretaries (with the exception of those whose positions confer bureau membership in some regions) who could be identified in these offices from 1958 through 1973.* Well over half of the 345 middle elite still held some elected or appointed post after 1964. While not bureau members, the middle political elite have almost all been members of the oblast committee and thus constitute a political level directly below the obkom bureau in the regional political hierarchy. In several tables their characteristics are compared to those typical of bureau members to assess the relative adaptiveness of the bureau to a succeeding middle elite.

Bureau characteristics are correlated in each table with regime and environmental variables.† Bureau members are first independently correlated with the regime period in which they served and with the level of social mobilization in each region. Social mobilization is operationalized as the percent urban change in regional populations between 1939 and 1970, the index in Chapter 3 that most sharply distinguished the concern of regional parties with cadre policy in 1970. From the analysis employed in previous chapters, the regions are dichotomized into low and high urban change regions. The level of urban change is then simultaneously controlled for regime change to measure the exact amount and direction of variation explained by each independent variable over the 19-year period.

---

*Career-biographic characteristics for the 345 middle elite were derived from the same sources used in identifying and compiling data on the 763 bureau members. In addition, detailed obituaries on 45 defined middle political elite appeared in the regional newspapers during 1970.

†As the unit of comparative analysis in tables is more the 25 collective bureaus than individual bureau members per se, 19 individuals elected to two of the 25 bureaus in the 1955-73 period were coded separately for each of the regional parties and counted twice in the total derived sample of 763. The separate coding of these 19 individuals on several characteristics varied, dependent on the changing nature of their career and background at the time they were elected to either one of the obkom bureaus. For example, a native bureau member in one region, transferred to another region, would be coded the second time as an outsider; the age of the same individuals would be computed differently the second time he is elected to another bureau, and so on.

171

Regional environment could also be defined as the Union-republic setting in which each regional party is located. Armstrong and Bilinsky, among other students of the Soviet Communist Party, have contended that cadre policies for regional parties in the Ukrainian Republic may have at times followed a pattern distinct from policies dominant throughout the rest of the Soviet Union.[14] Neither scholar has argued that Ukrainian regions are actually independent of central policy direction emanating from Moscow nor would either scholar go so far as to assume a uniform cadre policy for all 25 Ukrainian regions, marked by sharp contrasts and problems of political control alone between the more integrated Eastern regions (populated by Ukrainians) and the more recently incorporated Western border regions (comprised of divergent non-Ukrainian nationalities). Yet, if the Ukraine as a political subsystem in the Soviet Union has any viable autonomy in policy and cadre selection, Russian and Ukrainian bureaus may differ in certain background and career characteristics, or the regions within each republic may have been particularly affected by the regime change in 1964. To test these effects, bureau characteristics are simultaneously controlled in each table for Union-republic and for regime change.*

Two subgroups are also distinguished in each table. As previously shown, the obkom bureau actually includes distinct groups and individuals with varying political status. One of the most conventional group distinctions emphasized by Western scholars is the Party apparatchiki, who are represented on the bureau by the obkom secretaries. Other bureau members may have been Party secretaries at some point in their careers, but those who have been obkom secretaries within a specified time period are the only full bureau members authorized to administer the obkom apparat by their official positions.† A further distinction could be made even among all obkom secretaries. By his title and actual policy role in the region, the obkom first secretary is the dominant political figure in obkom bureaus. As a consequence, the two subgroups of obkom first secretaries and obkom secretaries in the total universe of bureau members are factored out separately for each time period. Of primary interest will

---

*Although there are more Russian than Ukrainian regions in the sample, the number of regions as a proportion of all nonautonomous regions in both republics is roughly equivalent. The 25 regions include 18 of the 50 nonautonomous Russian regions (36 percent) and 7 of the 25 Ukrainian regions (28 percent).

†While also an official of the obkom apparat, the obkom Party organizational director is usually only a candidate member of the bureau.

be to compare characteristics typical of both subgroups within each time period with those of all bureau members. In particular, how representative of the obkom bureau are obkom first secretaries and obkom secretaries?

In interpreting the significance of percentages in the following tables, we will be concerned with four essential questions:

1. What have been the typical characteristics one can identify with membership on obkom bureaus since 1955?

2. How have those characteristics been influenced by changes in the central political regime and by inherent environmental differences among regions?

3. What opportunities have been available for officials in the middle political elite to rise into the obkom bureau during this 19-year period?

4. If political adaptation means the recruitment of an elite both responsive to and representative of changing social forces and groups in a region, how would one evaluate the adaptive capacity shown by obkom bureaus over the 19 years?

TURNOVER IN OBKOM BUREAUS

Leadership change at the regional level has very likely become a major topic of internal Party debate in recent years. From a careful reading of Brezhnev's report to the 24th Congress in 1971 and articles by regional leaders in the central Party journals, two divergent views can be seen. One view, committed to stability in leadership, has defended the present regional leadership and has cautioned against any rapid turnover in regional elites. Rapid turnover, so it is argued, would remove many "politically mature" and "tested" leaders at the regional level.[15] Another view, often expressed by the same author who warns against any rapid turnover, recognizes that some of the present regional leaders have proven unable to cope with changing economic and political demands in the country. The failure of the economy to meet projected quotas is singled out as a particular factor that would warrant some replacement of the present regional leadership.[16] Typically an ambiguous conclusion has accompanied such articles and speeches with an appeal to "continue" in leadership positions the "tested experience" and "worldly wisdom" (zhiteiskii mudrost') of the older current leaders with the better technical training and enthusiasm of a new leadership generation.

The extent of turnover is thus fundamental to an understanding of obkom bureaus. Change in the membership of obkom bureaus depends upon the opportunities available for nonmembers to be elected. Granted, turnover in itself need not signify any equivalent change in the actual makeup of bureau members. Those newly recruited in the bureau may be exactly similar to those whom they replaced. Yet, as a minimum, no change can occur unless at least some bureau members are systematically elected for the first time. If the same bureau members are reelected every two years and hold on to their positions for several years, leadership is by definition unchanged. For the middle political elite in each region, such stability in the obkom bureaus forecloses any possibility to advance their careers. They are unlikely to find convincing any arguments that defend the continuity of bureau membership only because of "tested political maturity."

From the five alternative measures of turnover in Tables 5.1-5.4 below, the middle political elite would have good reason for any recent dissatisfaction. The analysis of turnover generally reveals a substantial retention rate of bureau members since the overthrow of Khrushchev in 1964.*

Tenure of Bureau Members

One such indication is the average tenure of bureau members, shown in Table 5.1. Over the 16-year period examined in the table, the typical member has been on the bureau a relatively short time. Of all bureau members, 58 percent have served only from one to five total years. Only 12 percent of all bureau members have remained in the same bureaus longer than a decade and might be termed an entrenched policy elite by total tenure. Nor can any significant variation be seen for those who have served in different kinds of regions over the 16 years. Between 1955 and 1970, low and high urban change

---

*Tables 5.1-5.4 calculate the turnover and tenure of obkom bureau membership only through the end of 1970, unlike the tables in Chapter 6, which include career-biographic data on all bureau members elected through the first six months of 1973. Because the names and positions only of 174 bureau members could be ascertained after 1970, it was decided that inclusion of their turnover and tenure through 1973 with the remaining bureau members for whom information was not available after 1970 would seriously distort the percentages in the tables. At the same time the tenure and duration of these 174 post-1970 members are presented independently in the text of this chapter to assess any modification, reversal, or continuation of the trends outlined in the four tables. In Chapter 6, the career-background variables in the tables are not distorted by including all known bureau members through 1973, because the variables do not change in value as significantly in a short span of time as those in Chapter 5.

174

TABLE 5.1

Total Years in Obkom Bureau, 1955-70
(percent)

	1-5 Years	6-10 Years	11+ Years	N[a]
Total bureau				
members, 1955-70	58	30	12	636
Urban change				
Low regions	56	32	12	337
High regions	59	27	13	299
Political regime				
1955-64	59	32	8	428
1965-70	53	29	18	387
Urban change (time)				
Low (1955-64)	59	32	8	228
High (1955-64)	60	30	10	200
Low (1965-70)	50	33	16	206
High (1965-70)	57	24	19	181
Union rep. (time)				
Russia (1955-64)	60	32	8	291
Ukraine (1955-64)	58	34	8	137
Russia (1965-70)	55	27	18	269
Ukraine (1965-70)	49	33	18	118
Obk. 1st sec's (time)[b]				
1955-64	48	42	9	95
1965-70	21	42	37	38
All other sec's (time)[c]				
1955-64	57	35	8	183
1965-70	42	40	17	149

[a]In all tables, percentages are expressed only for the total known universe of bureau members for each variable. There are actually 763 obkom bureau members in the sample. Bureau members include all individuals elected between 1955 and 1970 (1973 for tables in Chapter 6) to positions with potential full or candidate membership on the obkom bureaus. The sample includes all known obkom secretaries, chairmen and first deputy chairmen of the oblast capitals, chairmen of the oblast trade-union councils, first secretaries of the oblast Young Communist Leagues, chairmen of the oblast control commissions, editors of oblast newspapers, directors of obkom Party organization departments, chairmen of regional sovnarkhozy between 1957 and 1967, and first secretaries of other city and district Party organizations with positions on the obkom bureaus as of 1970 (Rybinsk gorkom in Yaroslavl', Krivoi Rog gorkom in Dnepropetrovsk, Sevastopol' gorkom in Crimea, Lenin raikom in Zaporozh'e). Not included are the oblast directors of the KGB, even though all of them are members of the obkom bureaus in 1970.

[b]Includes those obkom first secretaries elected to either one of the two obkom bureaus during bifurcation reform of 1963-64.

[c]All obkom secretaries with the exception of obkom first secretaries. Includes obkom secretaries elected to either one of the two obkom bureaus during bifurcation reform of 1963-64.

Source: Compiled by the author.

175

regions are almost identical in average tenure for bureau members; and Russian and Ukrainian regions fail to evidence any distinctive pattern by Union-republic.

In contrast, the average tenure has increased under the Brezhnev-Kosygin regime. One need only consider those who have been retained in the bureaus more than 10 years at the end of both time periods. In 1955-64, only 8 percent of all bureau members had remained over a decade; by 1970, however, that proportion has more than doubled to 18 percent. The pattern is confirmed even when regions are controlled for urbanization and Union-republic. In 1965-70, each of the four regional classifications increased by 8 to 10 percent in the number of officials over a decade in their bureaus.

It should be further noted that the percentages only count the total years through the end of 1970. Ten percent of those members in the category of 6-10 years in the table were actually elected to the bureaus in 1961. Regional Party conferences were held in early 1971 to elect new obkoms and obkom bureaus preparatory to the 24th Party Congress. Yet, even with the addition of new members at these elections and changes subsequent to the Party conferences, 64 of 174 bureau members (or 37 percent) who could be identified between 1971 and mid-1973 have remained a minimum of 11 years on the same regional bureaus.

Thus, the regime change has a very direct relationship to the increasing tenure of bureau members. The relationship is even more sharply drawn for the distinct subgroups of obkom secretaries and obkom first secretaries. During the Khrushchev regime, the tenure of both subgroups was almost identical to that of all bureau members. Almost half of those who became first secretaries and 57 percent of those elected obkom secretary served less than six total years in the bureau. The brief tenure of obkom secretaries during this period resulted in part from the bifurcation reform introduced by Khrushchev in 1963-64 supposedly in conjunction with a grander scheme to revitalize regional Party leadership. A second obkom secretariat was established in several regions. As a consequence, many individuals were elected obkom secretaries for the first time in the 1963-64 period. Several had never been on the obkom bureau before the reform or had served only briefly on the unified bureau prior to 1963. Almost immediately after the overthrow of Khrushchev, the Central Committee voted to dissolve the second obkom bureau, secretariat, and committee in each region.

The political significance of the reform and the consequence of its dissolution can now be observed. By the end of 1970, the percentage of obkom first secretaries less than six years in the bureau declined to 21 percent, and that of obkom secretaries to 43 percent. At the same time the proportion of first secretaries over a decade

176

in the bureaus increased over four times and the proportion of obkom secretaries over a decade has more than doubled. Obkom secretaries have also become much less representative of all bureau members since 1965. In 1955-64, average bureau members and obkom secretaries resembled each other by their total number of years on the bureau. By 1970, obkom secretaries are typically on the bureau a much longer period of time than other bureau members. Consider that, even in the 1965-70 period, 53 percent of all bureau members were still on the bureaus less than six years, well above the proportion of those elected obkom secretaries or first secretaries. Nor did the elections of new obkom secretariats in early 1971 significantly modify this pattern. Of 105 identifiable obkom secretaries in the 1971-73 period, 43 have a minimum of 11 total years on the same regional bureaus.

The disparity suggests that, even if an official from the middle elite has been elected to the bureau after 1964, he is now less likely than under the Khrushchev regime to become an obkom secretary and even less likely to become obkom first secretary. His channels of access into the bureau are more limited to the alternative bureaucracies with positions on the bureau. He will be elected to the bureau as oblast leader of a mass organization or chairman and first deputy chairman of the oblispolkom. The obkom secretariat in comparison is a more established elite and has changed very little in its composition during the interim.

The obkom bureau in the Ukrainian region of Zaporozh'e could be cited to illustrate the increasing average tenure among all bureau members and the greater continuity of obkom secretaries in regional leadership. From 1955 through 1964, the 24 members of the Zaporozh'e bureau, for whom sufficient career backgrounds could be developed, averaged 4.9 total years. Prior to the establishment of a second obkom bureau in January of 1963, only M. N. Vsevolozhskii (Party organizational director), F. Ya. Mokrous (oblispokom chairman), S. M. Timoshenko (agricultural secretary), and V. V. Skriabin (okbom first secretary) had been on the obkom bureau longer than eight years. The senior by total tenure in the regional Party leadership, Skriabin was a native of the region and had first been elected to the bureau as obkom second secretary in 1952,[17] two years prior to the time a major turnover of leadership in 1954 had elevated Vsevolozhskii, Mokrous, and Timoshenko to the obkom bureau as director of Party organs, obkom second secretary, and obkom agricultural secretary.[18] At least Vsevolozhskii and Timoshenko were recruited directly at that time in 1954 from positions they had held in the Zaporozh'e regional middle elite.[19] Skriabin, however, was replaced in August 1962 by A. A. Titarenko, a native of the Donets region who had never even been employed in Zaporozh'e prior to his election as first secretary;[20] and Timoshenko died in March 1963, allowing another formerly nonbureau member, V. G. Domshenko, to assume a major regional policy position as obkom agricultural secretary.[21]

The low average tenure in Zaporozh'e under Khrushchev was not just an immediate consequence of the second bureau. Actually, the second bureau incorporated several low ranking bureau members from the 1962 group; and, of eight obkom secretaries and two oblispolkom chairmen in 1964 right before the dual leadership pattern was rescinded, only three actually had not been members of the bureau prior to bifurcation.[22] Indeed, the period of greatest renewal in the Zaporozh'e bureau during the Khrushchev period occurred in late 1957 and early 1958, when, subsequent to Khrushchev's temporary consolidation of power and the removal of the "anti-Party" group in the Praesidium, seven new members were elected to the Zaporozh'e bureau for the first time, including three as obkom secretaries (two of whom were women).[23] The net effect of the second Zaporozh'e bureau in 1963-64 was marginal on the average tenure of bureau members, with the average of those by October 1964 actually rising slightly above the 10-year mean of 5.2 years. Rather, as several other regional bureaus, Zaporozh'e appears to have undergone a continuing pattern of turnover and replacement throughout the 10-year period under Khrushchev, with the peak reached between late 1957 and the middle of 1961.

The pattern of bureau tenure in Zaporozh'e after 1964 is also quite typical of several regional parties. The average tenure of the 17 bureau members in Zaporozh'e from 1965 through the end of 1970 increased to 7.4 years. Even the inclusion of new members during this period has not reduced the average tenure, with the median only for those in the bureau through 1970 still 7.4 years. Nor can any modification of the trend be found in the interim after the 1971 Party conference in Zaporozh'e. Of those nine Zaporozh'e bureau officials known to be in the region through 1972, the average tenure has reached 8.7 years.

Even more significant is the growing disparity in the median tenure for obkom secretaries in 1964 and in 1971. In 1964, the average of 6.1 years for obkom secretaries only slightly exceeded that of 5.2 years for all bureau members. By the end of 1971, however, the five obkom secretaries in Zaporozh'e averaged 12.4 years on the bureau, over 5 years above the 7.4 average for all bureau members through 1970. M. N. Vsevolozhskii, the obkom first secretary, has been a member of the bureau for 18 years since his election as Party Organs director in 1954.[24] While elected second secretary only in 1966 and released in November 1971, A. P. Trutnev had served at least 10 previous years in the bureau as Komsomol first secretary and chairman of the oblast trade-union council.[25] V. I. Petrykin,

the ideology secretary in 1971, was first elected to that position in
1961;[26] V. I. Skliarov, the industry secretary, has been a member
of the bureau also since 1961 at a time he was selected chairman of
the Zaporozh'e sovnarkhoz.[27] Indeed, the only secretary less than
a decade on the bureau through 1971 is the agriculture secretary,
V. G. Domchenko, who, as previously noted, was first elected to the
bureau in early 1963 only because the former agriculture secretary
Timoshenko had died.

Continuity has typified not only total tenure on the bureau, but
even the underlying pattern of replacement when it has occurred since
1964. Thus, six members have been elected to the bureau for the
first time between 1965 and 1972. Four of these new members were
elected from previous offices in the defined Zaporozh'e middle elite.
Two became first deputy chairman of the oblispolkom;[28] a third,
Komsomol first secretary;[29] and the fourth, capital gorkom first
secretary.[30] The fifth and sixth were M. V. Khorunzhii, elected to
the bureau for the first time in 1968 as oblispolkom chairman, and
N. A. Panteleev, elected to the bureau also for the first time in late
1971 as obkom second secretary. Not even an official in Zaporozh'e
prior to his election, Khorunzhii had been oblispolkom chairman of
the Odessa region through 1967;[31] Panteleev, a similar outsider,
had been gorkom first secretary of Lisichansk in the Lugansk region.[32]
Thus, if one were to assume the obkom second secretary and the
oblispolkom chairman constitute two of the most politically important
policy positions in Zaporozh'e, the trend since 1964 has obviously
been to reserve these positions for those already on the bureau or for
ones (like Khorunzhii and Panteleev) with "tested political maturity"
from the outside.

When bureau changes have occurred in Zaporozh'e since 1964,
they have more often resulted in former bureau members being reassigned back to the middle political elite. N. P. Kitsenko, formerly
editor of the oblast newspaper and ideology secretary through 1964,
is found as deputy chairman of the oblispolkom in charge of indoctrination problems in 1970.[33] B. N. Bazhenov, first deputy chairman of
the industrial oblispolkom in 1964, is director of the light and food
industry department of the obkom in 1970.[34] I. I. Khromykh, the
capital gorkom first secretary through at least 1959, is the director
of the industry-transport department of the obkom in 1970.[35]

This reverse pattern of reassignment out of the bureau to the
middle political elite is a quite common phenomenon in almost every
region of our sample. Agricultural secretaries in Saratov, L'vov,
and Khar'kov between 1955 and 1964 are the director of oblast agriculture, deputy chairman of the oblispolkom in charge of agriculture,
or even the rector of an agricultural institute in 1970.[36] The former
obkom second secretary and oblispolkom chairman of Odessa between

1958 and 1964 was reduced to rector of the Odessa Polytechnical Institute until late 1969.[37] The obkom first secretary and obkom industry secretary of Kemerovo through early 1960 are deputy chairman of the Kalinin oblispolkom and chairman of the Kemerovo Party Commission in 1970;[38] and the obkom second secretary of Kemerovo in 1966 is director of a coal combine in 1970.[39] The former obkom second secretary of Rostov, supposedly purged as a result of the Novocherkassk riot in 1962, has been retained as deputy director of a construction trust in 1970 and participates in a 1970 Rostov urban Party meeting.[40] A former Komsomol first secretary in Saratov has been reassigned in 1970 as secretary of the Saratov Aviation Plant;[41] and the former second secretary of the Kostroma region in 1959-61, to director of the Kursk oblast administration of commerce.[42] These examples are only in addition to several obkom secretaries (like Kitsenko in Zaporozh'e), appointed to the bureau for the first time during the bifurcation reform and subsequently returned to the middle political elite after consolidation of the bureaus in December of 1964.[43]

The actual significance of these demotions is far from clear. In his study of the Volgograd bureau during the 1950s, Stewart found similar examples of individuals returned to the middle elite after election to the bureau.[44] One would speculate that such demotions commonly typify the intense demands made upon bureau officials to perform satisfactorily and the great probability of fluctuations in career status dependent upon an individual's demonstrated merit, political maturity, or political influence with central Party officials. Nor, despite the absence of supporting evidence, can one overlook the even higher number of bureau members likely demoted (or purged) during the 1953-55 period in the wake of demands to upgrade the quality of agricultural leadership and break up bureaucratically entrenched interests at the regional obkom level.[45] It is not that uncommon even during the Khrushchev regime to find a former oblispolkom chairman reduced to the position of oblast agricultural director.[46]

On the other hand, the large number of demotions since 1964 could also represent an unusual situation. Not only would it further reflect on the restorationist and conservative tendencies in the political system, but the increasing tenure at the bureau level would now tend to freeze several of these former bureau members in major secondary posts of the obkom and oblast apparat. Consider that the former bureau members have already been demoted one stage. They occupy positions on what might be termed the second level of the regional political hierarchy. They would be next in line for any promotions into the obkom bureau. Yet, unless these former bureau members are elected once more to the bureaus,[47] they would probably be retained in the present second-level positions for a period of time longer than normal for such positions. Party-state cadres and officials at even a third lower level of the regional hierarchy would find fewer opportunities to advance higher in the same bureaucracies now dominated by the former bureau members. The increasing average tenure of bureau members and the simultaneous staffing of secondary positions by former bureau members would directly limit the career prospects of all lower cadres and officials at the same time it would preclude new policy initiatives from the lower rank-and-file Party cadres.

Consecutive Years

While the figures since 1964 show a higher percentage of the same individuals remaining in the obkom bureaus for a longer period of time, reassignment of individuals to different bureau positions has continued in all regions. In 1969-70 alone, 42 different bureau positions in the 25 regions were reassigned either to current bureau members or to new recruits. The turnover included among other offices four first secretaries, three obkom second secretaries, and nine obkom secretaries with specialist responsibilities in the apparat. Subsequent to the regional Party conferences in early 1971, reassignments of personnel also took place in 39 of 174 known positions through the first half of 1973. Thus, lower cadres and officials may have fewer opportunities to enter the obkom bureau after 1964, but not all individuals have held the same bureau positions. Even were bureau members merely to be rotated to another position, change among bureau positions could suggest an attempt to revitalize policy direction of the various functional interests represented on the bureau. The consecutive years an individual holds the same bureau position could provide an alternative indication of turnover and political adaptation in the obkom bureaus.

In this sense, the figures in Table 5.2 for consecutive years in the same highest bureau position tend to qualify some of the conclusions based solely upon average tenure in Table 5.1. The reader can see that officials have typically held the same high position for a short period of time. The turnover of bureau positions between 1955 and 1971 was very high, with only 28 percent of all bureau members remaining in the same position longer than five consecutive years. Nor has the change in political regimes or the rate of urbanization affected this rapid turnover. From 1965, the number of officials in the same position over 10 years is only 3 percent higher than in 1955-64, and bureau members in low and high urban regions during these six years have held the same highest position for almost an identical number of years.

181

TABLE 5.2

Consecutive Years—Same (Highest) Position in Obkom
Bureau, 1955-70
(percent)

	1-5 Years	6-10 Years	11+ Years	N
Total bureau members, 1955-70	72	25	3	652
Urban change				
Low regions	70	26	4	346
High regions	74	24	3	306
Political regime				
1955-64	74	24	2	353
1965-70	67	28	5	392
Urban change (time)				
Low (1955-64)	68	30	2	194
High (1955-64)	77	21	2	159
Low (1965-70)	65	29	6	206
High (1965-70)	66	30	4	186
Union rep. (time)				
Russian (1955-64)	75	23	2	218
Ukrainian (1955-64)	78	19	3	135
Russian (1965-70)	73	24	3	278
Ukrainian (1965-70)	58	34	8	114
Obkom 1st sec's (time)				
1955-64	47	46	6	97
1965-70	41	51	8	37
All other sec's (time)				
1955-64	64	33	3	193
1965-70	65	31	4	150

Note: For the purpose of analysis, the positions in the obkom bureau were broken down according to three descending rank orders of importance. Tentatively defined, the three rank orders included positions considered equivalent in political importance: (1) obkom first secretary, obkom second secretary, oblispolkom chairman; (2) obkom secretary, first secretary of the capital gorkom, first deputy chairman of the oblispolkom; and (3) first secretary of oblast Komsomol, chairman of oblast control commission, chairman of oblast trade-union council, editor of oblast newspaper, first secretary of gorkom and raikom Party organization with position on obkom bureau, director of Party organizational department. The individual position held for longest consecutive years at highest rank was counted in the table. If an individual held the same position before and after bifurcation, the years 1963-64 were included with the total consecutive years.

Source: Compiled by the author.

Some interesting differences can be observed when environmental factors are controlled for the change in political regimes. High urban change regions between 1955 and 1964 had a higher turnover rate, apparent by 9 percent for those in the same positions from one to five consecutive years. After 1964, the turnover rate in high regions has declined so that the proportion of officials is almost exactly identical in high and low regions. At the same time an important difference has emerged between Russian and Ukrainian regions. Ukrainian bureaus since 1965 have a higher percentage of officials in the same positions over five consecutive years (42 to 27 percent in Russian regions). The higher retention rate of Ukrainian officials is particularly unexpected. As Khrushchev had been the former Ukrainian First Secretary, Ukrainian regional bureaus in 1955-64 would have been expected at that time to benefit from a special status. If continuity in office would indicate any special status, just the opposite is now proven. The turnover of Ukrainian offices under Khrushchev was equivalent to the levels in Russian regions. It is only after his overthrow that turnover in the Ukrainian bureaus has declined.

This greater continuity after 1964 in the Ukrainian bureaus may indicate a compromise All-Union leaders had to reach with their Ukrainian counterparts in order to win support for the overthrow. Nominal protegés of Khrushchev from the Ukraine like Kirilenko, Yepishev, Poliansky, Podgornyi, Shcherbitsky, and Shelest' may have been a pivotal group in the Central Committee. As a result, Ukrainian regional leaders, many of whom may be protegés of these same central leaders, may have been granted even more independence in determining the selection and turnover of membership in their own regional bureaus. Whatever bearing central support may have upon continuity in office, the regional obkom secretariats in the Ukraine have changed very little in the interim since 1964. Indicative is the fact that only one of the 35 secretaries elected after the seven regional Party conferences in the Ukraine in 1971 did not already hold the same position in 1970.[48]

One can only speculate upon the reasons or the actual significance of the Ukrainian pattern under the Brezhnev-Kosygin regime, but a much clearer perspective of regime impact is gained by comparing obkom secretaries and obkom first secretaries before and after 1964. The consecutive years individuals have held positions in the obkom secretariat have not varied significantly from the Khrushchev period. True, first secretaries have remained a slightly longer period of time. In 1955-64, fifty-two percent had been first secretary over five years, while the comparable percentage since 1964 has risen to 59 percent. Yet the turnover of all obkom secretaries has not changed at all. Almost two-thirds of the 150 obkom secretaries between 1965 and 1970 have held the same relative position less than six years.

The turnover rate in the 25 regions is almost identical to that recently found by another Western scholar for all obkom first and second secretaries in the Soviet Union.[49] Between 1966 and 1971, by Hough's calculations, individuals in 43 percent of all obkom first secretary positions and 67 percent of all obkom second secretary positions in the Soviet Union have been replaced. By interpolation to Table 5.2, these percentages match the 41 percent of first secretaries and 65 percent of all obkom secretaries in their positions less than six years between 1965 and 1971. More specifically, counting two changes in obkom first secretaries reported at the 1971 regional Party conferences and two more in late 1972,[50] the obkom first secretary in 14 of the 25 regions at the beginning of 1965 has been replaced at least once by the middle of 1973.

The turnover rate in the obkom secretariat since 1964 is both significant and misleading. It is significant only if one considers the period against which turnover is compared in Table 5.2. Recall that several of the obkom secretaries included in 1955-64 had been promoted to the obkom secretariat only as a result of the bifurcation reform of 1963-64. Others had only recently been appointed to the bureau either in 1958 or in 1961-62, at a time the 22d Congress had passed resolutions requiring a mandatory turnover ratio in all elected Party organs. Thus, the turnover for 1955-64 could be considered particularly high for obkom secretaries. Yet, even though the Brezhnev-Kosygin leadership has not been identified with reforms of the regional party, the fact remains that the turnover of obkom secretaries by continuous years has been as high as the Khrushchev period.

The turnover rate by itself is also misleading. The turnover of obkom secretaries overlooks the increasing average bureau tenure characteristic of many of the same obkom secretaries. The reader need only contrast the identical percentages over time for the two subgroups in Table 5.2 with the quite dissimilar percentages and increasing tenure of both already shown in Table 5.1. Turnover has been as rapid as the Khrushchev period, but a distinct pattern has emerged in replacing more obkom secretaries with "politically mature" officials within the established bureau leadership itself. Even isolated examples of apparent attempts to revitalize obkom secretariats since 1965 seem more symbolic of the underlying conservative commitment in leadership selection. Thus, at an obkom plenum in Odessa that reviewed the work of trade organizations and communal associations in early 1972, the regional leadership followed up their formal concern in upgrading consumer welfare policy with the election of Z. P. Nazarenko as the new obkom secretary.[51] While Nazarenko had never been elected to the Odessa bureau prior to this time and could be tentatively identified as a consumer specialist before her election, she is also unlikely to provide radical new departures in this policy area, having served the previous 18 consecutive years as deputy chairman of the oblispolkom.[52]

Attrition Rate

Table 5.3 compares the rate of attrition among bureau members for the Khrushchev and Brezhnev-Kosygin periods. Even more exactly, the comparison bears out the interpretation of a post-1964 retrenchment in bureau membership. With the evident increase in average tenure and internal rotation since 1964, there has been a significant increase in those retained on the bureaus. The attrition rate among bureau members has declined from 63 percent between 1958 and 1965 to 35 percent between 1965 and 1971. Not only have a higher proportion of all members in 1965 remained on the bureau, but a secondary consequence has been to prolong the membership of those from the 1958-59 bureaus. Thus, while 63 percent of those elected to bureaus in 1958-59 had already been replaced by 1965, only an additional 18 percent of the 1958-59 group have left the bureaus since 1965. Almost one-fifth (19 percent) of all 1958-59 members

TABLE 5.3

Attrition Rate of Bureau Members, 1958-71*
(in percent)

	1958-59 in 1965	1965-66 in 1971	1958-59 in 1971
Total	63	35	81
Urban change			
Low regions	62	41	83
High regions	66	29	78
Union-republic			
Russian regions	64	33	79
Ukrainian regions	59	39	84

*The percent of individuals in obkom bureaus at the beginning of each time period not in obkom bureaus by beginning of terminal year in each time period.

Source: Compiled by the author.

continue to hold some bureau position through the end of 1970.* It is ironic to note that several of these bureau members themselves had been new recruits promoted in 1958-61. Their election at that time was heralded along with other Party reforms as an attempt by Khrushchev to rejuvenate regional leadership. Now many of them hold on to the most important bureau positions and, by their retention on the bureaus, testify to the limited opportunities available for a new generation of recruits to change the present regional leadership in 1971.

The decline in the attrition rate and its potential negative impact upon regional policy can be readily observed in the Russian region of Saratov. In Saratov, the attrition rate has declined from 6 of 13 members in 1958-65 to only 3 of 10 in 1965-71. Three of the seven original members through 1965 have also been retained in their same offices through the election of the new obkom bureau in early 1971. The dominant continuity of policy leadership since 1964 is even more evident by the importance of their policy positions: A. I. Shibaev, obkom first secretary since 1959;[53] V. Ya. Gerasimov, obkom second secretary since he replaced Shibaev in that position in 1959;[54] and A. P. Bochkarev, while apparently retired by mid-1971, oblispolkom chairman since 1955.[55] While formally no longer a member of the bureau by 1970, even V. I. Chebotarevskii, the former sovnarkhoz chairman of Saratov between 1958 and 1965, continues to exercise a direct influence in Saratov regional policy as chief of the Volga material-technical supply administration.[56]

Even those changes that have occurred in Saratov after 1964 have only tended to maintain bureau continuity. Two instructive examples are the capital gorkom first secretary and the chairman of the oblast trade-union council. P. G. Rodionov, capital gorkom first secretary since 1965, was replaced in 1970 by V. F. Trofimov, already a candidate member of the bureau at that time as director of the Party organizational department.[57] N. I. Fedulov, the 1970 chairman of the oblast trade-union council, was not included among the 10 identifiable bureau members in 1965-66 and had only been elected to this position in 1967-68.[58] Yet Fedulov had previously been a member of the Saratov bureau as far back as 1961. Ironically, as director of the Party organizational department, Fedulov at that time had written an article for Partiinaia zhizn' in which the Saratov region was cited as a model of constant leadership renewal to be emulated by other local Party organs.[59]

---

*Through 1973, only an additional 6 of 31 1958-59 bureau members who could be identified have been removed from the bureaus.

186

As Table 5.3 further indicates, the direction of change in the attrition rate has been constant within a certain range for all regional parties. The four regional classifications have a higher number of bureau members from 20 to 37 percent retained in 1965-71 than in 1958-65. Yet, within each regime period, at least some percent variation appears to be associated with particular environmental characteristics. Russian and high urban regions had a slightly higher attrition rate during the Khrushchev regime and by 1971 turned out a lower percentage of the original 1958 bureau members. Conversely, Ukrainian bureau members have been replaced at a higher rate during the Brezhnev-Kosygin regime. And, most significantly, low urban bureaus since 1964 have been replaced at a 12 percent higher rate than high urban bureaus.

The particular variation between low and high urban regions since 1964 deserves some guarded speculation on the intent and underlying significance of the attrition rate, for many of the defined low urban regions are at the same time the principal agricultural producing areas of the Soviet Union. Two assumptions could be made: The difference in the attrition rate for 1965-71 has been deliberate and not random; and the bureau change has been initiated to some extent in all regions by the collective Brezhnev-Kosygin leadership and has reflected their policy priorities. If these assumptions are valid, then, the concern for capable leadership in the agricultural sector and increased regime demands for grain and livestock production have appeared to override the general conservative reluctance to alter the composition of regional Party bureaus.

If we recall the conclusions reached in previous chapters, this proposition seems to be supported. In 1970, the same low urban regions considered 17 percent more cadre-organizational problems at obkom plenums than did high urban regions. In several regions, the replacement of directing Party leadership like the first secretary in Kursk and subsequent personnel changes were directly linked to agricultural failures. Indeed, on a comparative basis, the attrition rate of bureau members in such key agricultural regions as Kursk, Belgorod, Tambov, Orel, and Smolensk has almost been as high in 1965-71 as in 1958-64.* In Kursk alone, the attrition rate actually increased from 40 to 44 percent in 1965-71, and four different obkom agriculture secretaries have been elected to the bureau between 1965 and 1971. At the initial time of their election, the last three secretaries were recruited from positions outside the bureau or only after

---

*As a composite of the five regions, the attrition rate was 56 percent in 1958-64 and 50 percent in 1965-71.

a very brief tenure on the bureau.* Therefore, the higher 12 percent attrition rate in low urban regions would indicate a very major priority has been assigned to agricultural problems by the Brezhnev-Kosygin regime. The Party reforms introduced under Khrushchev, while affecting a much higher replacement of regional Party leadership, were implemented in a less selective manner, perhaps suggesting Khrushchev's preoccupation in revitalizing both agricultural and industrial policy guidance by the Party at the local level.

Under Khrushchev, the reforms were also implemented on a basis to favor Ukrainian over Russian bureaus by a lower attrition rate of 5 percent. Since his overthrow, though, the trend has actually reversed and Ukrainian bureau members have been replaced at a 6 percent higher rate than Russian bureau members. In two of the Ukrainian regions, Dnepropetrovsk and L'vov, the attrition rate has actually increased in 1965-71 over the comparable 1958-65 period.† At the same time the attrition rate of 1958-59 bureau members has been higher in Ukrainian than Russian regions (84 to 79 percent).

The higher attrition rate of Ukrainian bureaus in the post-Khrushchev period appears to contradict previous findings. In particular, the average tenure of Ukrainian bureau members (See Table 5.1) and their consecutive years in the same office (See Table 5.2) are both higher than in Russian regions. This seeming incongruity may be reconciled in part by examining more closely the actual impact of attrition since 1964. Sixteen of the twenty-nine 1965 bureau members replaced in the Ukraine entered the bureaus before 1960. In contrast, of those Ukrainian members from 1965 who remained on the bureaus through 1970, less than 30 percent dated their first election to the bureau before even 1962. Forty-six percent alone were new recruits elected to the bureau for the first time during the bifurcation reform of 1963-64 and retained in the bureaus after reunification in December 1964. Subsequently, many senior bureau members in the Ukraine have been replaced since 1964 with individuals whose medium tenure and consecutive years in office range from six to eight years by the end of 1970. In Russian regions, fewer 1963-64

---

*The last three agricultural secretaries with their tenure and position immediately prior to their election include A. F. Gudkov (1968-April 1970), director of Party organizational department (August 1967-January 1968); D. V. Kamynin (April 1970-April 1971), director of obkom agricultural department (1968-70); and I. Ye. Boiko (April 1971-), instructor of Central Committee agricultural department (1970).

†In Dnepropetrovsk, the attrition rate has increased from 50 to 56 percent; in L'vov, from 54 to 56 percent.

recruits were kept on after 1964, and a higher proportion of senior pre-1960 members have remained in office.

In Ukrainian regions, 1970 bureaus are typically more dominated by individuals originally recruited to regional leadership during or immediately prior to the 1963-64 bifurcation reform. In Russian regions, the 1970 bureaus are typically split in composition between a senior pre-1960 group and those whose first election is identified with the Brezhnev-Kosygin regime. The higher proportion of post-Khrushchev recruits in Russian regions will be quite evident in later tables. For, as we shall see, the greatest change in bureau composition between the two regimes has occurred in Russian regions.

Turnover and Change Indices

The increased proportion of new recruits in Russian bureaus after 1964 also raises several problems for the researcher in interpreting political adaptation at the regional Party level. One of the most difficult interpretative problems can be seen in the kinds of bureau positions with the highest turnover in the post-Khrushchev period. For, while several new Russian members have indeed been elected after 1964, many hold what could only be considered as the lowest-ranking positions in the obkom bureaus. In the Russian region of Saratov, as an example, 9 of the 11 new bureau members after 1964 were elected for the first time as oblast Komsomol first secretary, chairman of the oblast trade-union council, director of the obkom Party organizational department, and editor of the oblast newspaper. If the question for the researcher is turnover in the total membership of the obkom bureau, then the importance even of these lower-ranking positions should not be discounted. On the other hand, one could seriously question the actual extent of meaningful change in Russian bureaus since 1965. Very few of the same new Russian recruits were elected for the first time as obkom secretary, chairman of the oblispolkom, or first secretary of the industrial capitals. With due allowance for slight differences in status among regional bureaus, these seven positions would correspond in most regions to the highest-ranking offices by prestige and actual administrative importance.

An important distinction could be made between these seven positions and the remaining bureau members. The obkom secretaries control the regional Party apparat and through the appointment and supervision of lower Party cadres are ultimately responsible for the economic performance of the region; the chairman of the oblispolkom is the designated head of the regional government with its diverse agricultural, industrial, educational, and social welfare departments and administrations; and the first secretary of the capital gorkom directly supervises the largest number of industrial-construction enterprises in the regional economy. In contrast, the other bureau members have more limited responsibilities and political authority. As the leaders of the regional Komsomol or trade-union council, they supervise a narrowly defined constituency. Or, as the editor of the oblast newspaper, they occupy a position that gives them little direct administrative contact with the dominant economic policy concerns of the regional leaders. Because of the greater economic and political importance associated with these seven major positions,* individuals elected to them could be distinguished as a more relevant indicator of regional political adaptation. The proportion of bureau members newly elected to these seven positions would more clearly demonstrate the willingness of the regional party to recruit lower cadres directly into responsible positions of policy authority and regional influence. We might assume that lower cadres would evaluate their chances for career advancement not by the turnover in nominal bureau positions like the oblast Komsomol first secretary (a position in five regions with three or four different individuals elected between 1965 and 1971), but by the number of obkom secretaries, oblispolkom chairmen, or capital gorkom first secretaries who had never previously been elected to the bureaus or who were at a minimum promoted to these positions from lower bureau offices.

The problem is that the majority of these seven positions in 1970 are still held in Russian bureaus by senior bureau members, those previously defined as first elected to the bureaus before 1960. Only in Saratov we found that the obkom first secretary, obkom second secretary, and oblispolkom chairman have served continuously in

---

*A further indication of the comparative importance of these seven positions can be observed in the nonalphabetical rank listing of bureau members that accompanied 17 signed obituaries in the regional press of 1970. The individuals who held these seven positions were consistently listed as the first seven or eight signers on each obituary. The only apparent exception appears in eight of the obituaries in which the oblispolkom first deputy chairman is ranked seventh and the capital gorkom first secretary is dropped to eighth. Yet it is important to note that the remaining bureau positions (that is, Komsomol first secretary, chairman of the trade-union council, chairman of the control commission, director of Party organizational otdel, and so on) were consistently listed below these seven major positions. Given the very hierarchical nature of Soviet politics, the listing of officials in any set order would probably correspond to the considered importance of the positions.

the bureau at least since 1959. This concentration of senior members in the seven major positions is common in all Russian bureaus. Not only have the same individuals held these seven positions for several years, but also the tendency has been to recruit new individuals to these positions only from experienced members already on the bureau. The extent of internal rotation from the bureau into these positions conveys the general impression of a carefully regulated process of elite recruitment. Thus, Russian bureaus may actually have retained a high degree of leadership continuity by electing very few new recruits into the major policy-making positions in the region. The obvious question for the researcher is therefore twofold: How extensive has turnover in these seven positions been over the two regime periods, and, simultaneously, what proportion of bureau members have been elected for the first time to these seven positions? From this dual perspective, turnover and change are analytically distinct problems in interpreting regional bureau change.

Two composite indices of turnover and actual personnel change in the seven bureau positions are presented in Table 5.4. The turnover index measures on an interval scale the ratio of actual changes in each time period to the total number of potential changes. Potential changes are those that could have occurred if a new individual had been elected to each position in each year of the two time periods. The change index measures on a similar interval scale the ratio of outsiders elected to these seven positions for the first time against a denominator of potential new recruits. The denominator is based upon the total changes that occurred in each time period. The values of both indices range in value from 0.000 to 1.000. Higher numerical values on each scale indicate a higher turnover or personnel change in each time period.

The two scales provide a more exact basis from which to judge any change in obkom bureaus between the Khrushchev and the Brezhnev-Kosygin regime periods. Generally, the values on both indices strongly reaffirm the conservative trend identified with the post-1964 period in the previous tables. Both turnover and actual leadership renewal have declined to less than half the comparable ratios in 1958-64. Indeed, both indices actually underestimate the full extent of personnel change during the Khrushchev regime by excluding bureau members who already held one of the seven positions in 1962 but were merely reassigned another formal position during the bifurcation period. Similarly, although turnover and renewal have consistently declined in all four regional classifications, the higher ratio of renewal in low urban regions after 1964 again points to the major policy emphasis on the part of central leadership to recruit competent local leadership in the agricultural sector. Not only were one-tenth of all leadership positions in low urban regions

TABLE 5.4

Turnover and Change among Members in Seven Major
Bureau Positions, 1958-70

	Turnover Index[a]			Change Index[b]		
	1958/ 1964[c]	1965/ 1970	1958/ 1970	1958/ 1964[c]	1965/ 1970	1958/ 1970
Total	.233	.118	.178	.173	.084	.130
Urban change						
Low regions	.241	.141	.195	.182	.100	.144
High regions	.224	.096	.161	.163	.068	.116
Union republic						
Russian regions	.233	.120	.177	.169	.083	.127
Ukrainian regions	.232	.114	.181	.180	.085	.139

Note: Seven major bureau positions compared in all regions: obkom first secretary, obkom second secretary, three obkom specialist secretaries, oblispolkom chairman, first secretary of capital gorkom. Calculations include 369 total changes in these positions for 2,072 position-years from 1958 through 1970.

[a]The quotient obtained by dividing the actual changes in seven major bureau positions per year by potential changes that could have occurred in all seven positions per year. In each time period, the potential change was a product of seven times the number of years in the time period. For 1958-64, the denominator for each region would have equaled 57 position-years: 35 (7 x 5 years 1958-62) + 22 (8 obkom secretaries, 2 oblispolkom chairmen, and 1 capital gorkom secretary in 1963-64). For 1965-70, the total product for each region would have equaled 42 position-years: 7 x 6 years. For 1958-70, the total product for each region would have equaled 99 position-years: 57 + 42. The actual number of changes in all regions was then added and divided by the combined potential position-year changes to provide a quotient from 0.000 to 1.000 (turnover in each position for each year).

[b]The quotient obtained by dividing the number of individuals who had never held one of these seven positions prior to this election to the actual number of changes in the seven major bureau positions. Change index would range from 0.000 to 1.000 (total replacement of seven bureau positions by those who had never previously held one of these seven positions).

[c]Any individual elected to one of the bifurcated bureaus in January 1963 who had never been a member of the obkom bureau immediately prior to that appointment was considered a change between 1962 and 1963. All others were not considered a change if they were on the bureau in 1962 and were only elected to a different position on one of the two bureaus in 1963. Only 35 position-years were counted for regions not bifurcated in 1963-64 (Vologda, Trans-Carpathia, Tomsk, and Kaliningrad). In addition, only six offices were counted for Trans-Carpathia, the only region with four obkom secretaries between 1958 and 1970.

Source: Compiled by the author.

replaced from 1965 to 1971, but 23 percent of those newly assigned to these positions had never even been prior members of the obkom bureaus.

This seeming departure from rigid political stability already intimates a second contradictory dimension in the cadre policy of the Brezhnev-Kosygin leadership. The first dimension, quite clearly evidenced on a general basis in Tables 5.1-5.4, has shown a significant decline in the turnover of regional policy elites. By this sole criterion of turnover, the regional policy elites could be considered less potentially capable to formulate meaningful policy direction over problems arising in their immediate environments. The capability of regional leadership, however, cannot be prejudged solely on the basis of leadership turnover. If turnover has been more limited, perhaps the actual competency and background characteristics of those newly recruited to leadership after 1964 have been more carefully projected in terms of real policy needs and demands in their regions. However effective the wide-ranging turnover and renewal of the Khrushchev period may have been on the positive morale of lower cadres and officials, no less important would have been the ability of those newly elected leaders to understand and resolve policy problems and to cooperate with the same lower cadres and officials. In this sense, the higher turnover and renewal for low urban agricultural regions after 1964 in Tables 5.3 and 5.4 could suggest a second dimension of the Brezhnev-Kosygin period. While fewer new members as a total have been elected to the bureaus, have the backgrounds even of these few reflected a more calculated attempt to realign regional policy leadership with changing social forces and groups in their locales?

NOTES

1. Lt. General G. V. Sredin, LP, April 28, 1970, and candidate members of Ukrainian Central Committee, XXIV KPUkr. The director of Political Administration and candidate member of the Ukrainian Central Committee in 1966 was Y. Y. Mal'tsev. See XXIII KPUkr.

2. See biography of Admiral V. S. Sysoev upon nomination to the Supreme Soviet in KrP, June 3, 1970.

3. See biography of Admiral V. V. Mikhailin upon nomination to the Supreme Soviet in KaP, May 24, 1970.

4. See reference to G. N. Kiselev, deputy director of an unspecified sector of the All-Union Komsomol Central Committee, at oblast Komsomol conference reported in KaP, May 24, 1970.

5. With two exceptions (directors of the obkom agricultural and agitprop departments only in 1954-56), the official positions on the Volgograd bureau between 1954 and 1960 are the same as those

found for the 25 regional bureaus in 1970. See Philip Stewart, Political Power in the Soviet Union (New York: Bobbs-Merrill, 1968), pp. 98-99.

    6. Ibid., pp. 127-134.

    7. For documentation and an analysis of political dissent in the Ukraine since 1961 with specific reference to L'vov, Dnepropetrovsk, and the role of the KGB, see the review article by V. Swoboda in Soviet Studies 23, 4 (April 1972): 659-667.

    8. Jerry Hough, "The Party Apparatchiki," in H. Gordon Skilling and Franklyn Griffiths, eds., Interest Groups in Soviet Politics (Princeton University Press, 1971), pp. 47-92.

    9. Included among several examples of "agricultural" specialists in our sample are (1) A. F. Krivoshei (Belgorod), first deputy chairman of the oblispolkom (1955-64), obkom agricultural secretary (1965-70), and transferred back as deputy chairman in charge of agriculture (1970); for references, see delegates to Russian Supreme Soviet (I, March 3, 1955), agricultural conferences and articles (P, March 12, 1958; SKh, May 24, 1958 and May 22, 1959), articles as secretary (P, April 18, 1965 and PZh, July 13, 1968), and organizational change (BP, October 17-18, 1970); (2) Yu. V. Sedykh (Vologda), director of oblast agriculture (1965-66), first deputy chairman of the oblispolkom (1966), and obkom agricultural secretary (1968-71); for references, see articles (P, February 18, 1966 and I, September 28, 1966) and regional participation (KS, June 10, 1970); and (3) P. V. Guzenko (Kemerovo), obkom agricultural secretary (1956-62) and oblispolkom chairman (1963-72); for references, see biography (Kuz, May 19, 1970), award for agriculture (P, December 30, 1959), and articles (SKh, September 28, 1957 and SRos, July 26, 1972).

    10. Included among several examples of "cadre" specialists in our sample are (1) V. I. Popov (Yaroslavl'), oblast Komsomol first secretary (1959-61?) and director of obkom Party organizational department (1969-72); for references, see articles (KoP, February 23, 1960, SR, August 13, 1970, and P, April 9, 1969 and March 9, 1972); (2) A. P. Trutnev (Zaporozh'e), oblast Komsomol first secretary (1956-61), chairman of oblast trade-union council (1962-66), and obkom second secretary (1966-71); for references, see Komsomol plenums or articles (RU, January 19, 1957, PU, December 21, 1958), delegates at XXIII KPSS, and obkom plenums (PU, March 25, 1966, IZ, May 30, 1970, and RU, November 12, 1971); (3) A. K. Skomorokhin (Orel), director of obkom Party organizational department (1955-58) and chairman of the oblast trade-union council (1969-70?); for references, see PZh, no. 13 (July 1955), p. 29, criticism (CP, July 29, 1958), and regional participation (OP, July 31, 1970); and (4) F. P. Tkachenko (L'vov), director of Party organizational department (1961?) and director of the oblast MVD (1970?); for references, see article in PZh, no. 14 (July 1961) and regional participation in LP, September 22, 1970.

11. Included among several examples of "industrial" specialists in our sample are (1) M. Ye. Borodin (Yaroslavl'), first secretary of the Rybinsk gorkom (1957-59), first secretary of the Yaroslavl' gorkom (1959-62), and obkom industrial secretary (1963-65); for references, see V. Pavlov, Budni odnogo sovnarkhoza (Workdays of one sovnarkhoz) (Moscow: Profizdat, 1958), delegates at XXI and XXII KPSS, and articles (PZh, no. 16, August 1962, I, November 30, 1965); (2) L. P. Sidov (Rostov), director of the industrial-transport obkom department (1964? and 1970), first secretary of the Rostov gorkom (1965); for references, see Radio Rostov, January 19, 1965 and regional participation in VR, March 2, 1970; (3) K. A. Trusov (Khar'kov), first secretary of the Khar'kov gorkom (1954-63) and obkom industrial secretary (1965-71); for references, see Party conference (PU, December 29, 1954), delegates to Ukrainian Supreme Soviet (PU, March 3, 1955 and March 6, 1959), and obkom elections (PU, December 16, 1964, February 12, 1966, and January 31, 1971).

12. Included among several examples of "indoctrination" specialists in our sample are (1) V. Teslenko (Khar'kov), ideology secretary of the industrial obkom (1963-64) and editor of the oblast Russian-language newspaper (1965-70); for references, see articles (PU, July 9, 1964 and Sovetskaia kul'tura, June 27, 1963) and signature as editor (KrZ[Kh], February 1, 1965 and September 30, 1970); (2) N. Ye. Afanas'ev (Orel), director of obkom agitprop department (1958-60) and obkom ideology secretary (1961-70); for references, see criticism of Afanas'ev (SRos, July 29, 1958), participation in conference (SRos, September 8, 1961), and regional participation (OP, September 8, 18, and 29, 1970); and (3) N. R. Rumiantsev, obkom ideology secretary (1956-59) and oblispolkom deputy chairman in charge of indoctrination problems (1960?); for references, see Yaroslavl' reception (T, January 21, 1956), articles (SRos, October 16, 1957 and SKh, September 27, 1958), journalists' conference (Sovetskaia pechat', no. 3, 1959), and education award (UG, August 6, 1960).

13. As examples, (1) V. G. Furov (Novosibirsk), obkom ideology secretary (1956-60) (see articles in P, August 17, 1956 and Literaturnaia gazeta, November 23, 1957 and April 9, 1959) and deputy chairman of the USSR Council on Religious Affairs (appointment in I, February 13, 1966); (2) V. Ye. Malanchuk (L'vov), obkom ideology secretary (1963-67) (see ideological conferences in P, November 27, 1963 and PU, January 7, 1964), deputy minister of Ukrainian Republic Higher and Specialized Secondary Education (1967-72) and ideology secretary of the Ukrainian Central Committee (1972-   ) (see biography in PU, October 11, 1972); and (3) V. K. Grudinin (Kaliningrad), editor of the oblast newspaper (1958?) (see article in Sovetskaia pechat, no. 4, 1958) and first deputy chairman of RSFSR State Commission on the Press (1964-71) (see articles in CP, October 2, 1964 and Knizhnaia torgovlia, no. 8, 1971).

14. John A. Armstrong, The Soviet Bureaucratic Elite: A Case Study of the Ukrainian Apparatus (New York: Praeger Publishers, 1959), pp. 142-150; and Yaroslav Bilinsky, The Second Soviet Republic— The Ukraine after World War II (New Brunswick, N. J.: Rutgers University Press, 1964). See, in particular, Bilinsky's discussion of potential localist orientations among Ukrainian regional leaders, pp. 226-263.

15. Leonid Brezhnev, XXIV KPSS, vol. 1, p. 125; A. Vodolazskii, "Leninskie printsipy partiinogo rukovodstva v deistvii" (The Leninist principles of Party leadership in action), K, no. 2 (January 1971), p. 46; I. Koval, "Ulushat' podbora, podnimat' otvetstvennost' kadrov" (To improve the selection and to raise the sense of responsibility of cadres), PZh, no. 11 (June 1970), p. 32-33.

16. A. Skochilov, "Sobliudaia Leninskie printsipy podbora i vospitaniia kadrov" (Observing the Leninist principles of the selection and upraising of cadres), PZh, no. 3 (February 1971), pp. 21-24; P. A. Leonov, "Razvitie XXIV s"ezdom KPSS Leninskikh printsipov raboty s kadramia" (The development by the 24th Congress CPSU of the Leninist principles of work with cadres), K, no. 18 (December 1971), p. 52.

17. See biographies of Skriabin in 1958 Deputaty and 1962 Ezhegodnik. On early career in Zaporozh'e, see Istoriya mist i sil Ukrains'koi RSR: Zaporizhs'ka oblast' (History of the cities and villages of the Ukrainian Soviet Socialist Republic: Zaporozh'e Oblast) (Kiev: AN URSR, 1970), pp. 46-47.

18. For Vsevolozhskii, see biography in IZ, June 5, 1970; for Mokrous, see list of deputies to Ukrainian Supreme Soviet (PU, March 3, 1955), obkom election (PU, December 21, 1955), and article (PU, November 18, 1954); for Timoshenko, see obituary in PU, March 10, 1963 and election in PU, December 21, 1955.

19. Vsevolozhskii, as second secretary of the Lenin raikom in the capital Zaporozh'e (biography in IZ, June 5, 1970); and Timoshenko, as director of the obkom agricultural department (obituary in PU, March 10, 1963).

20. PU, August 17, 1962. For biography of Titarenko, see IZ, June 5, 1970 and 1966 Ezhegodnik.

21. See obituary in PU, March 10, 1963. Domchenko was agriculture secretary from October of 1963, according to U.S. State Department, Biographic Directory of Soviet Officials (Washington, D.C.: Government Printing Office, 1964).

22. Even of these three, N. P. Kitsenko, the ideology secretary in the agricultural obkom, had been a former member of the bureau prior to 1962 as editor of the oblast newspaper. Technically, he could be considered a new bureau member in 1963 only because he had been demoted from the bureau in 1961 to director of the obkom agitprop

department. See reference to Kitsenko among those awarded on commemoration of 50th anniversary of Pravda in Vedomosti SSSR (March-
May 1962).

23. The three obkom secretaries: L. F. Yefremova (fem.),
industry secretary (1958-64) (see specific elections in PU, February
7, 1960, September 16, 1961, and January 20, 1963); A. S. Sherstyuk
(fem.), ideology secretary (1957-60) (see ideological conferences,
articles, and reports in PU, July 28, 1957, December 12, 1957, May
17, 1958, October 11, 1958, August 26, 1959; election in PU, February
7, 1960); and V. A. Slobodchenko, second secretary (1958-64) (see
award by Brezhnev in Zaporozh'e in PU, May 17, 1958; delegates to
Ukrainian Supreme Soviet in PU, March 6, 1959 and March 7, 1963;
obkom elections in PU, February 7, 1960 and September 16, 1961).

24. See biography in IZ, June 5, 1970.

25. See report at Ukrainian CC Komsomol plenum (PU, January
19, 1957), article (PU, December 21, 1958), election (KoP, January
4, 1958), delegates at XXIII KPSS, and election as second secretary
(PU, March 25, 1966). Trutnev was reported to have been replaced
as second secretary in RU, November 12, 1971.

26. See obkom elections (PU, September 16, 1961 and January
20, 1963), articles and ideological conferences (UG, September 2,
1965; Krasnaia zvezda, December 31, 1965; P, October 18, 1966 and
January 8, 1969; IZ, August 7, 1970; I, June 20, 1973).

27. See election as sovnarkhoz chairman (PU, October 11, 1961),
as industrial oblispolkom chairman (PU, January 25, 1963), and as
industry secretary (PU, December 16, 1964, February 10, 1966).
Prior to his election, Skliarov was deputy chairman of the oblispolkom
(see deputies in Vedomosti SSSR, no. 12, 1956) and deputy chairman
of the sovnarkhoz (article in EG, July 19, 1961).

28. Yu. A. Ignatov (1967-70) and V. Solomakha (1970). Ignatov
was first secretary of the Tokmaksk raikom in 1966 (delegates at
XXIII KPSS) and was last cited as first deputy chairman on January
28, 1970 (IZ). Solomakha was released as first secretary of the
Kiubyshev raikom on June 8, 1970 (IZ) and identified as first deputy
chairman of the oblispolkom by an article on September 20, 1970 (IZ).

29. B. I. Ivanov, Komsomol first secretary from 1968 to 1972.
Ivanov was a Komsomol secretary of the oblast committee prior to
his election as first secretary and replaced G. P. Kharchenko, who
became first secretary of the Lenin raikom, retaining his position
as candidate member of the obkom bureau in that second position.
See KomZ (June 6, 1968) and IZ (January 25, 1970).

30. Ye. A. P'iankov (1968-   ). P'iankov was first secretary
of the Ordzhonikidze raikom in the capital Zaporozh'e and replaced
I. V. Malyi as capital gorkom first secretary in 1967-68 (for reference
to P'iankov see article in PZh, no. 1, January 1966, p. 49).

31. For oblispolkom chairman of Odessa, see article (SKh, March 22, 1958), election (PU, January 25, 1963), and address (PU, December 20, 1967). Khorunzhii replaced F. Ya. Mokrous (see above, note 18), who either died or retired soon after his last appearance at a plenum of the Ukrainian Central Committee (PU, December 30, 1967).

32. For election in Zaporozh'e, RU, November 12, 1971; as first secretary of the Lisichansk gorkom, delegates at XXIII KPSS.

33. See above, note 22. As obkom secretary, see U.S. State Department, Biographic Directory of Soviet Officials (Washington, D.C.: Government Printing Office, 1964); as deputy chairman, see participation in ideological conference (IZ, January 9, 1970).

34. See article in PU, May 10, 1964 and regional participation in IZ, March 15, 1970.

35. See PZh, no. 1 (January 1958), p. 25; list of delegates to Ukrainian Supreme Soviet in PU, March 6, 1959; and regional participation in IZ, February 14, 1970.

36. P. I. Krasnikhin, obkom agriculture secretary of Saratov in 1961 (article in SZh, October 14, 1961) and director of oblast agriculture from 1966 (delegates at XXIII KPSS; article in SZh, March 18, 1967; and K[S], June 6-7, 1970); V. F. Dzhugalo, obkom agriculture secretary of L'vov between 1954 and 1959 (criticism at L'vov plenum in RU, June 2, 1955; election in PU, December 20, 1955 and January 12, 1958) and agricultural deputy chairman (LP, September 21, 1970). M. K. Yevseev, obkom agriculture secretary of Khar'kov between 1955 and 1964 (elections in PU, December 13, 1955, January 14, 1958, February 9, 1960, and January 10, 1963; article in PZh, no. 13 [July 1955]) and rector of the Khar'kov Institute for the Mechanization and Electrification of Agriculture (KrZ[Kh], September 23, 1970).

37. See obituary of K. S. Kovalenko in PU, December 19, 1971.

38. S. M. Pilipets, first secretary from 1956 through early 1960 (election in P, February 4, 1956, award for agriculture in P, December 30, 1959) and deputy chairman of the Kalinin oblispolkom (award in Vedomsti RSFSR, February 4, 1971). N. A. Tregubov, industry secretary from 1957 to 1960 (article in SRos, April 18, 1957) and chairman of the obkom Party commission (award in Vedomosti RSFSR, March 6, 1968). On speculation of the January 1960 workers' riot that resulted in Pilipets's ouster as first secretary, see Michel Tatu, Power in the Kremlin: From Khrushchev to Kosygin (New York: Viking Press, 1970), p. 115, footnote 2.

39. V. S. Yevseev, obkom second secretary from 1964 through 1966 (punishment to coal mine director in P, November 11, 1964; article in T, July 31, 1965; and delegates at XXIII KPSS) and in 1970 director of the Southern Kuzbass Coal Combine (main reporter at obkom plenum in Kuz, June 10, 1970).

40. L. I. Maiakov, obkom second secretary in 1960-62 (obkom plenum in SRos, March 16, 1961; delegates at XXII KPSS; and M, June 26, 1962) and in 1970 deputy director of the North Caucasus Construction Administration (VR, July 22, 1970).

41. Y. P. Kochetkov, Komsomol first secretary in 1966 (delegates at XXIII KPSS) and secretary of the Saratov Aviation Plant Party committee (K[S], February 28, 1970).

42. G. D. Korotaev, obkom second secretary of Kostroma (delegates at XXI KPSS; article in Lesnaia promyshlennost', January 21, 1960) and oblast director of commerce in Kursk (KuP, January 7, 1970 obkom plenum).

43. As pertinent examples, (1) G. T. Fokin, obkom ideology secretary of Kirov (article in P, January 17, 1964) and chairman of the oblast committee on radio and television (KiP, January 27, 1970); (2) Z. F. Dubrovnina, obkom ideology secretary of Volgograd (Volgograd delegation in P, May 25, 1963 and article in I, September 16, 1964) and ideology secretary of the Volgograd gorkom (Sovetskaia Belorussiia, May 27, 1967, p. 1; reporter at ideological plenums in VP, June 27 and September 16, 1970); (3) A. F. Vasil'ev, chairman of the Briansk industrial oblispolkom (deputies to RSFSR Supreme Soviet in I, March 7, 1963) and industrial deputy chairman of the oblispolkom (industrial conferences and plenums in BR, January 15 and February 10, 1970).

44. Stewart, Political Power in the Soviet Union, pp. 96-97.

45. The campaign to send obkom officials down to work in the agricultural districts is reflected in one article during this period by P. I. Doronin, obkom first secretary of Smolensk in 1955, "Umet' dobivat'sia konkretnykh rezul'tatov" (Knowing how to achieve concrete results), PZh, no. 10 (1955). In the article, Doronin cites specific examples of obkom officials, including the obkom Party Organs director and the oblast chairman of the trade-unions council, reassigned as raikom first secretaries in order to increase agricultural production.

46. As an example, M. I. Sivolap, chairman of the Nikolaev oblispolkom in 1951-53 (P, August 1, 1951 article) and director of the Odessa oblast agricultural administration (PU, November 12, 1954 and April 19, 1956).

47. Which they have been on occasion in 1970. N. A. Seroshtan, ideology secretary of the Khar'kov agricultural obkom in 1963-64 (election in PU, January 10, 1963 and article in I, July 17, 1963) was demoted after 1964 to director of the obkom department of science and educational institutions. In 1970, he was reelected to the obkom bureau as obkom ideology secretary (KrZ[Kh], January 16, 1970).

48. For the Ukraine, the new obkom secretariats elected at 1971 Party conferences are listed in Digest of the Soviet Ukrainian

<u>Press</u>, no. 3 (March 1971), pp. 1-2. Of interest, the only change from prior secretariats in 1970 was the obkom ideology secretary elected in Odessa: L. V. Gladkaia was replaced by A. P. Cherednychenko, until that time director of the obkom science and educational institions department. See the discussion of the Odessa party in Chapter 2, pp. 82-87.

49. Jerry Hough, "The Soviet System: Petrification or Pluralism?" <u>Problems of Communism</u> 21, 2 (March-April 1972): 36.

50. According to <u>Pravda</u> (March 11, 1971), not reelected as first secretary at the January Party conferences were N. F. Vasil'ev of Belgorod and B. F. Petukhov of Kirov. Vasil'ev became first deputy chairman of the RSFSR Council of Ministers. In July 1972 (<u>PU</u>, July 5, 1972), G. I. Vashchenko of Khar'kov was promoted to first deputy chairman of the Ukrainian Council of Ministers. B. F. Korotkov of Perm' was replaced for reasons of "health," according to the plenum reported in <u>P</u>, November 24, 1972.

51. Kiev Radio, February 15, 1972 and <u>PU</u>, February 16, 1972.

52. For career references to Nazarenko, see Odessa conference in <u>I</u>, September 18, 1954 and article on housing in <u>I</u>, June 16, 1967.

53. See biography of Shibaev in <u>K(S)</u>, May 24, 1970.

54. See articles by Gerasimov in <u>EG</u>, August 7, 1960 and March 10, 1961; delegates at <u>XXII</u> and <u>XXIII KPSS</u>; regional participation in <u>K(S)</u>, March 29, 1970. Gerasimov was previously a member of the bureau as capital gorkom first secretary in 1954-55 (see citation in October, 1954 <u>PZh</u>).

55. See biography of Bochkarev in 1962 and 1966 <u>Deputaty</u>; oblast soviet reported in <u>SKh</u>, November 18, 1955; and regional participation in <u>K(S)</u>, March 1, 1970. Bochkarev was replaced in 1971 by N. S. Aleksandrov, the Party organizational director (see citation of Aleksandrov in <u>P</u>, June 4, 1971).

56. See articles and conference participation by Chebotarevskii in <u>P</u>, January 2, 1959; <u>EG</u>, March 16, 1961; <u>I</u>, June 25, 1964; delegates at <u>XXIII KPSS</u>; and participation in Saratov obkom plenum (<u>K[(S)]</u>, January 13-14, 1970).

57. See <u>K(S)</u>, February 27, 1970. For prior backgrounds of Rodionov and Trofimov, see delegates at <u>XXII</u> and <u>XXIII KPSS</u>.

58. Fedulov replaced V. I. Kiselev (himself a veteran <u>apparatchik</u> as former obkom first secretary of the Kalinin oblast through <u>1954</u>) sometime in 1967-68. The last reference to Kiselev appeared in delegates at the <u>XXIII KPSS</u>.

59. <u>PZh</u>, no. 15 (August 1961), pp. 113-119.

6

BACKGROUND AND
CAREER CHARACTERISTICS
OF OBKOM BUREAU MEMBERS,
1955-73

As the leader of the Soviet Communist Party, General Secretary Brezhnev would probably reject the interpretation that the Brezhnev-Kosygin regime has been less responsive in the recruitment of new members to local Party organs. Finding the conclusions on obkom bureaus in the previous chapter one-sided, Brezhnev would likely interject that the actual composition of local Party officials and not just the turnover of officials has been the principal concern in the period since he assumed direction of the Party. Indeed, a revitalized and strengthened local Party leadership was a dominant theme in the Central Committee report delivered by Brezhnev at the 24th Party Congress in 1971. Looking back over the report period between Congresses, Brezhnev in fact reviewed both problems and advances in the quality of local Party leadership.

On the negative side, Brezhnev criticized the slackening of Party discipline in some local Party organs, the decline of internal Party democracy, and the reluctance of Party leaders to take views into account from a broader spectrum of their fellow Party aktiv.[1] To Brezhnev, several examples could be cited of local Party leaders who had become isolated from their own Party organizations and had failed as a consequence to complete political and economic goals assigned to them. Passive or unwilling to assume initiative on their own, too many local Party leaders shirked personal responsibility, were intolerant of criticism by Party members of their actions, and were no longer representative of lower cadres and workers. Many local leaders actually seemed more concerned about the "external effect" of their actions than the successful completion of their responsibilities.[2] Among local Party leaders who had failed to meet expectations in the preceding six years, Brezhnev singled out for particular blame the secretaries of primary Party organizations, a Party level that had been under continuous criticism since the Central Committee resolution on Yaroslavl' in 1969.[3]

To remedy the economic and political problems of local Party leadership, Brezhnev proposed several reforms. One would continue to combine many primary Party organizations into enlarged or so-called unified Party organizations. Two consequences would be expected from the reform. For one, the unified Party organizations would parallel the restructuring of economic relationships in the industrial realm. Since 1968, several industrial and scientific enterprises with related productive responsibilities had been merged into production "agglomerates" (ob"edineniia). The agglomerates, often extending across nominal district or regional territorial divisions, coordinate under one single management the industrial production, research facilities, and marketing outlets of previously decentralized economic units. The restructuring of Party organization was therefore a logical extension on the political level of administrative-economic change: Party organizations have always paralleled the size and territorial dimension of administrative units they supervise.[4] A skeptic would also deduce a second underlying consequence. The positions of several criticized secretaries in industrial Party committees would be phased out by merging the local committees into the unified organizations.[5] As a second reform, Brezhnev announced the future recall of Party cards to review the qualifications of all Party members.[6] Closely tied to his criticisms of local Party leadership, the recall of Party cards, the first such action in the Soviet Union in 17 years, would provide a further pretext to screen out those local leaders considered unrepresentative of lower cadres or unable to fulfill economic tasks.

On the positive side, Brezhnev also perceived certain improved characteristics that had emerged among local Party leaders between Party Congresses. The average composition of local elected organs had changed significantly. Many cadres had been elected to local Party organs for the first time. A representative cross-section of Soviet society, the transformed local leadership was now made up of more workers and kolkhozniki, all social strata and groups, all nationalities, and all state, economic, cultural, and mass work sectors.[7] As the All-Union secretary for cadre policy Kapitonov later summarized the extent of personnel change, local Party organs had become a "personification" (olitsevorenie) of the Party's collective will, combining the most talented, politically mature, knowledgeable, and organizationally capable individuals from all strata and groups in Soviet society.[8] In his report Brezhnev cited two specific examples that illustrated the increased representative nature of local elected organs. By 1971, of all local Party secretaries, chairmen of central and republic ministries, and chairmen of local executive committees in the Soviet Union, 80 percent had begun their careers as workers and collective farmers. And, since 1966, new first secretaries of local Party organs were deliberately recruited from "local" natives in the same oblasts, krais, and Union-republics. Only in "exceptional cases" had outsiders been assigned as first secretaries in local Party organs.[9]

Not only were Party leaders more representative of Soviet society by their social and demographic origins, but, as reported in the central Party periodicals, the many new recruits had brought added youth, educational background, and professional-technical training to the local Party organs. Thus, of all new urban and district secretaries elected at the 1968 Party conferences in the Soviet Union, 70 percent were under 40 years of age.[10] In the Ukrainian Republic, 99 percent of all obkom, gorkom, and raikom secretaries in 1971 had at least some higher education; and the proportion of Ukrainian chairmen in local executive committees with higher education had increased from 84 to 88 percent in 1966 to 97 percent in 1971.[11] In articles that applied Brezhnev's analysis of greater representation to specific local Party organs, the first secretary in the Crimean oblast pointed out that 145 of the 164 members of the Crimean obkom in 1971 had either a middle or higher education. In addition, several technical specialists had been deliberately recruited into Crimean urban and district Party committees since the 23d Congress.[12] In the Belgorod oblast, the first secretary could emphasize that the average age of oblast Party apparatchiki was only 44 years and that of gorkom-raikom secretaries, only 40 years.[13] And, in the Ul'ianovsk oblast, the first secretary reported that the percentage of Party apparatchiki with higher education had increased from 42 percent in 1966 to 53 percent in 1971. Several of the new apparatchiki were former engineers, agronomists, teachers, and other technical specialists.[14]

Of course, some positive evaluation of local parties is only to be expected in any Congress report or in articles written by local first secretaries themselves. Yet evidence from the backgrounds of bureau members in our own sample does appear to confirm a steady advancement in the educational and technical qualifications typical of bureau members elected after 1964. Thus, of 158 bureau members from the 1955-73 period, the absolute number with only a middle teknikum or Party education declined from 37 in 1955-64 to 17 in 1965-73. Nine of 74 post-1964 bureau members have attained a minimum candidate degree, and 15 completed their higher education at institutes in the two decades after Stalin died. In the Tambov region, as one example, three of the current bureau members elected after 1964 hold candidate degrees in economics and history.[15] The agricultural secretary in the Orel obkom holds a candidate degree in economics and was elected to the bureau for the first time in 1969.[16] When he was promoted to obkom second secretary in April of 1970, he was replaced on the secretariat by V. M. Antonov. Antonov, formerly the deputy chief engineer of the major Cherepovets Metallurgical Plant in Vologda, was a skilled technician awarded a state prize in 1967 for his development of a 2,000 cubic meter blast furnace.[17] A graduate in metallurgy from the Leningrad Polytechnical Institute in 1955, Antonov assumed the duties of industrial specialist in the Orel bureau. The Orel leadership made very immediate use of his expertise, for his specific duties after April included the chairmanship of an Orel scientific-research conference organized to propose technical innovations in the regional industry.[18]

Brezhnev and other local leaders have also cautioned against any rapid turnover in Party leadership under the doctrinally unassailable tenet of the "continuity of old and new leadership." Yet, even qualified with the need for "continuity" and structured in a Marxist-Leninist framework, the frequent references by Brezhnev and others to the changing composition of local officials could be seen as a commitment to political adaptation in the Party, the principal theoretical concern of our own study. Brezhnev and other leaders seem to be particularly concerned in convincing any disillusioned younger rank-and-file Party members that their opportunities to become Party leaders have not diminished since 1964. Whether an increasing number of younger Party members have actually been elected lower Party officials would require comparable data on the ages both of officials and the total Party membership in each region. In lieu of information on rank-and-file Party members in each region, however, we could still examine the characteristics of obkom bureau members with those typical of middle elite officials, the succeeding leadership stratum in the regional Party hierarchy. And, if Brezhnev's analysis was not just an attempt to justify the low turnover observed in the previous chapter, we would anticipate an increasing convergence of characteristics typical of bureau members and middle elite officials after 1964.

Bureau characteristics that would possibly evidence any such convergence are shown in Tables 6.1-6.11. With some important qualifications, the figures generally support Brezhnev's analysis. Although the low turnover has affected the composition of obkom bureaus, more bureau members after 1964 have been recruited from later Soviet generations; they are more closely tied by demographic and career origins to the regions in which they have been elected; and at least obkom first secretaries are more technically qualified than they were during the Khrushchev period.

TABLE 6.1

Year of Party Entry, 1955-73

| | Year of Party Entry (percent) | | | | | |
	1925-38	1939-41	1942-45	1946-52	1953+	N
Total bureau members, 1955-73	22	26	24	15	13	389
Urban change						
Low regions	20	23	29	13	15	217
High regions	23	31	19	17	10	172
Political regime						
1955-64	29	34	25	9	3	284
1965-73	7	22	28	22	20	230
Urban change (time)						
Low (1955-64)	29	30	30	8	3	152
High (1955-64)	30	38	20	10	3	132
Low (1965-73)	6	19	33	20	23	132
High (1965-73)	9	27	22	24	17	98
Union-rep. (time)						
Russian (1955-64)	31	39	21	7	2	170
Ukrainian (1955-64)	27	26	31	12	4	114
Russian (1965-73)	8	29	26	18	18	125
Ukrainian (1965-73	7	14	30	26	23	105
Obk. 1st sec's (time)						
1955-64	42	42	14	2	—	84
1965-73	7	48	31	10	5	42
All other sec's (time)						
1955-64	10	40	33	12	5	109
1965-73	5	21	31	30	14	81
Total middle political elite, 1958-73*	9	9	27	24	32	186

*The middle political elite are not distinguished by regime period, because almost all of them held positions before and after 1964. Their composite characteristics for 1958-73 are compared against those typical of bureau members in either regime period.

Source: Compiled by the author.

TABLE 6.2

Year of Birth, 1955-73

	Year of Birth (percent)					
	1900-09	1910-19	1920-29	1930-39	1940+	N
Total bureau members, 1955-73	32	49	18	2	—	198
Urban change						
Low regions	32	50	17	2	—	101
High regions	32	48	19	1	—	97
Political regime						
1955-64	36	48	15	1	—	176
1965-73	11	59	26	3	—	91
Urban change (time)						
Low (1955-64)	36	48	16	—	—	89
High (1955-64)	36	48	15	1	—	87
Low (1965-73)	11	57	28	4	—	46
High (1965-73)	11	62	24	2	—	45
Union-rep (time)						
Russian (1955-64)	34	51	14	1	—	118
Ukrainian (1955-64)	40	43	17	—	—	58
Russian (1965-73)	10	63	23	5	—	62
Ukrainian (1965-73)	14	52	34	—	—	29
Obk. 1st sec's (time)						
1955-64	44	49	6	—	—	79
1965-73	8	68	20	5	—	40
All other sec's (time)						
1955-64	10	61	27	2	—	59
1965-73	4	44	40	12	—	25
Total middle political elite, 1958-73	25	32	38	4	2	56

Source: Compiled by the author.

PARTY ENTRY AND BIRTH

Two of the most evident changes that have occurred since 1964 are the Party entry and birth periods of members, shown in Tables 6.1 and 6.2. In Table 6.1, subsequent to the overthrow of Khrushchev, the proportion of postwar and post-Stalin Party entrants has increased from a combined 12 to 42 percent of all bureau members, a direct result of an equivalent decline of 34 percent in those who entered the Party prior to 1942. Among all bureau positions, the most dramatic change can be seen among those who have been elected capital gorkom first secretaries. The proportion of gorkom first secretaries from the postwar and post-Stalin Party eras has increased from 3 of 29 in 1955-64 to 23 of 30 in 1965-73. There are fewer bureau members for comparison by year of birth in Table 6.2; but, within a more limited absolute number, the same pattern of change is repeated. The proportion of members born in the first decade of the century has declined from 36 to 11 percent with an equivalent increase in those born in the second and third decades.

At the same time, there has not been any concurrent rejuvenation of regional leadership. As the figures in Table 6.3 indicate below, the average age of members when first elected to the bureaus has increased almost four years; and, in 1970, bureau members alone are 8.4 years older as a group than those elected in 1955-64. The reason for this increasing average age can be inferred from the previous chapter. With the significant decline in turnover since 1964, several senior bureau members have been retained in the same

TABLE 6.3

Average Age of Bureau Members, 1955-73*
(number of bureau members in parentheses)

	1955-64	1965-73	1970
Total bureau members	44.8 (176)	48.6 (91)	53.2 (62)
Ukrainian regions	44.7 (58)	48.5 (29)	52.6 (16)
Russian regions	44.9 (118)	48.7 (62)	53.4 (46)

*Age when elected to bureau position in first year of either time period.

Source: Compiled by the author.

positions. Nineteen percent of those elected in 1958-59 have still
been retained on the bureaus through at least 1970. Not only are
these senior members 10-15 years older than they were in 1958-59,
but, by their continuance on the bureaus, there are fewer positions
open to new recruits from outside the bureaus since they lack the
essential "political maturity." Because of the conservative retrenchment, even those added after 1964 have typically been elected to the
bureaus much later in their careers than were the present senior
members when first elected in the Khrushchev period.

The increased age and later recruitment of new bureau members can even be seen by comparing the ages of those elected to comparable bureau positions in the same regions before and after 1964.
Thus, M. V. Vinogradov was already the obkom ideology secretary
at the age of 37, when first elected to the Smolensk bureau in 1957.[19]
In contrast, T. N. Yarovaia, the current obkom ideology secretary
of Smolensk, had to wait until she was 48 years old before she was
first elected to the same position and to the obkom bureau in 1966.[20]
D. I. Aleshkin, who later succeeded to the apparat of the All-Union
Party Control Commission, was given his first major regional political
assignment, when he was elected obkom ideology secretary of Belgorod
at the age of 42.[21] M. G. Sukontsev was not assigned the same position in Belgorod until he had become 48.[22] D. P. Komarova was given
primary responsibility for agricultural policy in the Briansk region,
when she was elected oblispolkom chairman and a member of the
obkom bureau for the first time at the age of 40 in 1960.[23] When
Komarova became the RSFSR minister of Social Security in December
1967, through internal rotation, she was actually replaced on the obkom bureau by G. G. Kon'kov, who was now made first deputy chairman
of the oblispolkom at 48.[24] And, B. V. Malinin, while only 36 when
first elected the Vologda obkom industry secretary in 1955, remained
on the bureau through 1970 as chairman of the people's control commission.[25] As a result, Malinin exemplifies those senior bureau
members over 50 who were not replaced after 1964 and contribute
by their presence to the increased aging of all bureau members in
1973.

An even more valid basis from which to judge the potential
growing isolation of bureau members from lower cadres and officials
is the actual length of Party tenure shown in Table 6.4. Drawn from
a larger absolute number of 389 bureau members, the figures clearly
illustrate the contradictory dimensions of cadre policy in the Brezhnev-
Kosygin period. On the one hand, bureau members after 1964 with
less than 21 years in full-time Party work almost exactly parallel
the percentage of those recruited under Khrushchev. Brezhnev and
other Party leaders could emphasize these figures to support their
contention that cadre policy since 1964 has not discriminated against

TABLE 6.4

Party Tenure and Election to Obkom Bureau, 1955-72[a]

	Years in Party (percent)							
	1-5	6-10	11-15	16-20	21-25	26-30	31+	N
Total bureau members, 1955-72	—	4	6	22	21	27	20	389
Political regime								
1955-64	—	3	6	22	34	19	17	284
1965-72	—	4	8	18	16	32	20	230
Urban change (time)								
Low (1955-64)	—	3	6	21	36	19	15	152
High (1955-64)	—	3	6	23	30	19	18	132
Low (1965-72)	1	4	10	18	17	34	17	132
High (1965-72)	—	5	6	18	16	31	23	98
Union-rep. (time)								
Russian (1955-64)	—	2	5	24	29	20	20	170
Ukrainian (1955-64)	—	4	8	19	40	18	12	114
Russian (1965-72)	—	6	6	15	14	36	23	125
Ukrainian (1965-72)	1	3	11	23	20	28	15	105
All sec's[b] (time)								
1955-64	—	2	7	20	37	18	15	172
1965-72	—	—	4	18	19	34	25	115
Seven major bureau positions[c] (time)								
1955-64	—	2	6	21	35	20	16	239
1965-72	—	1	6	20	20	32	21	174

[a]Counted are the number of years between Party entry and the last year in either time period in which elected bureau member.

[b]All obkom secretaries, includes all obkom first secretaries.

[c]Includes obkom first secretary, obkom second secretary, three specialist obkom secretaries, oblispolkom chairman, and first secretary of the capital gorkom.

Source: Compiled by the author.

the less experienced Party workers. In isolated cases, they could even point to individuals like A. V. Romantsov, who was elected for the first time to the Belgorod obkom bureau as oblispolkom chairman in 1971 after only 12 years in the Party.[26] The three oblispolkom chairmen who had preceded Romantsov and had been first elected during the Khrushchev period had been in the Party 22 to 26 years at the time of their election.* On the other hand, senior bureau members, distinguished in the table by those over 25 years in the Party, have significantly expanded since 1964 from 36 to 52 percent. This finding is even more telling, if one further considers that, as a result, 59 percent of all obkom secretaries elected since 1964 have been in the Party for a minimum of 26 years and only 4 percent for less than 16 years.

If bureau members are typically older and more politically experienced after 1964, the change in average Party entry and birth periods can also not be discounted. Any generational differences between the regional middle elite and the obkom bureaus have at least narrowed considerably. As the reader can see by comparing the two groups in Table 6.1, almost an identical proportion of the 186 middle political elite and the 230 bureau members in 1965-73 entered the Party in the three periods of 1925-38, 1942-45, and 1946-52. It is true that the two groups still vary significantly in certain categories of Party entry and birth. Thus, a much lower proportion of post-Stalin Party members have been elected to the obkom bureaus in 1965-73 than their average in the middle elite would merit on an equal basis (20 to 32 percent); Party members from the 1939-41 period are still overrepresented on the bureau to their comparable level in the middle elite (22 to 9 percent); and, by age in Table 6.2, those born after 1919 on the bureaus are almost one-half (29 to 44 percent) their comparable level in the middle elite. With these exceptions, the obkom bureau members are at least a more representative cross-section of lower Party cadres and state officials after than before 1964.

By environmental characteristics, low urban regions consistently have recruited a higher proportion of members from the 1942-45

---

*G. P. Kovalevskii (Party entry, 1930), a former oblispolkom chairman of Kursk (I, January 28, 1951, and P, October 3, 1953), was elected oblispolkom chairman of Belgorod at the time of the region's formation in 1954. A. V. Kovalenko (Party entry, 1931) succeeded Kovalevskii as chairman in 1957. M. D. Khitrov (Party entry, 1940), was elected oblispolkom chairman in 1962. The Party entry date of V. G. Kobzev, who served as oblispolkom chairman in the interim between Kovalenko and Khitrov, is unknown.

war period. Even more significantly, lower cadres and officials in Ukrainian regions have a much better opportunity to be elected bureau members at an earlier stage of their political careers than their counterparts in Russian regions. By collapsing the Party categories of all bureau members through and after 1941 in Table 6.1, we can see that Ukrainian bureaus as a total have a younger composite Party membership by 17 percent in both regime periods. As a direct correlate, in Table 6.4, Ukrainian bureaus have a fourth fewer members than Russian bureaus over 25 years in the Party and, in 1965-72, eleven percent more members under 21 years in the Party.

A typical example of the relatively younger Ukrainian members can be found in the industrially key region of Dnepropetrovsk in the Southeast Ukraine. In 1955-64, eleven of the 21 bureau members in Dnepropetrovsk had originally entered the Party during the war and only 7 prior to 1942. After 1964, the proportion of members from the war period has declined to 8 of 20 members, but the three from the 1955-64 bureau were replaced by individuals who entered the Party in the postwar and post-Stalin eras. More significantly, only three of the 20 members after 1964 entered the Party prior to 1942, and five of the nine postwar recruits were first secretaries of the major industrial centers in Dnepropetrovsk.

The general shift to later periods of Party entry and birth has not been limited just to the lower-ranking positions on the 25 regional bureaus. Prior to 1965, only 16 percent of all obkom first secretaries had entered the Party either during the war or during the interim between the reconstruction of the economy and the death of Stalin in 1946-52. Only 6 percent of all first secretaries had been born after the Bolshevik final victory in 1920. Thus few would have been too young to have participated as young adults in the purges of the 1930s. Yet, by 1973, of all first secretaries elected in the post-Khrushchev period 46 percent date their Party entry after 1941 and a fourth were born after 1919.

While there is an insufficient number by birth in Table 6.2 to draw any meaningful comparison, in Table 6.1 the proportion of combined postwar and post-Stalin Party members among all obkom secretaries has similarly increased from 17 to 44 percent. Furthermore, if bureau members after 1964 are more representative of the middle political elite, there has also been a growing convergence of obkom secretaries to all obkom bureau members. Table 6.1 shows that in the Brezhnev-Kosygin period 44 percent of all obkom secretaries to 42 percent of all bureau members entered the Party after 1946, 31 to 28 percent in the 1942-45 period, and 26 to 29 percent in the years prior to the war. Not unexpectedly, from our previous analysis of ideological policy in 1970, the one position in the obkom secretariat that proves the exception is the ideology secretary.

Reflective of its more isolated political role and low potential for career advancement, only 3 of 21 known ideology secretaries elected between 1955 and 1973 entered the Party after 1945. In contrast, 44 percent (17 of 39) of all known obkom second secretaries in the Brezhnev-Kosygin period began their Party careers after the war or Stalin's death.

Reference to the events identified with particular eras of birth and Party entry already suggests a second meaning that could possibly be inferred from the tables. Even though bureau members were older and more politically experienced as an average in 1965-73 than in 1955-64, the differences in Party entry and birth periods could signify an equally important shift in the prevalent values and attitudes of regional leadership since 1965. As previously noted in our analysis of obkom first secretaries, Western scholars assert that values and attitudes of all Party leaders actually may differ according to the period in which leaders were born or first entered the Party. The early political maturation of the personality is the underlying assumption in such studies. They assume a common set of early socializing experiences would have similarly affected everyone who was born in a certain decade of Soviet history, reached maturity, and entered the Party at the same relative time. These socializing experiences, in turn, would have motivated individuals in their very decision to enter the Party in varying periods. The motivating characteristics of new Party members would vary by time and would later appear in terms of distinct personality types particular to Party recruits in different generations of the Soviet population. Thus, Party leaders who were born and entered the Party in any common life span will project those early initial experiences and motivating characteristics in their later values and attitudes. Particular stress is placed upon those Party leaders who first became active in the Party during the height of the purges in the late 1930s, during the nationalistic aura of World War II, during the reconstruction postwar phase, or during the technological post-Stalin era.

Of course, the concept of Party generations and age cohorts, hypothetically defined by common historical experiences, rather than actual age, greatly simplifies a complex process of political socialization for any individual. Not only does it assume that early adult experiences will automatically carry over and determine later political attitudes and values, but it overlooks the probable impact of late adult socialization upon the individual, varying role expectations in political positions, and general personality changes associated with aging.[27] Older individuals elected to the obkom bureau may be a more cautious group by the very fact of their new political authority and age, even though as young Party recruits they may have shared in common the dominant freer attitudes of that past historical era.

Indeed, if nothing else, the early political careers of many prewar Party recruits should have instructed them in the virtue of flexibility in adapting to demands made upon them by central leaders. More than other Party generations, prewar recruits may be able to read signals of change emanating from the center and respond, even when the new policy directions run contrary to their own basic values and beliefs. In this light, the reader is reminded that in 1970 social welfare problems were considered at the same level in regions with the oldest and youngest obkom first secretaries; and scientific-technical elites actually participated more frequently in obkom plenums convened by the oldest obkom first secretaries.

Yet, whatever the questionable assumptions in analyzing generations and cohorts for the Soviet Union, the findings in Tables 6.1 and 6.2 do indicate that a larger number of postwar and post-Stalin recruits have entered the bureaus after 1964. If these new members, particularly those elected obkom secretary, continue to reflect in any way their early experiences and motivations, the composite bureau membership after 1964 may be less ideological, more nationalistic, and more economically pragmatic. These traits may be especially characteristic of Ukrainian bureaus, in which 79 percent of all bureau members entered the Party after 1941.

The conclusion would also have to take into account a much slower change in the composition of obkom first secretaries. Even after 1964, of all first secretaries, 55 percent were still recruited from the prewar generation, and 76 percent were born before 1919 and were old enough as young adults to have participated actively in the purges of the 1930s. In addition to the increased age and Party tenure of all bureau members by 1973, this duality in the background of first secretaries and the other bureau members may be a further sign of what Brezhnev meant as the "continuity" of old and new regional leadership.[28]

DEMOGRAPHIC AND CAREER ORIGINS

On the basis of the percentages in Tables 6.1 and 6.2, the increasing similarity of post-Khrushchev bureau members and the middle political elite may also contribute importantly to a harmony of interests and working relationships in the regional work force. We could assume that, with common backgrounds formed by their early adult experiences, both groups may come to evaluate problems and to propose solutions from more identical orientations. Continuity in policy-making and daily implementation at all levels of the regional party would thus be assured. Moreover, with the influx of later age and Party generations into the regional bureaus since 1965, the middle elite may realistically identify their own future political careers more closely with those of the regional bureau elite. The middle elite at least may perceive that the regional bureau leadership is more conciliatory to their own policy views and more sympathetic to their own career aspirations. Despite differences that normally correspond to rank and position in a political bureaucracy like the regional party, both bureau members and the lower middle elite could share a more similar understanding of the region because of their common backgrounds.

However a common background may facilitate regional harmony and understanding, birth and Party entry periods of bureau members are only two of several relevant background characteristics. Equally important are the actual direct ties of the current bureau members with the middle political elite and with the very regional locales in which they have been elected. As previously noted, no less a political figure than General Secretary Brezhnev has explicitly recognized the importance of local recruitment into regional leadership positions. In his enumeration of positive changes in local Party organs at the 24th Party Congress, Brezhnev pointed to the number of "local" workers who had been deliberately elected as first secretary of Union-republic, krai, and oblast Party committees since 1966 with the "assignment" by the center of outsiders to these positions only in "exceptional cases."

For a Western scholar of regional parties, Brezhnev's specific reference to a cadre policy of more "local" workers is intriguing for its ambiguities. For one, what specific criteria does Brezhnev have in mind in defining a first secretary as a "local" worker? Is a "local" worker one who was born and educated in the same region in which he has been elected first secretary and could therefore qualify as an actual native of the region? Is a "local" worker one who has extensive occupational experience at lower positions in the regional hierarchy and is thus more familiar with local problems than an outsider? Or, in defining a "local" worker, does Brezhnev merely mean one who was originally assigned to the regional middle elite late in his career, was promoted to the obkom bureau, and can now nominally be considered a "local" first secretary only because he was recruited from within the region and the regional bureau? In this light, the tables in Chapter 5 and the figures in Table 6.4 have already revealed an increase in internal rotation among bureau members and a conservative trend to recruit obkom secretaries and first secretaries only from those with long political tenure on the bureaus. Thus, given the congenital distrust of "localism" by central authorities and the frequent geographical shifts of local leaders to prevent too close an association with a region, the first and second criteria would represent fundamental changes in Party cadre policy;

the third, by itself, would represent only a deceptive play on the term "local worker" and a justification for the already evident reduction in bureau turnover.

Nor did Brezhnev attempt to rationalize his statement by explaining what positive effects were perceived to follow from assigning more "local workers" to the position of first secretary in local Party organs. Indeed, Brezhnev was careful to limit his reference only to "local" first secretaries, not to all members of elected Party organs like the obkom bureaus. Therefore, by inference, is one to conclude that the other regional leaders in the obkom bureaus are not "local workers" and that the unstated circumstances dictating the recruitment of "local" first secretaries do not apply to all bureau members? Or, was the omission unintentional and has there been an equivalent change since 1965 in recruiting more "local" personnel to all obkom bureau positions?

While the specific rationale, definition, and extent of local recruitment remain unanswered by Brezhnev's brief reference in the Congress report, a trend toward local recruitment need not signify any real lessening of central control. With Brezhnev's qualification that outsiders may still have to be "assigned" to regions in "exceptional cases," it can still be safely assumed that all first secretaries will fall under the careful scrutiny and confirmation of the All-Union Secretariat before their election. Yet, if the Brezhnev reference does indicate a fundamental modification of traditional cadre policy in the regions, central authorities at least may now deliberately attempt to select bureau members only from those local middle elite officials.

In order to test Brezhnev's reference to "local workers," the demographic and career origins of all bureau members are shown in Tables 6.5-6.8. In an ascending order of significance, the tables correspond to what were previously delineated as the three alternative criteria Brezhnev may have intended in his definition of "local workers": the geographical location and occupation immediately prior to election on the obkom bureau; the prevalent occupational locale of bureau members; and the combined native origins by birth, education, and career experience of bureau members. By a comparison of the percentages on each of these criteria, we can judge the actual increase of local recruitment since 1965 and deduce a more specific meaning for the term "local workers."

Geographical Locale and Occupation

By the first criterion of previous geographical locale and occupation, the data in Tables 6.5 and 6.6 clearly evidence a greater

215

TABLE 6.5

Geographical Location Immediately Prior to First
Election to Obkom Bureau, 1955-73

	Location (percent)			
	Inside Region	Inside Regional Area[a]	Outsider[b]	N
Total bureau members, 1955-73	53	11	37	301
Urban change				
Low regions	58	10	32	165
High regions	46	12	42	136
Political regime				
1955-64	44	12	45	213
1965-73	65	10	25	171
Urban change (time)				
Low (1955-64)	51	10	38	115
High (1955-64)	35	13	52	98
Low (1965-73)	67	9	23	98
High (1965-73)	63	11	26	73
Union rep. (time)				
Russian (1955-64)	35	10	55	136
Ukrainian (1955-64)	60	14	26	77
Russian (1965-73)	64	10	26	105
Ukrainian (1965-73)	68	9	23	66
Obk. 1st sec's (time)				
1955-64	16	20	64	74
1965-73	39	12	49	41
All other sec's (time)				
1955-64	65	5	29	78
1965-73	71	12	17	66

[a]"Regional area" refers to historic-economic regions into which Soviet and Western demographers and geographers have traditionally grouped the territorial-administrative subdivisions in the Soviet Union (such as Central Black Earth, Northwest, North Caucasus, Southeast Ukraine).

[b]Individual neither in region nor oblast within surrounding regional area to present obkom bureau. All-Union or Union-republic officials were automatically classified "outsiders," even though Moscow or Kiev may be the region located in surrounding regional area to present obkom bureau.

Source: Compiled by the author.

TABLE 6.6

Position Held Immediately Prior to First Election to Obkom Bureau, 1955-73

	Sec. Gorrai[a]	Obkom Apparat[b]	Oblast Apparat[c]	Positions (percent) Obl. Kom.[d]	Sci.- Tech.[e]	All- Union[f]	N
Total bureau members, 1955-73	26	30	12	5	7	20	305
Urban change							
Low regions	26	30	13	6	7	18	169
High regions	26	30	11	3	6	24	136
Political regime							
1955-64	20	32	12	4	7	24	220
1965-73	34	29	13	5	4	14	167
Urban change (time)							
Low (1955-64)	21	31	13	6	8	21	121
High (1955-64)	20	33	11	2	6	27	99
Low (1965-73)	31	27	16	7	4	14	97
High (1965-73)	39	31	9	3	4	14	70
Union rep. (time)							
Russian (1955-64)	17	36	11	3	7	26	140
Ukrainian (1955-64)	26	26	15	6	8	19	80
Russian (1965-73)	35	33	10	4	4	15	101
Ukrainian (1965-73)	33	23	18	8	5	14	66
Obk. 1st sec's							
1955-64	9	43	8	1	6	32	77
1965-73	18	33	13	3	5	30	40
All other sec's (time)							
1955-64	31	29	6	8	6	19	78
1965-73	44	27	11	5	5	8	63

[a]Secretaries of urban, district, and borough parties.

[b]Instructors, deputy directors, and directors of obkom departments; secretaries of another obkom bureau.

[c]Deputy chairmen of oblispolkom, department directors and administrators of oblast government; chairmen and first deputy chairmen of another obkom bureau; deputy chairman regional sounarkhoz (1957-62).

[d]Oblast Komsomol: department directors or secretaries in the regional Komsomol; Komsomol first secretary of another obkom bureau.

[e]Scientific-technical officials: industrial enterprise directors, directors of scientific-research institutes, engineers in industrial enterprise, and so on.

[f]All-Union: official in All-Union or Union-republic Party apparatus, state apparatus, Komsomol, trade-union council, press; student in higher Party school.

Source: Compiled by the author.

local representation on obkom bureaus after 1964. Those "insiders" recruited from lower positions inside the very same region have increased from 44 to 65 percent of all bureau members, with the corresponding proportion directly assigned from outside the region and the regional area declining from 45 to 25 percent. The data also seem to bear out Brezhnev's conclusion that more "local workers" have been elected obkom first secretary. Obkom first secretaries originally recruited to the bureau from a position in the same regional middle elite have increased from 16 to 39 percent.

At the same time, the change in career origins has been more gradual for obkom first secretaries than for all bureau members. Even after 1964, almost half of all elected first secretaries continue to be "outsiders," a proportion twice as great as the 25 percent of all post-1964 bureau members. Brezhnev explicitly emphasized that first secretaries had been assigned from the center only in "exceptional cases." Yet, as Table 6.6 shows, exactly the same 32 and 30 percent of obkom first secretaries in the Khrushchev and Brezhnev-Kosygin periods have held All-Union or Union-republic offices immediately prior to their first position in the obkom bureau. By comparison, former regional middle elite are still underrepresented among obkom first secretaries to their proportion among all bureau members: 26 percent more bureau members than first secretaries have been "insiders" since 1965; and twice as many first secretaries as bureau members have been "outsiders" and were originally recruited from All-Union or Union-republic offices.

By previous occupations in Table 6.6, there has generally been less of a conclusive change in the career origins of obkom bureau members after 1964. Yet, even though a marginal difference, the 3 percent decline in scientific-technical officials recruited directly into obkom bureau positions could have some particular relevance. This decline in part results from the absence of sovnarkhoz chairmen in the 1965-73 bureaus, several of whom in 1957-63 had been directly reassigned from scientific-technical positions on the regional level. Despite exceptions like Antonov in Orel, who was directly recruited as obkom industry secretary in 1970 from deputy chief engineer of the Cherepovets Metallurgical Plant, no real attempt has been made to offset the technical expertise represented on the pre-1965 bureaus by the sovnarkhoz chairmen. The decline may well suggest a reluctance on the part of the Brezhnev-Kosygin leadership to entrust key regional policy roles to individuals with recent technical and non-Party backgrounds. In particular, a scientific-technical background has remained quite constant at a rather low level of 6 and 5 percent for obkom secretaries and first secretaries, the two key regional subgroups whose career origins will probably reflect the biases of the central leadership in recruitment even more exactly. By itself, this decline of recent scientific-technical officials on obkom bureaus could also tend to reduce their influences as an occupational sector in regional policy-making. Although the authority of industrial officials was supposedly raised as a consequence of the 1965 Liberman reform, regional industrial officials may be less likely to gain an empathetic response from bureau officials recruited even less frequently and recently from the same scientific-technical sector as the industrial officials.

If the pattern since 1965 shows little promise of an enhanced policy role for industrial officials, the recruitment of more "insiders" since 1965 has at the same time paralleled a very striking 14 percent increase in the number of former urban, district, and borough Party secretaries represented on the obkom bureaus. The addition of these local secretaries deserves further elaboration for three reasons.

First, as the reader can see in Table 6.6, former local secretaries are the only occupational sector that has appeared to benefit directly from the change in political regimes. In comparison to their levels in 1955-64, only two of the occupational sectors have gained even 1 percent, and the other three sectors have actually fallen from 3 to 10 percent. Thus, the additional local secretaries since 1965 alone account for two-thirds of the 21 percent increase in "insiders" noted in Table 6.5. The percentage of local secretaries recruited to obkom bureaus is particularly important because it probably serves as a more exact measure of political adaptation to regional interests. This is because former local secretaries are individuals recruited almost exclusively from an occupational sector in the same regional middle elite. In contrast, the other occupational sectors in Table 6.6 also include individuals laterally shifted from other regions and obkom bureaus or sent down from positions in the central apparat. As a rule, local secretaries have never been members of any obkom bureau until this initial election indicated in Table 6.6.* As such, the increased recruitment of local secretaries since 1965 directly contradicts the more conservative patterns of internal rotation and reduced turnover, generally confirmed by the findings in Chapter 5.

The change can even be specifically observed in the career origins of individuals recruited to the same bureau position in a

---

*With rare exceptions such as V. A. Artamanov, elected Odessa obkom second secretary in 1973 (Radio Odessa, April 6, 1973) from his previous position as first secretary of the Krivoi Rog gorkom in Dnepropetrovsk. Even here, however, as first secretary of Krivoi Rog, Artamanov was already a member of the Dnepropetrovsk obkom bureau, so the change could be considered as a lateral transfer on the bureau level between the two regions.

region before and after 1964. In the Odessa region, F. A. Stamikov, who served as capital gorkom first secretary during the Khrushchev period, had been appointed only after having first been director of the obkom Party Organs department.[29] L. Ya. Butenko, elected capital gorkom first secretary in 1970, in contrast was recruited as a former local secretary from a position outside both the central obkom apparat and the obkom bureau. As former first secretary of the Maritime raikom in Odessa, Butenko, indeed, had only been first elected to the Odessa gorkom bureau three weeks prior to his selection as capital gorkom first secretary.[30]

The contrasting backgrounds of Stamikov and Butenko also suggest a second relevance to the increased number of local secretaries after 1964. The previous occupational background of bureau members could well reflect the actual status and policy influence of the same sectors in the regional party. As such, any subsequent advantage in status or influence for local secretaries after 1964 has been achieved at the particular expense of central obkom apparatchiki, like Stamikov. As the data in Table 6.6 show, obkom apparatchiki were the single highest ranking sector by previous occupations among all 1955-64 bureau members (32 percent). Further indicative of their high status as a direct channel to the regional bureau may be the procedure by which obkom apparatchiki have consistently accounted for the highest proportion of all obkom first secretaries in both regime periods (43 and 33 percent). Even after 1964, a bureau member has almost twice as great an opportunity to become obkom first secretary if he had already been in an obkom apparat immediately prior to his first position on the bureau than if he had been a local secretary in the region. Yet, since 1965, the ratio of former obkom apparatchiki to all bureau members has both absolutely declined and been surpassed as the highest ranking occupational sector by local Party secretaries; and, among obkom first secretaries, former local Party secretaries have doubled from 9 to 18 percent.

The percentage of former local secretaries within the obkom secretariat has similarly risen from 31 to 44 percent. The increased number of local secretaries recruited as obkom secretaries could well be intentional. If administrative conflict exists between the obkom apparatchiki with "staff" functions and local secretaries with more direct "line" responsibilities, central leaders could anticipate that greater cooperation and mutual understanding would be fostered between the two groups by having former local secretaries assigned as obkom secretaries to head the regional departments.* This

---

*Cooperation between the "staff" obkom apparatchiki and the "line" local secretaries is also likely to be facilitated by the pattern

reasoning appears to have influenced in particular the recruitment of obkom industry secretaries, 52 percent of whom (14 of 27) have been local secretaries immediately prior to their bureau election. Indeed, as a subgroup in the bureau, all obkom secretaries have generally become more representative of the regional middle elite than individuals assigned to other bureau offices. Not only are 71 percent of all obkom secretaries insiders, but the percentage of obkom secretaries recruited to the bureaus from All-Union or Union-republic offices has declined from 19 to 8 percent, well below the level for all bureau members from 1965.

Finally, a careful analysis of Tables 6.5 and 6.6 reveals that the increased local origins of bureau members after 1964 are primarily associated with specific regions. Regional environment characteristics account for a large percentage of the increase that has appeared within the last nine years. Thus, the geographical and occupational origins of bureau members have changed most dramatically in high urban, Russian, and low urban regions. "Insiders" in high urban and Russian bureaus have increased by 28 to 29 percent from the comparable levels in 1955-64, and "insiders" in low urban bureaus, by 16 percent.

---

in which the former are almost exclusively recruited directly from the latter. As the background for obkom department directors between 1955 and 1973 indicates below, 36 of the 54 directors were former urban, district, and borough Party secretaries. Only 6 of the 54 could be considered full-time careerists in the obkom apparat by their position (secretary, deputy director, or instructor) in the obkom department immediately prior to their first assignment as a department director. On the other hand, only 3 of the 54 were recruited from positions outside the Party apparat (main engineer of a plant, director of an oblast Party school, editor of an oblast newspaper), and few occupational viewpoints other than those of Party officials are likely to be reflected in those who staff the regional secretariat on a full-time basis.

Occupational Positions before First Elected Obkom Department Director, 1955-73:

Gorrai Secs.	Obkom Apparat	Oblast Apparat	Raikom Apparat
36	6	5	1

Non-Apparat	Oblast Komsomol	All-Union
3	2	1

The changed composition of the three regional groups appears to represent a concerted attempt to establish closer ties between the regional bureaus and their regional middle elites. Parallel to the addition of "insiders," the proportion of "outsiders" has declined by an equivalent 26, 29, and 15 percent; at least 10 to 19 percent of all new "insiders" after 1964 are local Party secretaries (compare percentages in Table 6.6); and 7 to 13 percent fewer bureau members have been recruited from former All-Union or Union-republic officials.

The specific changes that have occurred particularly in Russian low urban regions also coincide with two distinct features in bureau turnover after 1964. As stressed previously in Chapter 5, although the absolute rate of turnover among major bureau officials in Russian low urban regions declined after 1964, a continuing high proportion of "outsiders" have been recruited to those positions that have opened at a rate similar to the 1955-64 period. Furthermore, fewer bureau members from the 1963-64 bifurcation reform were retained on Russian than Ukrainian bureaus after 1964. To replace those pre-1960 senior members who have transferred, retired, or died, Russian bureaus have consequently recruited a higher percentage of new bureau members from what we can now identify more precisely as the regional middle elite. The Russian bureaus by 1973 are typically split in composition between a senior pre-1960 group and those whose first election to the bureau coincides with the Brezhnev-Kosygin period. In Ukrainian regions, a much higher percentage of bureau members by 1973 still date their first election to the 1963-64 period and may not have yet attained their normal tenure on the bureaus. The change in bureau composition that was already initiated in Ukrainian regions during the 1963-64 period for some reason was delayed in Russian regions until after Khrushchev's overthrow.

Thus, paradoxical as it would normally seem, at the same time the top regional leadership has remained longer in all regions, the regional middle elite in Russian regions, in particular those who may be local secretaries in agricultural areas, actually have a greater relative opportunity to become bureau members and even a major bureau official after rather than before 1964. Only by considering these several factors can one hope to render any logical coherence to Brezhnev's seemingly contradictory references to leadership continuity and change at the 24th Party Congress.

The change in Russian low and high urban regions after 1964 contrasts sharply with the stability in bureau composition among Ukrainian regions. Approximately two-thirds of all bureau members in the Ukraine have been recruited from "insiders" during both regime periods; and, even prior to Khrushchev's overthrow, over a fourth of all Ukrainian bureau members were former local secretaries in their regions. Nor have Ukrainian bureaus only recruited more members directly from positions within the same region. As Tables 6.7 and 6.8 will further indicate (see next section), during the 1955-73 period, Ukrainian regions have consistently ranked 19 to 24 percent above Russian regions in the total proportion of bureau members who could be classified regional natives by prevalent occupational locale, birthplace, and education. In the three regions included within the Southeast Industrial Region of the Ukraine (Dnepropetrovsk, Khar'kov, and Zaporozh'e), 9 of the 14 individuals elected obkom first secretary since 1953 were actually born and educated in the very same region as the obkom bureau. Four of the other five were either born and educated in a neighboring oblast of the Southeast Industrial Region or had spent a major segment of their early careers within the same region before their election as first secretary.

It is of final interest to note that a very similar high percentage of Ukrainian bureau members after 1964 have been recruited both from the regional middle elite (68 percent in Table 6.5) and from those who entered the Party after 1941 (79 percent in Table 6.1). Therefore, if the attitudes of bureau members are determined by their similar background, the preconditions for "localism" at least could be said to be more prevalent among Ukrainian bureau members by these two background characteristics. With the predominance of post-1941 Party generations and local officials in Ukrainian bureaus, one could reasonably assume that most Ukrainian bureau members would be characterized by a distinct and more uniform set of political attitudes. As attitudes logically deduced from their similar Party and career background, Ukrainian bureau members may project more local or sectional biases in their political orientations and may identify their own political careers more closely with local regional problems and friendships. Less dogmatic and motivated primarily by material incentives, Ukrainian bureau members may also be more receptive to consumer demands among their own regional population. Even though this may be mere speculation, if carried to a logical conclusion, it implies that these attitudes would tend to transform the highly ideocratic regional party in the Ukraine into an organization better described as a local political machine. And, even if mere speculation, the rapid increase of local recruitment in Russian regions after 1964 raises the prospect that all regional leadership in the USSR may come to resemble the localist biases more typical of the Ukraine.

Prevalent Locale and Recruitment Typology

Significant as the changes in Tables 6.5 and 6.6 could portend, they only meet the very elementary first criterion of what could be defined as a "local worker" in obkom bureaus. If Brezhnev and other central Party leaders seem committed to a policy change of more local workers in obkom bureaus, it seems equally unlikely that they would either welcome or intend cadre policy changes so radical as to transform the nature of regional parties and the Soviet political system. On the contrary, the preservation of vested political interests and Party orthodoxy has almost been a hallmark of the conservative leadership since 1965. While making some symbolic gestures to fundamental reform, the conservative Brezhnev-Kosygin regime has more often seemed very cautious and compromising in domestic policy areas. They have not attacked policy problems in the grand innovative (if chaotic) style of their predecessor Khrushchev, but they have accommodated limited reforms to more conventional approaches.

In this sense, even an examination of more fundamental demographic and career origins of bureau members after 1964 reveals a similar commitment to traditional Party cadre policy in the selection of regional leadership. If more local secretaries and insiders have been recruited from lower ranks of the regional party, very few bureau members as yet could actually be termed "regional natives" by more rigid criteria of extended career backgrounds in the same region or their place of education and birth. By these two criteria in Tables 6.7 and 6.8, little difference can be found in the background of most bureau members before and after 1964.

One such indication is the prevalent occupational locale of bureau members before their first election to the bureau, shown in Table 6.7. Indicative of a commitment to the status quo in regional cadre policy is the fact that a very similar proportion (32 and 39 percent) of all bureau members in the two periods have been recruited from those with prevalent careers in the region. Perhaps still distrustful of too close an identification of regional leaders with their own regions, the Brezhnev-Kosygin leadership has followed the more traditional policy in selecting almost half of all bureau members from "outsiders," those whose careers were spent primarily outside the region and even surrounding regional area.

A second and even more telling indication of the status quo in cadre selection can be observed in the cumulative ties of bureau members with their regions by birth, education, and total career, distinguished along a recruitment typology in Table 6.8. As in Table 6.7., the data in Table 6.8 generally fail to evidence any substantial departure in establishing closer grass-roots ties between obkom bureau members and their locales during the years 1965-73. A very similar 26 and 32 percent of all bureau members (for the two periods) could be classified "regional natives" by birth, education, and extended career in the same region. An additional 13 and 6 percent

TABLE 6.7

Prevalent Occupational Locale before First Elected
to Obkom Bureau, 1955-73*

	Occupational Locale (percent)			
	Inside Region	Inside Regional Area	Outsider	N
Total bureau mem- bers, 1955-73	32	15	53	179
Urban change				
Low regions	37	13	50	92
High regions	26	17	56	87
Political regime				
1955-64	32	16	52	154
1965-73	39	14	47	90
Urban change (time)				
Low (1955-64)	37	14	49	79
High (1955-64)	28	17	55	75
Low (1965-73)	44	8	48	48
High (1965-73)	33	21	45	42
Union rep. (time)				
Russian (1955-64)	25	14	61	105
Ukrainian (1955-64)	49	18	33	49
Russian (1965-73)	33	18	49	61
Ukrainian (1965-73)	52	7	41	29
Obk. 1st sec's (time)				
1955-64	18	25	57	68
1965-73	36	19	45	42
All other sec's (time)				
1955-64	50	6	44	54
1965-73	52	11	37	27
Total middle political elite				
1958-73	74	2	24	50

*Prevalent refers to regional locale in which at least a plurality of career was spent. For middle political elite, the "major position" was substituted for election to obkom bureau. "Major position" refers to highest achieved or last held position by middle elite. Career for all officials was computed to include all occupational experiences accumulated from age 21 or (if date of birth is unknown) the year of Party entry.

Source: Compiled by the author.

TABLE 6.8

Typology of Recruitment Origins into Obkom Bureaus,
1955-73[a]

	Recruitment Origins			
	Native[b]	Intermediate[c]	Outsider[d]	N
Total bureau mem-				
bers, 1955-73	29	12	60	168
Urban change				
Low regions	34	14	52	88
High regions	23	10	68	80
Political regime				
1955-64	26	13	61	152
1965-73	32	6	62	97
Urban change (time)				
Low (1955-64)	33	15	51	78
High (1955-64)	19	11	70	74
Low (1965-73)	39	6	55	49
High (1965-73)	25	6	69	48
Union-rep. (time)				
Russian (1955-64)	19	13	69	102
Ukrainian (1955-64)	42	14	44	50
Russian (1965-73)	25	6	69	65
Ukrainian (1965-73)	47	6	47	32
Obk. 1st sec's (time)				
1955-64	23	18	59	61
1965-73	41	8	51	39
All other sec's (time)				
1955-64	35	5	60	60
1965-73	27	10	63	30
Total middle				
political elite,				
1958-70	55	8	37	60

[a]Period of career includes total years spent in obkom bureau positions. For regional middle elite, "major position" was substituted for election to obkom bureau.

[b]"Native": (1) born or educated (university or middle teknikum) in same region or contiguous regional area of obkom bureau; and (2) a minimum 75 percent of total career in region of obkom bureau.

[c]"Intermediate": born or educated in region or regional area, but with less than 75 percent of total career in region of obkom bureau.

[d]"Outsider": (1) neither born nor educated in region or regional area; and (2) has spent less than 75 percent of total career in region of obkom bureau. In reality, most "outsiders" have spent much less than half of their total career in present region.

Source: Compiled by the author.

in both regime periods could be classified as "intermediates," also
born or educated in the regional environment but with careers more
interspersed between assignments in other local parties and the
center. Most significantly, though, the overwhelming majority of
62 percent of all bureau members in both periods continue to be
recruited from "outsiders." Neither born nor educated in the regional environment, most "outsiders" were assigned to the bureau
at an advanced stage of their political careers from the center or
another region. As a result, the typical bureau member in both
periods has been relatively unfamiliar with regional problems before
his first election to the obkom bureau.

The policy of limited local recruitment has created a wide
disparity between the background of typical bureau members and the
middle political elite in any region. While only a third of all bureau
members are "insiders" in Table 6.7, almost three-fourths of the
known middle elite have spent the plurality of their careers at positions in the same regions. In Table 6.8, of all bureau members,
32 percent are classified as "regional natives," in sharp contrast
to 55 percent of all regional middle elite. Thus, the middle elite in
any regional party are probably more oriented to regional problems
and their political careers may be more dependent upon regional
cohorts than their superiors in the obkom bureaus.*

The continued disparity in career background between the two
levels of regional leadership cannot be ignored by central authorities
responsible for selecting bureau members. More than likely, the
exact balance between regional natives and outsiders in a bureau is
carefully weighed in the central Party secretariat. On one hand,
simple administrative-political efficiency would dictate to central

---

*Given the Russian penchant to give proper names to collective
political phenomena, it might be more appropriate to describe the
extended regional ties of most middle elite officials not as "regionalism" or "localism" but as "Nikolaevism"—for the closely linked
career and name of Nikolai Nikolaevich Kutsak is almost a humor-
ous parody of the extended regional backgrounds found among regional middle elite officials. Born of poor peasants in the Nikolaev
raion of Odessa, Nikolai Nikolaevich returned to his native region
after the war to work in the Nikolaev kolkhozes. From 1948, he
held the following political positions: department director and second
secretary of the Nikolaev raikom Komsomol; instructor, director
of the organizational department, and second secretary of the Nikolaev Party raikom; and first secretary of the Nikolaev raikom, the
position he held from 1962 until his death in early 1970. See ZK,
February 10, 1970.

authorities that at least some bureau members should have extended prior background in the same region as the obkom bureau. With greater authority than middle elite officials, bureau members are collectively responsible for coordinating the details of industrial and agricultural production in a region, satisfying consumer demands, and resolving local discontent. A primary source of discontent would be the very resentment of the regional middle elite itself. The very identification of a native bureau member would thus benefit him in his current position because the middle elite will know him personally, will be able to anticipate his policy initiatives, and will be able to link their own political aspirations for advancement with his own successful career.

On the other hand, central authorities must also anticipate that recruiting too many regional natives into a bureau would maximize the opportunities for "localist" distortions such as corruption, profiteering, and false reporting of completed economic quotas. Too great a familiarity with a region, it could be reasoned by central authorities, breeds a contempt toward the perceived broader interests of the country. Regional bureau members will become overprotective of regional interests and will sacrifice interregional shipments of goods in order to satisfy local industrial demands. Not only may regional natives be considered by central authorities to be less politically reliable than outsiders, but they would probably be deemed less politically useful or capable in the long run. All bureau members may be assumed by central authorities to possess specialized administrative and political talents that can be successfully applied in any of several different locales or contexts. As such, the "generalist," laterally shifted between bureaus or from the center to the regional locales, is probably both the ideal of the obkom bureau official and the pattern of apprenticeship by which bureau members are prepared to assume later major positions on the Union-republic and All-Union level.

On a general quantitative level, these considerations have appeared to guide Party cadre policy in both regime periods, evidenced by the lateral recruitment of most bureau members in Table 6.7 and the limited ties most have with their regions in Table 6.8. More specifically, these considerations can be seen by the reader to have influenced the careers of typical bureau members in both periods like I. S. Chirva, N. V. Golubev, V. D. Babich, I. V. Bondaletov, G. D. Lapchinskii, L. P. Lykova, and V. T. Duvakin. Chirva, obkom ideology secretary of the Crimean oblast throughout the Khrushchev period, had actually been recruited from the L'vov obkom bureau, where he had been at least the oblast Komsomol first secretary as far back as 1948.[31] Golubev, capital gorkom first secretary of Briansk from 1954 through 1959, and Babich, obkom industry secretary and later chairman of the Briansk control commission from 1958 through 1970, had been demoted to Briansk from their previous positions as obkom first secretaries of the Kursk and Kabardinsk oblasts.[32] Bondaletov, capital gorkom first secretary of Zaporozh'e between 1960 and 1962, was reassigned as an "industrial" specialist to the Latvian Republic, where he has served through 1971 as deputy chairman of the republic council of ministers.[33] Lapchinskii, obkom ideology secretary of Tambov between 1958 and 1961, had never held a known prior position in Tambov but had been recruited as the former secretary of the Krasnoiarsk kraikom in distant Eastern Siberia.[34] Indeed, as an equivalent trade-off of generalists, Lapchinskii was assigned to Tambov in 1958 at the same time P. F. Morozov, the Tambov oblispolkom chairman, was transferred to Krasnoiarsk as the new kraiispolkom chairman.[35]

The careers of Lykova and Duvakin may even better typify the "generalist" ideal sought by central authorities for bureau members. Lykova is currently deputy chairman of the Council of Ministers in the Russian Republic and was one of only two female bureau members from the 25 regions promoted from the regional level to a central position between 1955 and 1973. A youthful recruit to the central Party apparat in 1947-49, Lykova was sent down to the regional level, where she became secretary and then second secretary of the Ivanova obkom for six years. Importantly, from Ivanova, she was laterally shifted to the Smolensk region, where she held the identical position of obkom second secretary for four years before returning to the center as Russian minister of Social Security in 1961.[36] Duvakin's career to date has been equally divided between youth and agricultural specialization. First secretary of the Kirov oblast Komsomol in the early 1960s, Duvakin was elected All-Union Komsomol secretary in 1962 and served continuously in the Komsomol Secretariat for nine years.[37] Besides his frequent attendance at youth rallies and festivals,[38] Duvakin appears to have been an agricultural "trouble-shooter," responsible for Komsomol-sponsored agricultural projects in the locales of Kazakhstan, Central Asia, and the Caucasus.[39] Dismissed from the Komsomol Secretariat in 1970, Duvakin was elected obkom agriculture secretary in the Saratov region, a position for which he may be eminently qualified by his Komsomol background; it must be noted, however, that he has no specific familiarity with agricultural problems in the Saratov region itself.[40]

Obkom First Secretaries

However similar in background most bureau members like these have remained before and after 1964, the data in both tables also reveal a very specific change in the background of obkom first secretaries. By prevalent occupational locale, insiders have doubled from 18 to 36 percent of all first secretaries. Even more importantly, by the combined factors of career, birth, and education, the proportion of first secretaries who could be classified as actual regional natives in Table 6.8 has increased from 23 to 41 percent. In addition to the change by previous occupational locale and sector in Tables 6.5-6.6, all three criteria thus definitely tend to support Brezhnev's analysis that more "local" obkom first secretaries were elected between the 23d and 24th Party Congresses.

If Brezhnev's analysis is consistently supported by the data, a less precise conclusion can be offered for the actual significance or meaning of the change itself. From one perspective, it would seem highly unlikely that Brezhnev would have mentioned this specific change unless central authorities had themselves recognized its potential significance and had arrived at some mutual consensus on its need. Any consensus probably formed around concerns with the quality of regional Party leadership in the economy and the related economic failures of the last nine years. Central leaders may have reasoned that native first secretaries by background would generally be more capable regional administrators than outsiders because of their more direct familiarity with local economic problems. Moreover, the change could have been defended since 1965 as consistent with economic decentralization and greater local initiative, both key principles urged since adoption of the economic reform of 1965. Thus, overweighing the traditional apprehension many central leaders would feel toward localism in regional parties, the break in precedence, at least in selecting native obkom first secretaries, may now have been considered necessary in the short run to spur economic effectiveness at the regional level.

In restructuring regional-center Party relationships, the effect of the change could extend beyond the level of regional parties. Consider that at another level several obkom first secretaries are simultaneously elected members and candidate members of the Ukrainian and All-Union Central Committees. We could reasonably assume that the same native first secretaries in central committees are more likely to sense a primary obligation to their own regional political base and are more likely to advocate vigorously their own exclusive regional interests. With more native first secretaries in central committees since 1965, some allowance may thus have been made for the channeling of discrete regional interests into central decision-making.* The context of political bargaining at the

_____

*On an agenda of future research, it would perhaps be useful to compare by content analysis the advocacy role of native and nonnative

central level, which already may involve several affected interest groups on particular domestic issues, would be further complicated by the addition of more native first secretaries to central committees. On a broader dimension, the native origins of first secretaries could reflect upon important trends in the Soviet political system toward greater decentralization and increasing local influence on the central policy-making process.

From a second alternative perspective, however, the change by itself could be considered insignificant, if not highly misleading. For one reason, while insiders and regional natives have both increased as a total proportion of all first secretaries, the percentage of outsiders by both criteria has declined more gradually. Even after 1964, almost half of all first secretaries were still recruited from outsiders on the obkom bureaus. Secondly, by combining the native and intermediate classifications in Table 6.8, the total percentage of native first secretaries by birth and education in the same regional environment has not increased significantly since 1965; 41 percent in the 1955-64 period and 49 percent in the 1965-73 period. Rather, any change in background appears to be associated with the longer political careers in the same regions typical of obkom first secretaries elected after 1964. Thirdly, to explain the longer political careers of first secretaries in the same region, we need only reconsider the structural dimensions of bureau membership, carefully outlined in the previous chapter. In particular, with the reduced turnover and increased tenure of senior members since 1965, fewer new members have been elected. As a direct consequence, by internal rotation, first secretaries have been elected more frequently from those senior members already on the bureau for a long period of their career. Thus, the only objective reason that more defined native first secretaries by total career have been elected after 1964 may be that the central Party leadership has been less willing to alter the general membership of obkom bureaus. The increased proportion of native first secretaries could signify less of a deliberately initiated cadre policy than a mere post-hoc justification for the conservative retrenchment in regional Party leadership.

In order for the reader to appreciate both the extent and the limitations of the change, let us merely examine the different background of the four obkom first secretaries elected to the Volgograd

---

first secretaries at the central political level. Analysis of their speeches delivered at central committee plenums, Party congresses, and sessions of the Supreme Soviet could reveal important differences in the extent they argue for policy from the perspectives of their own regional interests.

region since 1948. The tenure of the first three secretaries—I. T. Grishin (1948-55), I. K. Zhegalin (1955-60), and A. M. Shkol'nikov (1961-65)—either overlapped Khrushchev's ascendancy to Party leadership or were direct products of the Stalinist cadre policy maintained more consistently between 1955 and 1964. Grishin, for one, was born in the Riazan oblast and spent his entire career both in Komsomol and Party assignments in Moscow and his native oblast. Following three years in the central apparat, a four-year period as oblispolkom chairman of Novosibirsk during the war, and three years at the higher party school, the "outsider" Grishin was assigned to Stalingrad (Volgograd) as obkom second secretary in 1948 and nine months later was elevated to obkom first secretary.[41]

Zhegalin would be classified as an intermediate on the basis of the recruitment typology in Table 6.8, for he had actually been born in the region of Saratov, which borders Volgograd in the surrounding Volga Regional Area.[42] Yet, subsequent to the completion of his higher education in the Urals region of Orenburg, Zhegalin's entire political career between 1939 and 1955 was spent in positions outside both Volgograd and his native Volga Regional Area: Party work in the Orenburg region; gorkom first secretary in Turkmenistan; secretary and second secretary of the Rostov obkom; and first secretary of the Gronzy region in the Caucasus.[43] Born and educated in the Moscow region, Shkol'nikov, unlike his predecessor Zhegalin, could not even claim some early origins in the Volga Area. Like Zhegalin and Grishin, though, Shkol'nikov's career prior to his election as Volgograd first secretary in 1960 typified the generalist ideal. After early industrial and Party positions in the Perm' oblast, Shkol'nikov between 1941 and 1960 was assigned in turn by the center as Central Committee Commissioner of Party Control for the Vladimir and Voronezh oblasts, obkom second secretary of the Kaluga oblast, inspector of the Central Committee apparat, and first secretary of the Tambov and Voronezh oblasts.[44] Except for Grishin's nine months as obkom second secretary and Zhegalin's nominal birthplace in neighboring Saratov, therefore, none of the first secretaries during the Khrushchev period had any prior demographic or career ties to Volgograd before his election as obkom first secretary of the region.

The break in precedence occurred with the election of the fourth first secretary, L. S. Kulichenko, in November of 1965 during the Brezhnev-Kosygin regime. A regional native, Kulichenko was born in the Volgograd city of Tsarshchyne and graduated from the Volgograd Mechanical Institute in 1936. Following his graduation and except for the brief period Volgograd was occupied by the German army during the war, Kulichenko has never held any non-Party or Party position outside his own native region of Volgograd. Prior to his election as first secretary, Kulichenko had been oblispolkom chairman and had already accumulated 13 consecutive years on the Volgograd bureau as chairman, obkom second secretary, and first secretary of the Volgograd gorkom. Kulichenko's total career identification with the obkom leadership extends even further back to 1945, when he was director of an unspecified (Party organs?) obkom department.[45]

Despite the change evident with Kulichenko's election as first secretary, regional middle elite officials in Volgograd are likely to view it as something of a mixed blessing for their own careers. On the positive side, Kulichenko, both as a regional native and a product of the lower Party ranks in Volgograd, would obviously serve as a more relevant success model for current middle elite officials. Middle elite officials could contrast the situation with that in which outsiders like Grishin, Zhegalin, and Shkol'nikov were first secretary and conclude that their own opportunities have remarkably improved to become future bureau members or even obkom first secretary in Volgograd. Indeed, as previously noted, there is some reason to conclude that Kulichenko is aware of his advantageous position as a native first secretary for inspiring current behavior among the regional middle elite. Kulichenko himself coined the term "poor morale problem" among lower Party cadres and state officials at a 1970 Volgograd plenum in arguing the necessity for continued rapid mobility in the Volgograd region. While not referring to himself directly, Kulichenko cited several examples of Volgograd officials born and educated in the region who by merit had achieved higher political positions in Volgograd. What is particularly important to bear in mind is Kulichenko's own native background and the consequently greater credibility the theme of native success addressed by him would have on an audience of the Volgograd middle elite.

Nor would Kulichenko's audience in the middle elite require any further proof of his sincerity than to consider the parallel career of V. P. Borodin, the current oblispolkom chairman of Volgograd. Born in a peasant village in Volgograd and a 1952 graduate of the Volgograd Agricultural Institute, Borodin had advanced rapidly from lower Party ranks into major regional leadership positions: instructor of the obkom agricultural department in 1952; chairman and first secretary of rural Volgograd districts in 1956-61; director of the obkom agricultural department in 1961; and obkom agriculture secretary in 1962-65. At the relatively young age of 41, Borodin was elected oblispolkom chairman in November 1965, replacing Kulichenko when the latter was elevated to the position of obkom first secretary.[46]

On the negative side, the Volgograd middle elite could also be quite cynical about the supposed significance of the change. They will be aware that, at the same time regional natives like Kulichenko and Borodin have risen to leadership of the region, turnover in all major bureau offices since 1965 has decreased from 0.25 in 1955-64 to 0.14 and the attrition rate of all bureau members has shrunk from 54 to 31 percent. Whatever resentment middle elite officials may have harbored with the election of outsiders like Grishin, Zhegalin, and Shkol'nikov under Stalin and Khrushchev would also seem less significant now than the fact that the average tenure of individuals elected to the major bureau positions in Volgograd has risen from 5.8 years in 1955-64 to 9.5 years in 1965-70. And, while Kulichenko might inspire regional Party pride and identification among middle elite officials, he is also one of four senior bureau members by 1971 who have been on the Volgograd bureau for a minimum of 15 consecutive years, preventing election of the same middle elite officials to the obkom bureau after 1964.* Thus, middle elite officials by right could question the symbolic importance in having regional natives as first secretary and oblispolkom chairman when their own individual opportunities to be elected to the obkom bureau have been reduced so drastically as a parallel development.

CAREER TYPES AND LEADERSHIP CHARACTERISTICS

Until this point of our analysis, we have distinguished the career origins of bureau members almost solely as a measure of prior association with a regional party. However relevant this perspective, both Western scholars of the Communist Party and Soviet leaders themselves have traditionally been less concerned with the geographical locale than the actual nature of prior occupational training among Party leaders. As we noted in analyzing the impact of first secretaries in 1970, Western scholars have in particular often employed such conceptual terms as "coopted" and "recruited" to characterize differences in the level of specialized or political background in the careers of Party leaders. "Coopted" officials with more extensive nonpolitical and professional-technical background are viewed as a positive advancement in the capabilities of Party leaders and the adaptation of the Party to societal demands.

---

*The others are N. I. Chmutov, A. M. Mon'ko, and N. A. Nepokupnoi. Only by the end of 1973 was Nepokupnoi replaced as obkom second secretary by S. Y. Krylov, a new bureau recruit as the former director of the obkom industry-transport department (See VP, May 8, 1970, and regional conference report in K, no. 18, December 1973, p. 121).

While objecting perhaps to the negative view of recruited Party apparatchiki by Western scholars, even central authorities have increasingly come to recognize the merits of electing local Party officials with more diversified and specialized backgrounds outside the Party bureaucracy. Thus, in his report to the 24th Party Congress, General Secretary Brezhnev concluded that an increasing number of newly elected local first secretaries had "fine political and specialist training."[47] Significantly, this reference occurred at the same point of his report in which Brezhnev described the newly elected first secretaries as "local" workers. The juxtaposition appeared to be deliberate. The very definite impression is conveyed that the new local first secretary elected since 1965 is now typically a native of his region and one with specialized background.

However accurate Brezhnev's description of the specialist background of first secretaries, it unfortunately is as ambiguously stated as his description of the same first secretaries as "local workers." Particularly unclear are the criteria upon which Brezhnev might have based his analysis of the specialist background of first secretaries. For one, if he meant that an increased number of specialists had been directly coopted as obkom first secretary, this contention was already partly disproved by the data in Table 6.6. Actually, by previous occupational position, the proportion of obkom first secretaries recruited from former scientific-technical officials has remained quite low at 6 and 5 percent in both regime periods from 1955 to 1973. On the other hand, Brezhnev was also careful to stress that the new first secretaries had both "political and specialist training." Some form of satisfactory parity between specialist and Party career for first secretaries is essentially implied by Brezhnev's description, a parity that heightens the technical-administrative proficiency of the obkom secretariat without abandoning regional Party leadership to unassimilated group views other than Party orthodoxy.

From this concept of parity in occupational background, Table 6.9 is an attempt to operationalize Brezhnev's reference by comparing the balance of occupational experience of all bureau members. All bureau members have been distinguished by their resemblance to one of three occupational career types: recruited, intermediate, and coopted officials. The occupational types correspond to the level of political and nonpolitical specialized background attained by bureau members before their first elected position on the regional bureau.

On a first level of analysis, the number of combined intermediate and coopted first secretaries actually increased by 17 percent in the nine years after Khrushchev was overthrown. Indeed, as a consequence of the increasingly specialized background of first secretaries, a higher proportion of bureau members than of first secretaries are

TABLE 6.9

Typology of Career Origins before First Election to
Obkom Bureau, 1955-73

	Career Origins (percent)			
	Recruited[a]	Intermediate[b]	Coopted[c]	N
Total bureau members, 1955-73	62	21	17	174
Urban change				
Low regions	64	18	17	92
High regions	60	24	16	82
Political regime				
1955-64	62	20	17	157
1965-73	61	22	16	85
Urban change (time)				
Low (1955-64)	65	16	19	81
High (1955-64)	59	25	16	76
Low (1965-73)	65	20	15	46
High (1965-73)	56	26	18	39
Union-rep. (time)				
Russian (1955-64)	58	25	17	104
Ukrainian (1955-64)	72	11	17	53
Russian (1965-73)	58	25	18	57
Ukrainian (1965-73)	68	18	14	28
Obk. 1st sec's (time)				
1955-64	67	22	11	72
1965-73	50	31	19	42
All other sec's (time)				
1955-64	67	15	19	54
1965-73	65	19	15	26
Total middle political[d] elite, 1958-73	43	18	39	49

[a]"Recruited" officials: more than 55 percent of accumulated careers in Party or political positions immediately prior to first election to obkom bureau. Party or political positions were defined to include offices in the Party, Komsomol, trade-union, and state bureaucracies.

[b]"Intermediate" officials: almost equivalent (45-55 percent) proportion of career immediately prior to first election to obkom bureau in both non-Party and specialist positions.

[c]"Coopted" officials: more than 55 percent of accumulated careers in direct specialized non-Party and nonpolitical positions (industrial enterprise director, foreman in plant, agronomist, mechanizer, collective farm chairman, teacher, jurist, and so on) immediately prior to first election to obkom bureau.

[d]For regional middle elite, "major position" was substituted for election to obkom bureau.

Source: Compiled by the author.

comprised of the more traditional full-time Party apparatchiki in the 1965-73 bureaus. Bureau members whose career patterns approximate recruited officials after 1964 thus find themselves at a greater disadvantage to become obkom first secretary than they would have under Khrushchev. As it would be too late for the same Party apparatchiki to leave the obkom bureaus and accumulate some more specialized background, the structure of career opportunities has now balanced in favor of those who entered full-time Party work at a later stage of their specialized or professional careers. The shift has been dramatic enough so that obkom first secretaries are actually closer in occupational profile to the current middle elite than are other bureau members. Incentives to become obkom first secretary among the same current middle elite may now dictate they acquire some direct experience in specialized positions outside the Party bureaucracy or consider delaying entry into full-time Party work for a longer period of time after their graduation from a higher technical institute.

Not only have more native and specialized first secretaries been elected since 1965, but, as Table 6.10 further indicates, there is some reason to anticipate a growing convergence between career and recruitment origins among all bureau members. The dichotomy between recruited outsiders and coopted natives tends to confirm in part the implied linkage between recruitment and career backgrounds made by Brezhnev at the 24th Congress. Of all bureau members with extensive careers solely in the Party bureaucracy, 59 percent were born and educated outside the region or regional area in which they have been elected. Conversely, 57 percent of all native bureau members by birth and education have entered full-time Party work only after having spent the majority of their careers in specialized occupations outside the Party bureaucracy.

If the trend to recruit more actual natives as obkom first secretaries continues, are we then witnessing a major transformation in Party leadership at the locales in the Soviet Union? Table 6.11 suggests that the emergence of the "native specialist" hybrid could fundamentally alter the quality of regional leadership. More bureau members who are natives and coopted officials have entered the Party after 1941, have served in the Party between 11 and 30 years, have received a higher education in an industrial institute, and have been recruited from the middle elite inside the same region as the obkom bureau. Outsiders and recruited officials have more typically entered the Party before 1942, have served in the Party a minimum of 21 or over 31 years, have as likely received only a higher agricultural degree or may never have attended a higher educational institution other than the Higher Party School, and have been unfamiliar with regional problems by their direct assignment to the bureau from

TABLE 6.10

Career and Recruitment Types
in Obkom Bureaus, 1955-73
(percent)

Career Types	Recruitment Types			
	Native and Intermediate[a]	Outsider	Total	(N)
Coopted and intermediate[b]	57	43	100	(54)
Recruited	41	59	100	(85)

[a]For parsimony in bivariate analysis, natives and intermediates are collapsed as one equivalent classification: that is, bureau members born or educated in region or contiguous region of obkom bureau as a minimum.

[b]For parsimony in bivariate analysis, coopted and intermediate officials are collapsed as one equivalent classification: that is, bureau officials with almost half or more of their total careers in specialist positions immediately prior to first obkom bureau election.

Source: Compiled by the author.

outside the region. Since 1965, the differences by Party entry, Party tenure, and geographical locale between native and outsider bureau members have increased, while the relative proportion of coopted officials with industrial degrees now far surpasses an equivalent absolute number of recruited officials.

Native members are younger than outsiders. Of 67 regional natives, 21 were born in the decades after 1919 contrast to 6 of 70 outsiders. Nor is the difference in age merely a reflection of the later recruitment to the obkom bureaus of native members. Even after 1964, almost half of the regional natives (16 of 36) were born after 1919 in contrast to less than 15 percent (5 of 34) of all outsiders. Thus, more native members would have been too young to have participated directly in the purges of the late 1930s. Their attitudes and maturation are identified with the war and postwar periods of Party recruitment and adulthood. While the same age differences are not as sharply drawn between coopted and recruited officials, recruited officials tend to be a decade older than coopted officials, with 36 alone born between 1900 and 1909. By prior

TABLE 6.11

Career and Recruitment Typologies of Bureau Members by
Associated Characteristics, 1955-73

	Native and Intermediate[a]	Outsider	Recruited	Coopted and Intermediate[b]
Party entry	67	87	101	65
1925-38	14 (2)[c]	29 (7)[c]	42 (9)[c]	8 (1)[c]
1939-41	22 (13)	30 (20)	27 (16)	25 (12)
1942-45	17 (10)	18 (13)	19 (11)	19 (10)
1946+	14 (11)	10 (8)	13 (11)	13 (9)
Birth	67	70	94	63
1900-09	27 (3)	23 (6)	36 (6)	14 (2)
1910-19	29 (17)	41 (23)	41 (22)	35 (18)
1920-29	20 (15)	6 (5)	15 (10)	12 (9)
1930-39	1 (1)	—	2 (1)	2 (2)
Higher education	66	61	86	64
Industrial	25 (15)	18 (9)	16 (8)	31 (17)
Agricultural	18 (8)	17 (6)	27 (13)	13 (4)
University	12 (7)	7 (3)	16 (7)	10 (4)
Only Party or middle	11 (6)	19 (9)	27 (9)	10 (7)
Geographical locale prior to obk. bureau	65	72	98	58
Inside region	40 (23)	26 (17)	38 (23)	29 (15)
Inside reg. area	8 (5)	7 (3)	13 (5)	5 (3)
Outsider	17 (7)	39 (17)	47 (18)	24 (13)
Position prior to obk. bureau	67	72	99	62
Sec. Gorrai	15 (8)	12 (8)	14 (10)	15 (8)
Obkom apparat	18 (11)	29 (14)	43 (15)	15 (10)
Oblast apparat	7 (6)	9 (6)	10 (7)	4 (3)
Oblast Komsomol	3 (1)	—	6 (3)	—
Sci-tech.	7 (2)	4 (2)	—	15 (4)
All-Union	17 (8)	18 (6)	26 (10)	13 (6)
Total years obk. bureau[d]	68	99	105	68
1-5 years	26 (10)	33 (9)	41 (11)	29 (10)
6-10 years	22 (12)	29 (15)	37 (18)	26 (13)
11+ years	20 (15)	37 (35)	27 (22)	13 (10)
Party tenure[e]	68	85	99	64
1-10 years	—	1 (0)	2 (0)	—
11-20 years	22 (7)	15 (6)	23 (10)	21 (6)
21-30 years	34 (21)	41 (22)	42 (19)	34 (19)
31+ years	12 (8)	28 (17)	32 (17)	9 (6)

[a] For parsimony in bivariate analysis, natives and intermediates are collapsed as one equivalent classification: that is, bureau members born or educated in region or contiguous region of obkom bureau as a minimum.

[b] For parsimony in bivariate analysis, coopted and intermediate officials are collapsed as one equivalent classification: that is, bureau officials with almost half or more of their total careers immediately prior to first election to the obkom bureau in specialist positions.

[c] Absolute numbers in parentheses are those bureau members elected between 1965 and 1973.

[d] Total years in obkom bureau only through the end of 1970.

[e] Party tenure only counted through 1972.

Source: Compiled by the author.

occupational position, 30 of 62 coopted officials and 22 of 67 regional natives were local Party secretaries or scientific-technical officials immediately prior to their first bureau election. Sixty-nine of 99 recruited officials and 47 of 72 outsiders were obkom apparatchiki or were sent down to the regional bureaus from previous All-Union and Union-republic positions.

Despite these differences, two important qualifications should be pointed out. The prior positions of seven regional natives even after 1964 were outside the regional environment before they were first brought back to assume a position on the obkom bureau; and eight natives after 1964 also held All-Union or Union-republic offices immediately prior to their first bureau position. As such, there appears to be at least a lingering apprehension on the part of central authorities about entrusting all regional natives with major political responsibilities in their own regions. By broadening the geographical experiences and orientation of some regional natives, central authorities may hope to offset the negative characteristics of "localism" and to prevent too close a career and policy identification among all natives with their own regional cohorts and more parochial regional concerns. Finally, there is little if any difference in the table at all in the total years coopted natives or recruited outsiders have spent on the obkom bureaus either before or after 1964. The question thus remains whether even the potential benefits of assigning highly skilled natives will outweigh the negative costs of retaining the same bureau members in policy-making roles so long that they actually become isolated from younger regional natives and come to feel threatened by new technical advances in the specialized professions in which they were first trained over two decades ago.

CONCLUSION

In conclusion, Brezhnev's optimistic reappraisal of advances in local Party organizations at the 24th Congress cannot be totally dismissed. The gap in Party generations and birth periods between bureau members and the regional middle elite has narrowed considerably in the last nine years; an increased percentage of local middle elite officials are represented on the obkom bureaus; local Party secretaries (especially in Russian regions) have found a greater opportunity to be elected obkom bureau members than they had under Khrushchev; and more highly trained obkom first secretaries with greater direct knowledge of problems in their own regions have been elected for the first time.

Yet, overshadowing the changes in bureau composition is a second contradictory dimension in the reduced turnover of bureau membership. The attrition rate for all bureau members and the renewal of members in the major policy positions are one-half the levels under Khrushchev; bureau members have remained for a much longer period of time or have been elected for the first time at a later stage of their political careers than they would have under Khrushchev; the average bureau member is four to eight years older than he would have been in 1955-64; and the cadre policy to recruit more actual regional natives has benefited only those bureau members eventually elected obkom first secretary.

Comparing the composition of bureaus before and after 1964, middle elite officials would appreciate the greater representation of their own former political cohorts. Yet those middle elite officials who have spent their entire career in the Party bureaucracy might question the fairness or logic of a policy that now awards the leadership of the regional party to obkom first secretaries who themselves have spent much less than half of their careers as Party apparatchiki. Middle elite officials in regions like Volgograd would also see little utility in electing more native obkom first secretaries. Because of the drastic reduction in bureau turnover, the same native first secretaries like Kulichenko have typically been elected only after a long continuous period in the obkom bureau leadership.[48] If they are more familiar with regional problems by the fact of their native origins, these senior bureau members by tenure and age may also represent the one segment of bureau leadership most out of touch with the changing attitudes and aspirations of younger middle elite officials. Only in regions like Kursk, where a young native first secretary like Gudkov has been recruited from the current middle elite and after a brief time on the obkom bureau, may lower Party cadres and officials perceive a meaningful and positive advance in the regional party.

To return to the theoretical alternatives posed at the beginning of our analysis of obkom bureaus, the data in the last two chapters have definitely proven a direct relationship between the regime change in October 1964 and changes both in the rate of bureau turnover and the types of individuals represented on obkom bureaus. Turnover was more rapid in the Khrushchev period; more native and postwar recruits have been elected bureau members in the Brezhnev-Kosygin period. While less significant a factor, the impact of regional environment can also be shown by the consistently higher proportion of younger native bureau members elected in Ukrainian regions during both regime periods and by the higher turnover of bureau membership in low urban regions since 1965.

Have regional parties become more or less politically adaptive during the period 1954-73? On one hand, the retrenchment in bureau turnover definitely supports the position of Western scholars who have characterized the Brezhnev-Kosygin regime as a conservative bureaucracy. On the other hand, the infusion of new bureau members even after 1964 from postwar and native strata within the regions also substantiates the contentions of Party leaders like Brezhnev who view the years 1965-73 as a period both of "continuity" and positive "change." It will be our task in the final chapter briefly to assess these two alternative positions from a broader perspective of political change in the Soviet Union.

NOTES

1. Leonid Brezhnev, XXIV KPSS, vol. 1, pp. 118-126.
2. Ibid., p. 121.
3. Ibid., p. 122.
4. Ibid., pp. 81, 92-94, 122. In early 1973, a decision was made to move the agglomerates from their experimental stage to full-scale application throughout the Soviet Union. See "On Some Measures to Further Perfect Industrial Administration," Resolution of the Central Committee CPSU and the Council of Ministers USSR, in PZh, no. 8 (April 1973), pp. 3-7.
5. That both local economic and Party leaders are sensitive to such underlying political implications in the reform is indicated by the resistance and charges of "departmentalism" and "localism" leveled in articles like G. V. Romanov, "Sovershentsvovanie proizvodstva i upravleniia—delo partiinoe" (The perfecting of production and administration—A Party matter), PZh, no. 6 (March 1971), p. 14; and "Sovershenstvovat' upravlenie, povyshat' effektivnost' promyshlennogo proizvodstva" (To perfect the administration and to raise the effectiveness of industrial production), K, no. 11 (July 1973), p. 33.
6. Brezhnev, XXIV KPSS, pp. 120-121.
7. Ibid., p. 119.
8. I. Kapitonov, "Nekotorye voprosy partiinogo stroitel'stva v svete reshenii XXIV s"ezda KPSS" (Some problems of party construction in light of the decisions of the 24th Congress CPSU), K, no. 3 (February 1972), p. 38.
9. Brezhnev, XXIV KPSS, p. 124.
10. B. Moralev, "Podgotovka i perepodgotovka rukovodiashchikh kadrov" (The training and retraining of directing cadres), PZh, no. 1 (January 1971), p. 31.
11. I. Lutak, "Kadry partii—provodniki ee politiki" (Cadres of the Party—Conductors of its policy), PZh, no. 5 (March 1972), p. 32.

12. N. Kirichenko, "Povyshaetsia rol' organov kollektivnogo rukovodstva" (The role of collective leadership organs is raised), PZh, no. 19 (October 1971), pp. 29-30.

13. M. Trunov, "Kakoi nam nuzhen spetsialist" (What kind of specialist we need), I, September 20, 1973.

14. A. Skochilov, "Sobliudaia Leninskie printsipy pdbora i vospitaniia kadrov" (Observing the Leninist principles on the selection and upraising of cadres), PZh, no. 3 (February 1971), p. 20.

15. A. I. Pomogaev (historical sciences), editor of oblast newspaper); O. K. Sazonova (economic sciences), obkom ideology secretary; A. P. Zavgorodnii (economic sciences), obkom agriculture secretary. See TP, March 18-19, 1970. Pomogaev's candidate degree may not have been as impressive to other Party leaders. On August 11, he was summarily dropped as oblast editor and replaced by the former director of the obkom science and educational institutions department. There was no official notification of the dismissal or an explanation of Pomogaev's future assignment.

16. N. P. Rusanov, OP, June 30, 1970. Until 1969, Rusanov had been first secretary of the Kolpiansk raikom (see signatures of socialist obligations in Orel in SRos, September 17, 1957, deputies to Russian Supreme Soviet in SRos, March 6, 1959, delegates at XXII KPSS) and and the Livensk gorkom (delegates at XXIII KPSS).

17. See biography of Antonov in 1968 Ezhegodnik.

18. OP, July 2, 1970.

19. See articles by Vinogradov in SRos (August 25, 1957), UG (December 19, 1959); award for educational achievements as obkom secretary in UG (August 2, 1960); and citation of birth in Vedomosti RSFSR, no. 25 (June 18, 1970).

20. See report at plenum in P (January 9, 1966), award by Supreme Soviet (Vedomosti RSFSR, December 26, 1968). For present responsibilities, see ideological conferences in RP (January 27, February 20, and April 4, 1970).

21. See obituary of Aleshkin in I (April 1, 1973) and references-articles in P (August 9, 1954), Sovetskaia Kul'tura (April 27, 1957), Sovetskaia pechat' (no. 3, 1959).

22. See oblast conference in SROs (September 20, 1968), award in Vedomosti RSFSR (December 12, 1968), and regional participation in BP (January 27, October 17-18, 1970).

23. See biographies of Komarova in 1962 and 1966 Deputaty, 1966 and 1971 Ezhegodniki.

24. See new deputies to Russian Supreme Soviet cited in SRos (April 13, 1967), award to Kon'kov in Vedomosti RSFSR (February 13, 1969), and article in BR (June 18, 1970).

25. See plenum in P (November 12, 1955); articles in G (February 28, 1956) and T (May 27 and October 11, 1958); award in

Vedomosti RSFSR (November 13, 1969); and regional participation in KS, June 10, 1970.

26. See deputies to Russian Supreme Soviet in SRos (June 17, 1971), delegates at XXIV KPSS. Until that time Romantsov had been first secretary of the Shebekinsk agricultural raikom (BP, July 10, 1970).

27. On these points, see the articles in Carl Beck et al., Comparative Communist Political Leadership (New York: David McKay, 1973).

28. Another Western scholar has recently emphasized a similar duality in age between an older generation of superiors at the intermediary political level of the Soviet Union and their considerably younger subordinates. See Jerry Hough, "The Soviet System: Petrification or Pluralism?" Problems of Communism 21, 2 (March-April 1972): 38. Hough's analysis is based upon the average ages of officials in 5 republics and 20 oblasts of the RSFSR for 1967 and 1971.

29. See article by Stamikov in PZh, no. 16 (August 1958), list of delegates at XX KPUkr and XXII KPSS.

30. ZK, January 30 and February 21, 1970. While Butenko's election illustrates a general pattern for all regional bureaus after 1964, his specific appointment may have been more closely related to the mounting criticism of Odessa cultural officials in 1970. During the same capital gorkom plenum at which he was first elected to the gorkom bureau, Butenko was also one of the cited participants who discussed problems of indoctrination and cultural officials in the city.

31. See article in P (October 29, 1948); meeting of French delegation in P (September 9, 1957); elections in PU (December 17, 1957, February 7, 1960, September 19, 1961); article in PU (September 5, 1961); Central Committee ideological conference in PU (June 1, 1958); and U.S. State Department, Biographic Directory of Soviet Officials (Washington, D.C.: Government Printing Office, 1964).

32. Golubev was reported to have been dismissed for poor agricultural leadership of Kursk in P, March 22, 1950. He had held the position since P, December 26, 1948. Golubev's career in Briansk can be identified by his article in PZh, June 1955, and the delegates to Russian Supreme Soviet in SRos, March 6, 1959. For Babich's career in Kabaradinsk, see members, Central Auditing Commission, XIX and XX KPSS, deputies to Supreme Soviet in T (March 15, 1950); award as Briansk secretary in P (December 30, 1959) and obkom plenum in SRos (December 14, 1960); regional participation in BR, January 15, 1970.

33. See delegates at XXI KPUkr, XXII KPSS; articles and references as deputy chairman of the Latvian Industrial Bureau for

Construction (Sovetskaia Latvia, February 28, 1963) and deputy chairman of Latvian Council of Ministers (Sovetskaia Latvia, January 18, 1964 and July 10, 1971).

34. See references and articles in P (May 6, 1955), K (August 1957), SRos (June 9 and July 28, 1960), and UG (October 7, 1961).

35. See biography in 1962 Deputaty; citation as chairman in P, February 26, 1950; article as Kraiispolkom chairman in P, March 19, 1958.

36. See biography in 1962 Ezhegodnik. As a graduate of the Vologda Pedagogical Institute and a former gorkom secretary of Vologda, Lykova was tied by career neither to Ivanova nor Smolensk. Also see deputies to Russian Supreme Soviet in I (January 25, 1951) and SRos (March 6, 1959).

37. See election to Mandate Commission at 14th Komsomol Congress and identification as Kirov oblast Komsomol first secretary in Kop (April 17, 1962); for election as Komsomol Secretary, see Kop (April 21, 1962).

38. See addresses to Polish and Mongolian youth delegations in KomZ (May 31, 1967), youth delegation at Expo '70 in P (August 8, 1967), address at 9th World Festival of Youth and Students in Kop (July 23, 1968).

39. As examples, see participation at conferences and plenums reported in Kazakhstanskaia pravda (March 1, 1963 and April 24, 1965), KoP (January 18, 1963; January 4, 1966; March 18, 1966; January 27, 1967), articles and awards for agriculture in SZh (January 11, 1967) and I (May 24, 1967).

40. K (S), June 5, 1970.

41. See biography from VP, cited in Philip Stewart, Political Power in the Soviet Union (New York: Bobbs-Merrill, 1968), p. 136. Grishin most likely had succeeded A. S. Chuianov, obkom first secretary "for more than 10 years of Stalingrad during the war period," according to the reference to Chuianov, who participated in a 1970 commemorative celebration of the Stalingrad Battle (see VP, May 5, 1970). Also, for Chuianov, see Candidates of All-Union Central Committee elected at XVIII VKT(b) and article by Chuianov on the war years in Oktiabr', no. 2, 1968.

42. Stewart, Political Power in the Soviet Union, p. 137.

43. See biography in 1962 Ezhegodnik.

44. See biography in VP, May 22, 1970. Shkol'nikov is currently first deputy chairman of the Council of Ministers in the Russian Republic.

45. Ibid.

46. Ibid.

47. Brezhnev, XXIV KPSS, p. 124.

48. For evidence that obkom first secretaries have been elected at a much later stage of their political careers since 1965, see Robert E. Blackwell, "Career Development in the Soviet Obkom Elite: A Conservative Trend," <u>Soviet Studies</u>, 24, 1 (July 1972): 24-40.

CONCLUSION:
ALTERNATIVE REALITIES
IN THE SOVIET UNION

Speculation on the prospects and direction of change in the Soviet political system has become more commonplace among Western Soviet-area scholars during recent years. The queries seem prompted as much by a cautious reassessment of conventional assumptions in the Western academic field as by the appearance of contradictory tendencies in the Soviet system itself. While show trials of Soviet Jews in 1970-71 and the mock confessions of Pyotr Yakir and Vikor Krasin in 1973 indicate the real limits to change, traditional models of the Soviet system like totalitarianism also seem wholly inadequate to explain the inability of the police state to suppress or intimidate dissident ethnic groups and intellectuals. The physicist Andrei Sakharov still outspokenly defends Soviet scientists against Party intervention in their work and bluntly warns the West against trade and political détente with an incorrigible Soviet leadership bent on the West's destruction; Zhores Medvedev was released from confinement in a mental institution apparently in response to pressure mounted by Soviet and international scientists; Soviet Jews staged a sit-down protest inside the Kremlin on the eve of the 24th Party Congress, and other Jewish scientists in Leningrad and Moscow are reported to have engaged in a work boycott against the government's refusal to grant their requests for emigration to Israel; Lithuanian students in Kaunas rioted following the political suicide of a Lithuanian who protested anti-Catholic policies; and an organized political underground, before its suppression in 1972, published a bimonthly periodical that reported on conditions in forced labor camps and criticized current Soviet policies. These events suggest either that the scope of permissible dissent has been extended in the Soviet Union or that (more likely) a highly bureaucratized secret police can no longer effectively monitor or coerce into silence larger numbers of politically conscious groups in the Soviet Union.

While claiming legitimacy from their Leninist heritage, the cautious, bureaucratic, and aging Party leadership at all levels also seems to be almost a parody on the model of the Soviet Union as a "Permanent Revolution." How, indeed, reconcile the supposedly imperative need of the system for one-man rule with the persistent stability of the current collective leadership in the Politburo? The years since 1964 have not witnessed any continuous turnover and renewal of cadres or any extensive mobilization of the Soviet population. Rather, the Party leadership has remained firmly ensconced in leadership positions and appears content to base its support in the Party on a defense of the political status quo and in Soviet society on a platform of increased consumer goods and services.

In policy-making, the system-dominant elitist model is probably still the most accurate general description of the distribution of political power in the Soviet Union. Yet, in individual issue sectors, there are irrefutable signs of growing decentralization and a willingness to accommodate alternative views from a broader spectrum of lower political and specialist elites. On the other hand, a visitor to the Soviet Union soon becomes aware of the very pragmatic and consumer-oriented nature of Soviet youth. He only wonders how these attitudes among similar younger Party cadres and specialist elites can be reconciled with the orthodox ideological stance and sanctimonious appeals for personal self-sacrifice of an aging Party leadership.

If these tendencies do not signify any imminent collapse of the Soviet political system, they at least suggest a potential growing crisis of confidence and legitimacy in the system among larger segments of the Soviet population. No longer can the Party leadership presume a common sense of commitment in Soviet society. For that sense of commitment in the past derived from an unquestioning acceptance of Stalinist values and regimentation. Despite the partial rehabilitation of Stalin under the Brezhnev-Kosygin leadership, those values have been discredited since Khrushchev's secret speech in 1956 and the following period of questioning and painful disillusionment with the past, which was not suspended in 1964; and regimentation is impractical and counterproductive in a highly sophisticated economy dependent less upon the constraint of an undisciplined work force than upon the voluntary initiative and inventiveness of professional technicians. Even more significantly, that sense of commitment rested upon the ability of the system to renew itself by inspiring and channeling the enthusiastic idealism of mobilized strata and groups in the Soviet population. With an aging and firmly entrenched Party leadership unwilling to recognize or adapt to changing conditions but unable to rekindle that enthusiasm by the example of their own dour corporation personalities, both the commitment and idealism would remain in doubt. Perhaps a new basis of political support can be found. The sober low profile of the current leadership and its primary emphasis on consumer welfare and political stability may well be a welcome relief for the overwhelming Soviet "silent majority," who could have expected in the past only grandiose schemes of impossible transformation and sudden lurches in domestic and foreign policy. Yet, for a society in which the political belief system has even more been transmogrified into a bureaucratic rationale of conformity to vested interests, political dissidents like Sakharov and Andrei Amalrik may constitute less of a minority by the extremity of their political views than by their continuing ability to believe in idealistic alternatives or possibilities at all.

If the Soviet leadership has reached an uncertain period of transition, with greater diversity in the system, more Western scholars at the same time have begun to reevaluate their own assumptions on the nature of the Soviet political system. Importantly, this self-critical analysis on the part of some Western scholars has paralleled an increasing rigor in their methodological approaches to the study of Soviet politics. From an inconsistent phase of fact-gathering or deductive model-building, more Soviet-area scholars are redirecting their efforts to the rigorous operationalization of concepts, the accumulation of data, and the verification of explicitly formulated hypotheses.

If this trend could be characterized as a quantitative or behavioral revolution in Soviet-area studies,[1] it is also one with direct continuity to the previous major works written on the Soviet political system. The only basic difference is that generalizations and assumptions first described in these major works are now being subjected to exacting quantitative analysis within the limits of data available on Soviet politics. Thus, in a seminal article on the Soviet system written in 1966, Zbigniew Brzezinski first described the post-Khrushchev leadership as a degenerating political elite.[2] To test Brzezinski's conclusions in an exacting fashion, Robert Blackwell has recently examined by quantitative analysis the recruitment patterns of obkom first secretaries elected before and after 1964. Deriving his hypotheses from Brzezinski's article, Blackwell finds that, by all controlling factors, obkom first secretaries at least have been elected at a much later stage of their political careers than they would have been before 1965.[3] Similarly, Philip Stewart and other scholars at Ohio State University have recently attempted to test the most prevalent explanations of political mobility in the Soviet Union for the universe of obkom first secretaries in Russian oblasts who were reassigned from their regions between 1955 and 1968. Carefully defining and measuring the exact relationship between their independent variables, they find that different factors appear to account for the mobility of obkom first secretaries at different periods of time between 1955 and 1968.[4]

The significance of studies like Blackwell's and Stewart's may be less the additional knowledge they have provided on the Soviet political system than their attempt to confront implicit assumptions and theories on the Soviet system with hard data. By focusing upon a specific area of political reality, their research approach also explicitly allows for the possibility of diversity and change in the Soviet political system over time or within any similar time period. As such, the quantitative approach could eventually necessitate revision of unquestioned tenets on the Soviet political system in Western scholarship. Sweeping generalizations on the monolithic nature of the Soviet system may require important modifications as more hard data become obtainable and are systematically analyzed.

Perhaps any merit to this detailed examination of regional parties must also be judged against the evident transition in Soviet politics and in Western scholarship on the Soviet Union. Our very framework was drawn to the potential range of diversity and change that may have appeared among regional parties since 1955. Questioning the model of the Communist Party structure as uniform and inflexible, we have attempted to delineate the exact extent of decentralization and adaptive capability shown by regional parties since that year. Whereas Western scholars have often assumed that the same problems are considered in all regional parties and that the same kinds of individuals participate in local policy-making, we have devised specific measures of regional issue concern and group participation; and we have examined the probable reasons for any variation among 25 regional parties in 1970. Whereas Western scholars have described the leadership of the Communist Party as an elite isolated by background and outlook from Soviet society, we have attempted to identify characteristics of background and outlook for comparable regional elites over an 18-year period; and we have developed specific hypothetical linkages between these characteristics and a succeeding elite in the regional environments.

Our study allows us to make the following conclusions:

1. Regional parties in the Soviet Union are granted at least some autonomy to direct their concerns selectively to local problems; while social mobilization has no consistent relationship to regional policy, particular issue areas, such as cadre-organizational problems, social welfare, and substantive industrial and agricultural problems, indicate some adaptation to environmental characteristics.

2. Regional parties have much less autonomy in deciding what occupational sectors will participate in policy-making; some local allowance, however, is made in highly industrialized regions for scientific-technical officials, who have a greater opportunity to participate at lower policy-making levels such as capital gorkom plenums and regional industrial conferences.

3. Obkom first secretaries have little independent impact upon what issues are considered in a regional party or what occupational sectors participate in obkom plenums; different first secretaries in the same regional environment, however, will vary in their concern with cadre-organizational policy and in the proportion of scientific-technical officials who participate in obkom plenums.

4. If regional parties have some local discretion in determining policy and participation, central officials still have the greatest direct influence upon the political process in regional parties; this can be evidenced by the consistent changes in turnover and composition for all obkom bureaus since the overthrow of Khrushchev in 1964; yet, as certain characteristics of bureau members continue to differ by environmental factors after 1964, even central officials appear to take into account local circumstances before selecting regional bureau members.

5. The present Brezhnev-Kosygin leadership is committed to a cadre policy of recruiting more regional bureau members from local regional natives; but the actual significance of the policy cannot be clearly ascertained because total bureau turnover has declined in the interim and more natives as yet cannot be identified in any position other than obkom first secretary.

Finally, the reader could ask if the analysis or conclusions in this study have brought us any closer to an understanding of the Soviet political system or the alternative directions of political change most likely in the immediate future. The analysis in the study was often interrupted with qualifications, the variation on all regional issues and sector participation could not be considered significant, and regional bureau members could be characterized as both more and less politically adaptive since 1964. Yet the very question itself may be wrongly conceived. For the question presumes an underlying consistency, if not inflexibility, in the very analytical framework that alone could assure definitive and preordained answers. Caution, tentativeness, skepticism, and a critical awareness of limitations in a study of Soviet politics may be the most positive attributes that a Western Soviet-area scholar can offer at the present time to his reader.[5] Scholarship based upon hard data and carefully formulated hypotheses can help us avoid the worst aspects of circular reasoning and polemics in evaluating and interpreting the Soviet political system. But, with the questionable and limited kinds of information still obtainable on the Soviet Union, even the most explicit hypotheses and exacting data must eventually be given a subjective meaning and order that all too often will only come to reflect the scholar's own implicit values and biases. Even more at the present time, in a period of uncertain transition and redirection in the Soviet Union, consistency would be a mark not of academic achievement but of the limited relevance of one's findings.

NOTES

1. The principal groundbreaking studies are included in Frederick A. Fleron, ed., Communist Studies and the Social Sciences (Chicago: Rand McNally, 1969); Roger E. Kanet, ed., The Behavioral Revolution and Communist Studies (New York: Free Press, 1971); and Carl Beck et al., Comparative Communist Political Leadership (New York: David Kay, 1973).

2. Zbigniew Brzezinski, "The Soviet Political System: Transformation or Degeneration," Problems of Communism 25, 1 (January-February 1966): 1-15.

3. Robert Blackwell, "Career Development in the Soviet Obkom Elite: A Conservative Trend," Soviet Studies 24, 1 (July 1972): 24-40.

4. Philip Stewart et al., "Political Mobility and the Soviet Political Process: A Partial Test of Two Models," American Political Science Review 66, 4 (December 1972): 1269-1290.

5. Perhaps the most eloquent appeal to date for these attributes among Western Soviet-area scholars has been sounded by Jerry Hough, in "The Soviet System: Petrification or Pluralism?" Problems of Communism 22, 2 (March-April 1972): 25-45.

SELECTED BIBLIOGRAPHY

This is a list only of the most extensively used sources in the present book and does not include additional periodicals and books examined for biographical and career data on a less systematic basis.

NEWSPAPERS AND JOURNALS

All-Union and Union-republic

Ekonomicheskaia gazeta (Moscow), 1958-72

Gudok (Moscow), 1954-72

Izvestiia (Moscow), 1948-73

Kommunist (Moscow), 1952-73

Komsomolskaia pravda (Moscow), 1954-72

Komsomolskoe zania (Kiev), 1954-72

Partiinaia zhizn' (Moscow), 1952-73

Pravda (Moscow), 1948-73

Pravda Ukrainy (Kiev), 1950-73

Radianskaia Ukraina (Kiev), 1950-73

Sel'skoe khoziaistvo (Moscow), 1954-59

Sel'skaia zhizn' (Moscow), 1960-72

Sovetskaia kul'tura (Moscow), 1957-72

Sovetskaia Rossiia (Moscow), 1957-73

Trud (Moscow), 1954-72

Uchitel'skaia gazeta (Moscow), 1954-72

Vedomosti Verkhovnogo Soveta RSFSR (1955-72)

Vedomosti Verkhovnogo Soveta SSSR (1955-72)

Urban and Region

Belgorodskaia pravda (Belgorod), 1970

Brianskii rabochii (Briansk), 1970

Dneprovskaia pravda (Dnepropetrovsk), 1970

Industrial'noe Zaporozh'e (Zaporozh'e), 1970

Kaliningradskaia pravda (Kaliningrad), 1970

Kirovskaia pravda (Kirov), 1970

Krasnoe znamia (Khar'kov), 1970

Krasnoe znaimia (Tomsk), 1970

Krasnyi sever (Vologda), 1970

Krymskaia pravda (Crimea), 1970

Kommunist (Saratov), 1970

Kurskaia pravda (Kursk), 1967 and 1970

Kuzbass (Kemerovo), 1970

Leningradskaia pravda (Leningrad), 1955-65

L'vovskaia pravda (L'vov), 1970

Molot (Rostov), 1962, 1966, and 1967

Moskovskaia pravda (Moscow), 1955-65

Orlovskaia pravda (Orel), 1970

Rabochii put' (Smolensk), 1966 and 1970

Severnyi rabochii (Yaroslavl'), 1970

Sovetskaia sibir' (Novosibirsk), 1967

Tambovskaia pravda (Tambov), 1970

Vechernii Novosibirsk (Novosibirsk), 1967 and 1970

Vechernii Rostov (Rostov), 1967 and 1970

Volgogradskaia pravda (Volgograd), 1970

Zakarpatskaia pravda (Trans-Carpathia), 1970

Znamia (Kaluga), 1967 and 1970

Znamia kommunizma (Odessa), 1970

Zvezda (Perm'), 1970

OFFICIAL PARTY DOCUMENTS

Vneocherednoi XX s''ezd Kommunisticheskoi Partii Ukrainy 16-17 ianvaria 1959 goda: stenograficheskii otchet. Kiev: Gospolitizdat Ukr SSR, 1959.

Materialy-XXI s''ezd Kommunisticheskoi Partii Ukrainy 16-19 fevralia 1960 goda: stenograficheskii otchet. Kiev: Gospolitizdat Ukr SSR, 1960.

Materialy-XXII s''ezd Kommunisticheskoi Partii Ukrainy 27-30 ianvaria 1961 goda: stenograficheskii otchet. Kiev: Gospolitizdat Ukr SSR, 1961.

Materialy-XXIII s''ezd Kommunisticheskoi Partii Ukrainy 15-18 marta 1966 goda: stenograficheskii otchet. Kiev: Gospolitizdat Ukr SSR, 1967.

XXIV Z'izd Kommunistichnoi Partii Ukraini 19-21 marta 1971 goda: stenograficheskii otchet. Kiev: Gospolitizdat, 1972.

XIX s"ezd Vsesoiuznoi Kommunisticheskoi Partii (b) 5-14 oktiabria
1952 goda: stenograficheskii otchet. Moscow: Gospolitizdat,
1953.

XX s"ezd Kommunisticheskoi Partii Sovetskogo Soiuza 14-25 fevralia
1956 goda: stenograficheskii otchet. Moscow: Gospolitizdat,
1956.

Vneocherednoi XXI s"ezd Kommunisticheskoi Partii Sovetskogo Soiuza
27 ianvaria-5 fevralia 1959 goda: stenograficheskii otchet.
Moscow: Gospolitizdat, 1959.

XXII s"ezd Kommunisticheskoi Partii Sovetskogo Soiuza 27-31 oktiabria 1961 goda: stenograficheskii otchet. Moscow: Gospolitizdat,
1962.

XXIII s"ezd Kommunisticheskoi Partii Sovetskogo Soiuza 29 marta-8
aprelia 1966 goda: stenograficheskii otchet. Moscow: Gso-
politizdat, 1966.

XXIV s"ezd Kommunisticheskoi Partii Sovetskogo Soiuza 30 marta-9
aprelia 1971 goda: stenograficheskii otchet. Moscow: Gospolitizdat, 1971.

Spravochnik partiinogo rabotnika. Volumes 10-12. Moscow: Politizdat, 1970, 1971, and 1972.

Biographical and Statistical Sources

Bondarenko, P. T. "Deiatel'nost' Khar'kovskoi oblastnoi partiinoi
organizatsii po vospitaniiu rabochikh promyshlennosti v dukhe
kommunisticheskogo otnosheniia k trudu, 1959-1961." Unpublished Candidate dissertation précis, Moscow State University,
1963.

Buznitskaia, V. M. "Deiatel'nost' Khar'kovskoi oblastnoi partiinoi
organizatsii po ukrepleniiu sviazi ideologicheskoi raboty s
zhizn'iu v period razvernutogo stroitel'stva kommunizma, 1959-
1963." Unpublished Candidate dissertation précis, Khar'kov
State University imeni Gor'kii, 1965.

Deputaty Verkhovnogo Soveta SSSR. Sessions V-VIII. Moscow:
Izvestiia Sovetov Deputatov Trudiashchikhsia SSSR, 1958, 1962,
1966, and 1970.

Ezhegodnik bol'shoi Sovetskoi entsiklopedii. Volumes 1958-72.
    Moscow: Gosudarstvennoe nauchnoe izdatel'stvo, 1958-71.

Istoriya mist i sil URSR v dvadtsiatishesti tomkah: Dnipropetrovs'ka
    oblast', Kharkivs'ka oblast', Kryms'ka oblast', Lvivs'ka oblast',
    Odes'ka oblast', Zakarpats'ka oblast', and Zaporizhs'ka oblast'.
    Kiev: Ukrains'ka Radians'ka Entsiklopediia, 1969-70.

Itogi vsesoiuznoi perepisi naseleniia 1959 goda: SSSR, RSFSR, and
    Ukr SSR. Moscow: Statistika, 1962.

Itogi vsesouiuznoi perepisi naseleniia 1970 goda. Volumes I-IV.
    Moscow: Statistika, 1972-73.

Kolosha, I. M. "Bor'ba KPSS za ukreplenia soiuza rabochego klassa
    i kolkhoznogo krest'ianstva v period semiletki, 1959-1965"
    (Na materialiakh Brianskoi oblastnoi partiinoi organizatsii).
    Unpublished Candidate dissertation précis, Moscow State Peda-
    gogical Institute imeni Lenin, 1967.

Narodne gospodarstvo Ukrains'koi RSR. Kiev: Gosstatizdat, 1957-70

Narodnoe khoziaistvo RSFSR. Moscow: Gostatizdat, 1956-70.

Ocherkii istorii Brianskoi organizatsii KPSS. Bransk: Prioskoe
    Knizhnoe izdatel'stvo, 1968.

Ocherkii istorii Yaroslavskoi organizatsii KPSS. Yaroslavl':
    Verkhne-Volzhskoe knizhnoe izdatel'stvo, 1967.

Ocherkii po istorii razvitiia Sovetskogo Khar'kova. Khar'kov:
    Khar'kovskoe oblastnoe izdatel'stvo, 1956.

Pavlov, V. I. Budni odnogo sovnarkhoza. Moscow: Profizdat, 1958.

Pervie shagi novykh partiinykh organov na sele. Briansk: Brianskii
    rabochii, 1963.

Prominent Personalities in the USSR. Metuchen, N.J.: Scarecrow
    Press, 1968.

Rabotat' i zhit' po kommunisticheskii, 1958-1962 (Na materialiakh
    Khar'kova). Khar'kov: Khar'kovskoe knizhnoe izdatel'stvo,
    1963.

Titov, V. N. Khar'kovshchina nakaune sorokaletii Velikogo Oktiabria. Khar'kovskoe oblastnoe izdatel'stvo, 1957.

U.S. Department of State. Biographic Directory of Soviet Officials. Washington, D.C.: Government Printing Office, 1957, 1960, 1963, and 1966.

gorkom first secretaries, 207;
ideology secretary, 212; impact
of political change, 170-173; indices of turnover, 191-193; internal rotation and turnover,
165, 173-174, 179-181, 189-191;
local recruitment and middle
elite, 221-222, 227-228; Party
entry and birth period, 207-208;
party tenure, 208-209; prescribed membership, 160-161;
previous All-Union and Union-
republic offices, 240; recruited
and coopted compared, 238, 240;
and theory of social mobilization,
169; Ukrainian versus Russian
turnover, 187-189
obkom first secretaries: background, 19, 147-148, 218-219,
220, 229-230; coopted, 138-141,
153; delivery of plenum reports,
33, hypotheses and problems,
128-130, 131; influence of Party
generation, 133, 134, 137, 213-
214; "local" workers and specialist background, 146-147,
218-219, 235; and Party effectiveness, 66; Party entry, 211;
political and environmental
variables, 151, 153-154; recruitment origins, 141-147, 149, 150,
231-232; role analysis, 126-128,
130, 155; turnover rates, 184
(see also Kulichenko, L. I.)
obkom leadership: and relationship with subsystems, 64-65
obkom plenums: and cadre-organizational problems, 43, 44,
66; and determination of important issues, 22, 24-25, 30-31,
32; and issue adaptation, 101-
102, 103; and Jewish question,
50-51; and participation, 53-54,
104
obkom secretaries: level of, 387;

recruitment of, 220-222
oblast parties: local leadership,
2-4, 8; measurement of participation and themes, 54-55
occupational group categories,
110-111
Odessa region: first secretaries
Stamikov and Butenko, 220
ideological conferences, 98;
Jewish question, 50-51; virtual
representation, 91-92
omitted policy themes; anti-Zionist
campaign, 48-51

Party leadership: recruited Party
apparatchiki, 235, 236, 241;
status quo and potential crisis,
248-249
Party membership: concept of
generation and age cohorts,
212-213
Party organization: criticisms,
67-68; restructuring on production agglomerates model, 202
plenums: cadre-organizational
problems, 65; "expanded"
agricultural, 34; group participation and impact on policy-
making, 106, 107, 159-160; on
oblast newspaper, Smolensk, 46;
occupational sectors, 33, 34;
as political forums, 130; raikom,
37-38; reports by obkom first
secretary, 31-33; scientific-
technical elite, 35-38; urban and
district secretaries as participants, 34
policy-making: analysis of intensity factor, 53; impact of plenum
participation, 106, 159-160;
participation of occupational
sectors, 130; quantitative factors
of analysis, 53-54; system-
dominant elitist model, 248
political adaptation: alternative

views, 241-242; Brezhnev commitment, 204; power struggle, 50, 51
political culture, 93-94
political participation: direct and indirect, 13-14
productivity problems, interpretations of, 107

regional kolkhoz councils: background, 74-75
regional newspapers, 44-45; criticisms, of, 46-48; and Jewish issue, 49-50
regional parties: importance, 16, 22; effect of social mobilization and political adaptation, 17-18; "expanded" plenums, 105; issue adaptation, 61; leaders and ideology, 90; leadership conflict, 101; "local" workers, 214-215 officials and agricultural production, 76-77; participation in obkom plenums, 104; problems of analysis, 38-40; proportion of of groups in plenums, 111-112; variation with urbanization, 65; role of production goals, 103, shablonism, 118; social welfare policy, 81-89; women in leadership roles, 90-91
regional policy-making: concepts, 155; determinants, 151, 153-154; elite recruitment, 165; influence of first secretaries, 128-129; plenum participation, 165
regional work force: density of, 70-71, 72
research problems, 110
Rostov: ideological conferences, 98; social welfare policy forum, 85-87; virtual representation, 91-93
Russian Republic: Lykova, L. P.,

228-229 (see also Ukrainian Republic)

Saratov region: Obkom bureau attrition, 186; turnover in obkom bureaus, 189-191
scientific-technical elite: classifications, 115-117; decline in obkom bureaus, 218-219
shablonism, 22, 118
Shelepin, Aleksandr, 42
Smolensk: plenum on oblast newspapers, 46
social mobilization (see theory of social mobilization)
social welfare: and oblast party, 84; and obkom plenums, 83; as regional issues, 81-83; role of industrial ministries, 82; urban example, Rostov, 85-87
Soviet political elites: career backgrounds, 137-141
Soviet studies: changing methodology, 249-250

tenure analysis: first and second secretaries, 184-185; obkom bureau, 180-181; Ukrainian example, 183
theory of social mobilization, 17-19, 65; absolute educational levels, and indices, 103; and cadre organizational issues, 100; effect of urbanization, 70; and ideological conferences, 98-99; and obkom bureaus recruitment, 169; and occupational group participation in plenums; 106; occupational sectors, 116
Tomsk: group participation in obkom plenums, 107-109
24th Congress: CPSU, 42-43, 146-147, 201-203

Ukrainian Republic: attrition rate,

obkom bureaus, 187-189; average tenure, obkom bureaus, 183; comparison of obkom bureaus with middle elite, 210; comparison with the Russian Republic, obkom turnover, 187-189, 222-223

urban density: methodology, 69-70, 71

urbanization, 62, 70; cadre-organizational problems, 65; substantive and nonsubstantive, 103

Volgograd region: comparison of obkom first secretaries, 231-234; middle elite, 233-234

Vologda: group participation in plenums, 107, 108-109

virtual representation, 91-92; concern for, 106; group interests in conferences, 94, 105, 109; for specialized work sectors and Party cadres in conferences and seminars, 104-105; thesis of, 91-92

women's role: in regional parties, 90-91; and Lykova, L. P., 228-229

Zaporozh'e region: cadre conferences, 44; obkom bureau tenure, 177-179

JOEL C. MOSES is Assistant Professor of Political Science at Iowa State University. During the winter of 1970 he traveled and conducted research in the Soviet Union and returned to Europe in the summer of 1973 to update his findings. His current research interests concern Soviet domestic politics.

Dr. Moses holds a B.A. from Beloit College and an M.A. and Ph.D. from the University of Wisconsin at Madison.

RELATED TITLES
Published by
Praeger Special Studies

THE POLITICS OF MODERNIZATION IN
EASTERN EUROPE: Testing the Soviet Model
edited by Charles Gati

SOVIET AGRICULTURAL POLICY: Toward the
Abolition of Collective Farms
Stephen Osofsky

THE SOVIET ECONOMY IN REGIONAL
PERSPECTIVE
edited by V. N. Bandera
and Z. L. Melnyk

THE SOVIET WEST: The Interplay between
Nationality and Social Organization
edited by Ralph S. Clem

6 00 019867 7   TELEPEN